MEN AND CITIZENS

A STUDY OF
ROUSSEAU'S SOCIAL THEORY

Cambridge Studies in the History and Theory of Politics

MEN AND CITIZENS

A STUDY OF
ROUSSEAU'S SOCIAL THEORY

BY

JUDITH N. SHKLAR

Harvard University

CAMBRIDGE
AT THE UNIVERSITY PRESS
1969

Published by the Syndics of the Cambridge University Press
Bentley House, 200 Euston Road, London N.W.1
American Branch. 32 East 57th Street, New York, N.Y. 10022

Library of Congress Catalogue Card Number: 75—75828

MAY 8 '72

Standard Book Number: 521 07574 2

Printed in Great Britain by
Alden & Mowbray Ltd
at the Alden Press, Oxford

CONTENTS

v

PREFACE

Since the title of this book announces its contents quite accurately, I shall not detain the reader with any further explanations. It is far more agreeable to tell everyone how much I owe to those of my friends who helped me write this book by reading it and talking to me about it or by just being good enough to listen to me, hour after hour, go on and on about Rousseau. Among them, George A. Kelly, because he disagrees with me so profoundly, has a special claim on my gratitude. I thank them all and hope they will like this book as much as I enjoyed writing it.

It is, however, to those Harvard and Radcliffe students, both undergraduate and graduate, with whom I have read and discussed Rousseau that I feel most thankful. Their response to Rousseau was an inspiration to me. I wrote this book for them, and it is to them that it is inscribed.

Chapters 1 and 4 appeared originally in somewhat different form as articles and are here reprinted with permission from the *Political Science Quarterly*, LXXXI (March, 1966) and the *American Political Science Review*, LVIII (December, 1964), respectively.

July 1968   J.N.S.

LIST OF ABBREVIATED WORKS

C.G.	*Correspondance Générale de Jean-Jacques Rousseau.*
Hachette	*Œuvres Complètes,* Hachette, Paris, 1905.
Inégalité	*Discours sur l'Origine et les Fondements de l'Inégalité Parmis les Hommes.*
Lettre à Voltaire	Lettre à M. de Voltaire.
N.H.	*La Nouvelle Héloise.*
O.C.	*Œuvres Complètes.*
Poland	*Considérations sur le Gouvernement de Pologne.*

I

TWO JOURNEYS TO UTOPIA

UTOPIAS OLD AND NEW

Jean-Jacques Rousseau was not a professional philosopher. He never pretended that he was. His great claim was that he alone had been 'the painter of nature and the historian of the human heart'.[1] It was an art that did not demand great logical rigor or systematic exposition of abstract ideas. Rousseau did not even aspire to these accomplishments. He did not think that perfect consistency was really very important. What did matter was always to be truthful.[2] By truthfulness he meant what we generally tend to call sincerity, and in his case it involved an overriding will to denounce the social world around him. It made him one of the greatest of the nay-sayers. His denial was comprehensive, embracing civilization as a whole. And in his tone of undeviating contempt for all he saw around him, he was singularly consistent. Moreover, if he was the very prototype of the *homme revolté*, he was not without a deep sense of order, and his ideas found expression in a form of social criticism that was both formal and traditional in its structure.[3]|For Rousseau was the last of the classical utopists. He was the last great political theorist to be utterly uninterested in history, past or future, the last also to judge and condemn without giving any thought to programs of action. His enduring originality and fascination are entirely due to the acute psychological insight with which he diagnosed the emotional diseases of modern civilization.| Both the radical new ideas and the tradition of utopianism were essential to his critical task.

The classical utopists, of whom Sir Thomas More was both the first and greatest, were not visionary reformers. Their aim was to

---

[1] *Rousseau Juge de Jean-Jacques* in *Œuvres Complètes* (ed. Pléiade, Paris, 1959), I, 728 (hereafter cited as *O.C.*). (Unless translations are attributed, they are my own.)

[2] *La Nouvelle Héloise* (hereafter cited as *N.H.*), 'Seconde Préface', *O.C.*, II, 27.

[3] For Rousseau as 'homme revolté', see Sven Stelling-Michaud, 'Rousseau et l'Injustice Sociale', Samuel Baud-Bovy *et al.*, *Jean-Jacques Rousseau* (Neuchâtel, 1962), 171–86, and Eric Weil, 'Jean-Jacques Rousseau et sa Politique', *Critique*, VII (1952), 4–28.

picture the awful distance between the possible and the probable by showing in great detail how men *could* live, even though they *always* refuse to do so. Utopia is an attack on both the doctrine of natural sin, which imposes rigid limits on men's social potentialities, and on all actual societies, which always fall so short of men's real capacities. The object of all these models, however, was never to set up a perfect community, but simply to bring moral judgment to bear on the social misery to which men have so unnecessarily reduced themselves. For the fault is not in God, fate, or nature, but in ourselves—where it will remain. To recognize this, to accept it, to contemplate and to judge: that was the function of the classical utopia. Utopia was neither in space nor in time. It was designed solely to induce moral recognition in the reader.[1] If one thinks that the only purpose of political philosophy is to provide serviceable guides to action for politicians and political groups, then indeed utopia was a useless enterprise. If critical understanding and judgment, however, are also real ends, then the construction of such models is not only justifiable, it is a perfect instrument.[2] In neither case is the commonplace contrast between 'realism' and 'utopianism', as one between the practical and the impossible, relevant.[3] Whatever value this distinction may have in discussing the political thinking of the nineteenth and twentieth centuries, it is pointless when applied to classical utopianism, which was neither historical nor activist in its concerns.

In Rousseau's case utopia was a perfect way to express ideas that were dictated by personal imagination and by a profound need for self-revelation and self-vindication. Of metaphysics he knew little, nor did he care. There is no sign that he took an interest in history as the study of man's actual development in time. Neither his correspondence nor his public writings show the least concern with current affairs. Only when he was personally involved did he finally turn to a serious investigation of Genevan politics. It has

[1] For a more general account of utopian political thought, see the author's 'The Political Theory of Utopia: From Melancholy to Nostalgia', *Daedalus*, XCIV (1965), 367–81.
[2] This point has been especially recognized by the distinguished anthropologist and ardent admirer of Rousseau, Claude Lévi-Strauss, *Tristes Tropiques*, trans. by John Russell (New York, 1964), 61.
[3] Jean Fabre, 'Réalité et Utopie dans la Pensée Politique de Rousseau', *Annales Jean-Jacques Rousseau*, XXXV (1959–62), 181–216.

indeed been well noted that Voltaire had his Calas affair and many like it, but that Rousseau was interested in only one case: his own.[1] The result of this self-absorption was, however, not just a quantity of autobiographical writing. It also led to an outraged awareness of the distance between the self and the hostile external social world which he could express in quite impersonal terms. The utopian form was ideally suited to convey his concern for the contrast between what is and what ought to be. With it came the characteristic indifference to history.[2] Moreover, Rousseau shared the typical utopian sense of the distance between the probable and the possible. He also knew that suffering was not necessary since he 'had discovered that the source of all men's miseries and wickedness was in their false opinions'.[3] The task, therefore, was to show men models of what they could be, if only they were to abandon their chains—an eventuality he did not in the least expect.

One difficulty presented by Rousseau as a utopist is that he offered two models rather than one. One model was a Spartan city, the other a tranquil household, and the two were meant to stand in polar opposition to each other. Most of Rousseau's interpreters have felt that somehow or other these two should be reconciled.[4] In fact there is nothing astonishing about his proposing these two models, rather than a single utopia. It had often been done before. Plato and Seneca have never been accused of being half head and

[1] Jean Starobinski, *Jean-Jacques Rousseau: La Transparence et l'Obstacle* (Paris, 1957), 25. However, even this egoism can be defended as the necessary stance of a self-aware observer; see, for example, Claude Lévi-Strauss, 'Jean-Jacques Rousseau, Fondateur des Sciences de l'Homme', in Baud-Bovy *et al.*, 239–48.

[2] 'Lettre au Prince de Wurtemberg', 10 novembre 1763, *Correspondance Générale de Jean-Jacques Rousseau* (ed. Théophile Dufour, Paris, 1924–32), X, 205–17 (hereafter cited as *C.G.*). The only discussions of historical events occur in his commentaries on the writings of the Abbé de Saint-Pierre and these were commissioned articles which he found uncongenial work. *Confessions*, IX, *O.C.*, I, 407–8, 422–4. Certainly he presented no alternative, more 'realistic' plans, nor did he investigate any historical examples other than those mentioned by the abbé. C. E. Vaughan, *The Political Writings of Jean-Jacques Rousseau* (Oxford, 1962), I, 359–422 (*La Paix Perpetuelle et la Polysynodie: Extraits et Jugements*).

[3] *Lettres à Malesherbes, O.C.*, I, 1136.

[4] For example, J. H. Broome, *Rousseau* (London, 1963), 103; Robert Derathé, 'L'Unité de la Pensée de Jean-Jacques Rousseau', in Baud-Bovy *et al.*, 204–18; Bertrand de Jouvenel, 'Théories des Formes de Gouvernement chez Rousseau', *Le Contrat Social*, VI (1962), 343–51. Some writers have, of course, suggested that Rousseau was simply incapable of choosing a consistent model; for example, Albert Schinz, *La Pensée de Jean-Jacques Rousseau* (Paris, 1924), 24–45, 102–6, 247.

half heart, part classical and part romantic, yet both used two models, an age of innocence and an age of conscious virtue, to illuminate actual corruption. To be sure, both argued that the age of reason must absorb and rise above the virtues of the lost natural state.[1] However, other writers, most notably Fénelon, did not use the two models in this way, but rather treated them, as Rousseau was to do, as two equally valid, though different utopias. And Fénelon was one of the few authors of whom one can say with some assurance that Rousseau had read him. Certainly he admired him.[2] One must, to be sure, be very cautious in linking Rousseau to Fénelon, or to any other religious moralist of the century preceding his own. No superficial similarities can hide the fact that Rousseau was concerned with earthly felicity and they with eternal salvation. Moreover, Fénelon's *Télémaque* is a 'mirror of princes', and that is something Rousseau could not conceivably have wanted to imitate. However, the 'mirror of princes' has the same function as utopia: to judge the actual by confronting it with the perfect. Moreover, Rousseau fully understood the aim of Fénelon's *Télémaque*. Fénelon prepares Emile to recognize the evils that he will meet on his travels. Emile is taught how to observe, not how to act.[3]

The most significant aspect of *Télémaque* is not its possible direct influence on Rousseau, but simply that it illustrates a tradition of

---

[1] Plato, *The Statesman*, 217b–277a; Seneca, *Letters to Lucilius*, Nos 90 and 95. There is no particular reason, however, to suppose that Rousseau was a close student and follower of these two, or any other, classical authors. Tracing his sources would seem to be both futile and impossible. See George Pire, 'De l'Influence de Sénéque sur les Théories Pédagogiques de J.-J. Rousseau', *Annales Jean-Jacques Rousseau*, XXXIII (1953–5), 57–92, and 'Du Bon Plutarque au Citoyen de Genève', *Revue de Littérature Comparé*, XXXII (1958), 510–47. A similar neo-Stoic 'solution' to Rousseau's models was presented by Ernst Cassirer, *The Question of Jean-Jacques Rousseau*, trans. by Peter Gay (New York, 1954), 65, 98–99, 104–5, 122. However, it has been just as plausibly argued that, far from preferring Sparta, Rousseau *really* chose domestic bliss as his ultimate model; for example, see H. Gaston Hall, 'The Concept of Virtue in *La Nouvelle Héloise*', *Jean-Jacques Rousseau, Yale French Studies* (Fall–Winter 1961–2), 20–33.

[2] Albert Cherel, *Fénelon au XVIIIe Siècle* (Paris, 1917), 143–4, 321, 393–8, 466–8. For Rousseau's admiring remarks about Fénelon, see *Confessions*, VI, 229, XII, 620; *Rousseau Juge de Jean-Jacques*, II, *O.C.*, I, 863–4; *Les Rêveries du Promeneur Solitaire*, III, *O.C.*, I, 1013; *Emile*, trans. by Barbara Foxley (London, 1948), 367, 376–7, 431.

[3] *Emile*, 431.

4

using different utopias together without suggesting any contradiction. *Bétique*, the utopia of spontaneous rural simplicity, illuminates all the vices of a denatured civilization.[1] *Salante*, the creation of a single legislator, is a model of organized civic virtue, which serves to show up the social degradation of France under Louis XIV.[2] Although Rousseau did not choose to adopt Fénelon's thin mythological disguises, the purpose of his two utopias was quite similar, and certainly no more mystifying. His quiet village, and golden age, also held a message addressed to all men, while his Spartan city was a damning mirror held up to the élite of Paris. What is strikingly novel is his insistence that one must choose between the two models, between man and the citizen. This necessity for choice, moreover, is not a call for a decision, but a criticism. It contains the core of Rousseau's diagnosis of mankind's psychic ills. All our self-created miseries stem from our mixed condition, our half natural and half social state. A healthy man, the model for any system of education, would have to adhere consistently to a single mode of life. Nature is no longer an option open to men. Education as a conscious choice is a social experience. The alternatives are therefore not nature or society, but domestic or civic education. Is a man to find his maturity in a recreated Golden Age or as a citizen of a Spartan republic? He cannot have both, but he must try one or the other if he is to escape from his present disorientation and inner disorder. To find self-fulfillment, a child must be educated against society, in isolation from and rejection of all prevailing customs and opinions. Then he may be fit to found a family and live with it in rustic peace. It is the least harmful of social possibilities. The only other soul-satisfying choice is to lose oneself in a collectivity, in a Spartan order where a totally artificial environment recreates for each citizen the conditions of nature's regularity and harsh disciplining order. Both utopias are unnatural, but each meets the psychic needs of men for inner unity and social simplicity. Indeed because both are consciously created social structures, both eliminate those disturbing natural impulses

[1] Télémaque, *Œuvres Choisies de Fénelon* (Paris, 1879), VII, 78–83. See also the tale of the good savages, the Manduriens, *ibid.* IX, 94–6.
[2] *Ibid.* X, 112–27; XVII, 215–19.

which make it impossible for men to accept society long after they have become unfit for nature.

Negatively, both models show up the painful consequences of our actual failure to choose: war between men, conflict within each soul.[1] Above all, because they are incompatible, the attempt to pursue both enhances the strain under which men actually labor. That is why it is so intensely demoralizing. For there is no compromise that can be worked out between self-repression and self-expression. Each has its rewards and penalties, but the two cannot be reconciled. That is why one *ought* to choose, even if no one has, or is likely to do so.

The possibility of making this choice is not impaired, any more than is its rightness, by the fact that it has never been and is not going to be made. Rousseau was, to be sure, simply not interested in the past as such and he looked to the future with fear and trembling. He was always ready to 'put the facts aside'.[2] The Golden Age is not an early stage of man's development. It is a condition which he has never known and never will enjoy.[3] However, it is necessary to know both it and the state of pure nature, if one is to have a clear vision of man's present life, and if one is to judge the latter properly.[4] To abandon the Golden Age, to say that it is a mere chimera is, above all, to renounce forever the belief in human virtue.[5] The Golden Age of domestic happiness is both a moral necessity and a possibility. Rousseau had seen intimations of it in rural Switzerland. And even if he had never known a happy family or true friendship, he found it so easy to picture them in his imagination, and felt so profound a longing for them that he could never doubt that psychologically they were feasible. Historically they were never achieved. However, history itself is for the wise man but 'a tissue of fables whose morals are well adapted to the human heart.'[6] He did not really believe that Lycurgus' Sparta or men as virtuous as Brutus and Cato had actually existed. He did, however,

---

[1] *Emile*, 6–10; Vaughan, I, 305 (*L'état de guerre*); II, 128–9 (*Contrat Social*).
[2] Vaughan, I, 141 (*Discours sur l'Origine et les Fondements de l'Inégalité Parmis les Hommes*, hereafter cited as *Inégalité*).
[3] *Ibid.* I, 448–9 (*Première Version du Contrat Social*).   [4] *Ibid.* I, 136 (*Inégalité*).
[5] *Réponse à M. Bordes* (*Œuvres Complètes*, Hachette, Paris, 1905, hereafter cited as Hachette), I, 54; *Emile*, 438.   [6] *Emile*, 120–1.

6

think that the ancient historians had known men sufficiently like these heroes to make their portraits seem at least plausible.[1] Again, he found it so easy in his imagination to identify himself, a citizen also, after all, with these types, that their psychological possibility could not be denied.

To revile his contemporaries it was not necessary to prove more than the mere possibility of ancient virtue. What would the Parisian scribblers not give for that fatal Sparta never to have existed? For the most virtuous of Greek cities had no philosophers![2] As long as such civic virtue was a possibility, they stood condemned. As long as those Swiss peasants seemed content in their vegetative life, how could Voltaire, or any other champion of civilization, compensate the victims of urban complexity for their lost bliss?[3] As instruments of condemnation the models were more than adequate. Rousseau never meant them to be anything more. 'I intend to attack error rather than to establish new truths.'[4] 'I am an observer, not a moralist. I am the botanist who describes the plant. It is for the physician to order its use.'[5] Let the states of Europe run to their ruin, Rousseau was convinced that reform was useless and impossible.[6] Even Geneva, in the days when he still cared for it, was not a place in which he expected to see Sparta resurrected.[7] Rousseau went well beyond disdaining the very idea of historical progress.[8] He made passivity his central principle, and a necessary one. For nothing less was compatible with the total condemnation of his age. To make his rejection complete and to justify his sustained attack, he had only to show that the ills of actuality were as irreparable as they were unnecessary. They were too immense to be altered, yet

[1] Vaughan, I, 320 (*Fragment*).   [2] *Réponse à M. Bordes*, 55–6.

[3] 'Lettre à M. Voltaire', 18 août 1756, *C.G.*, II, 303–24 (hereafter referred to as *Lettre à Voltaire*).   [4] Vaughan, I, 342 (*Fragment*).

[5] *Mon Portrait*, III, *O.C.*, I, 1120; *Réponse à M. Bordes*, 65.

[6] 'Je vois tous les Etats de l'Europe courir à leur ruine.' Vaughan, I, 425–6 (*Considérations sur le Gouvernement de Pologne*, hereafter cited as *Poland*). As for the futility of reform, it was a constant theme; see, for example, Vaughan, I, 489–91 (*Première Version*).

[7] *Politics and the Arts: Letter to M. d'Alembert on the Theatre*, trans. by Allan Bloom (Glencoe, 1960. Hereafter cited as *Letter to d'Alembert*), 67. '*Préface' à Narcisse*, *O.C.*, II, 971–2.

[8] *Rousseau Juge de Jean-Jacques*, II, 805–6; 'Lettres Morales', *C.G.*, III, 351–3; 'Lettre à M. de Mirabeau', 26 juillet 1767, *C.G.*, XVII, 155–9. This denial was, moreover, the essence of both of the two *Discourses* and the attending correspondence.

not so inevitable as to make outrage seem foolish. Utopias were genuine portraits of the human heart, but they were not photographs of actual people.

Rousseau did not apply the word utopia to his own work. He associated utopia too much with futile dreams of perfect cities to recognize its critical functions.[1] The *Social Contract* was, perhaps, too abstract to seem obviously a part of the utopian tradition. Rousseau thought of this work as grounded in actuality because it was meant to warn the citizens of Geneva against the despotic designs of their magistrates. If Rome was his model, Geneva, though far from perfect, was still worth saving from ultimate corruption.[2] In fact, of course, Plato and More had not been oblivious to the injustice that prevailed around them and their assaults upon their fellow citizens were no less powerful than Rousseau's. If he and they believed that good laws might make good men, the sickening sight of the wicked men created by worthless government was the immediate and common inspiration of all. Utopia is the present political order reversed. That hardly requires a sense of hope for the future. A recognition of the fragility of even the best of republican institutions is far from incompatible with utopia as a device for condemnation. Neither Rousseau nor anyone else has much to add to Plato's ample account of the psychology of moral and political degeneration.[3] Indeed Rousseau's pervasive sense of the inevitable decline of both Sparta and the Golden Age only illustrates his affinity for the philosophers, poets and historians of classical antiquity. It is not difficult to see why he wanted to translate Tacitus, nor why his experiences in Venice and Geneva gave rise to that wish.[4] These two republics, both in a state of degeneration, formed a single image in his mind. Both demonstrated the end to which all republics must sooner or later come. To warn them against further corruption was a duty, really to alter their downward path, impossible.[5] As for the Golden Age it had never been anything but the expression of nostalgia. It is, as it were, defined by its irretrievable joys. Rousseau had been reminded of it in rural Switzerland. To remember it was to

---

[1] *Lettres Ecrites de la Montagne*, Hachette, III, IV, 204-5. [2] *Confessions*, IX, 404-5.
[3] *Republic*, 545-80. [4] *Confessions*, VIII, 394.
[5] Vaughan, II, 75, 89, 107-8, 117, 119 (*Contrat Social*); *Confessions*, IX, 404-5.

long for it. Again personal experience and classical literature were at one in moving his imagination.

There is, however, an intellectual chasm that does separate Rousseau from Plato and More and one that certainly marks their respective utopias. What Rousseau chose to regard as their unfounded dreams of perfection was nothing less than the metaphysical structure of their thought. Human nature and the city that might be are grounded in the noumenal realm. Both have contours that reason can recognize. Perfection is not in history, but that does not render it, for Plato or More, unreal. Utopia is not here and now, but it is to be found in the rational cosmos which it reproduces. Man as a rational being is more than the sum of his reactions. Thus, both human nature and society must first be recognized as conceptual realities, which set goals, no less than they describe the patterns of which both are merely reflections. Both would remain unintelligible without a prior grasp of utopia which is primarily the *true* model of man and polity. All this Rousseau rejected utterly and completely. His sense of disaster was correspondingly total. Degeneration was the law of life. Utopia was an imaginative interruption of that process and a painful awareness of it. That was all.

For Rousseau had left the theory of a stable human nature behind him with the rest of the Platonic tradition. As a book on public education the *Republic* was admirable.[1] The philosophy which it expressed he entirely rejected. The cave is where we must always remain, he noted explicitly, and it was 'puerile' of Plato to think that man could ever have the knowledge needed to leave it. No such knowledge was even conceivable. Plato was a mere dreamer, however pleasant. In fact, however, we can know nothing and can see nothing. 'We run after shadows which escape us. Some fleeting spectre, some vain phantasm flits before our eyes and we think we see the eternal chain of being.' All that we can possibly grasp, in fact, is a sense of our own selfhood and we must end where Descartes began, with 'I think therefore I am.'[2] Introspective psychology therefore necessarily replaces every other possible way of describing men, and its revelations are far from comforting.

First of all, the notion of a structured human nature was dispelled

---

[1] *Emile*, 8.   [2] 'Lettres Morales', 358–9.

by the variety of psychological possibilities. To Rousseau that meant that men were doomed to be displaced persons, moving without a compass from one unsatisfactory situation to another. Since everything is possible, nothing is right or suitable. The state of nature is man's original condition, but not one in which he could remain or in which he is truly a man. On the contrary he is a 'stupid and limited' creature, scarcely different from the animals.[1] He does not suffer, but neither does he really live as a human being. His freedom, which separates him in his potentialities from the animals, must lead him out of nature to manhood. His 'perfectibility', that is his human faculties, imagination and memory, are bound to develop.[2] And freedom, in this context, means that there are no set limits to what he can do with and to himself. What he does is to abuse his powers and to make himself miserable. The growth of his faculties, responding to an infinity of stimulants, takes any number of directions, and none of them brings him the felicity he seeks. Association with other men breeds artificial emotional needs, dependence, weakness, vanity, competitiveness, inequality and an unlimited number of other ills. For men can imagine anything at all, and their fantasies multiply until the cave is a veritable museum of the absurd. As for God, what has He done for man? If He exists, He says, do not blame me. 'I have made you too weak to leave the abyss, because I made you strong enough not to fall into it.'[3] Nothing could express the divine indifference more perfectly.

Men cannot return to nature. Nature is a state that in Rousseau's account is explicitly a starting-point that men, as their own creators, must leave in order to become men at all.[4] It is not their home. And indeed there is no resting place anywhere for men. There is not even a moment in their lives when they can say, 'I wish this instant might last forever'.[5] Flux is our only constant experience.

Fantasy-ridden, torn by inner conflict, at odds with each other, distracted by memory and hope men err from misery to misery. The worst of these are created cooperatively. Inequality, the expression of *amour-propre* and competition, is at the very core of every social organization except the immediate family. Both of

---

[1] Vaughan, II, 36 (*Contrat Social*).   [2] *Ibid.* I, 147–52 (*Inégalité*).
[3] *Confessions*, II, 64.   [4] Vaughan, I, 207 (*Inégalité*).   [5] *Rêveries*, V, 1046.

Rousseau's utopias are interruptions of the progress of inequality. Social inequality begins when villagers compete innocently in their holiday games. It ends in due course with despotism. The Golden Age is a picture of the state of men before inequality has become a serious concern. Sparta arrests its growth at a crucial moment: at the founding of civil society when inequality might be averted by law, if a semi-divine law-giver should appear. Both utopias are essentially preventive. They forestall, they halt the normal course of history. Sooner or later change overwhelms both. What unites the two models is Rousseau's aversions, his contempt for actuality and also his outraged sense of men's helplessness in the face of change and mutability. In his utopias history does briefly stop—until it begin to roll over them as it sooner or later must.

Change was not for Rousseau as for Plato or More the opposite of eternity, of that timeless perfection that makes the rational order. It was for him a part of that restlessness which was the very mark of man's freedom, of his psychological development. Change was also the essence of the modern age. Rousseau was well aware that the rate of social change was quickening and he dreaded it, because he knew that it could only cause further dislocation and greater hostilities than those altogether intolerable ones which he already knew. Emile flees not only injustice in general, when he tries to retreat to the Golden Age. He is also running away from the modern world. 'The crisis is approaching, and we are on the edge of a revolution. . . What man has made, man may destroy.' The 'great [will] become small, the rich poor and the king a commoner'. Emile will have a carpenter's skills to protect him against the 'inscrutable changes' which will destroy the 'present order of society'.[1] The Spartan utopia is no less a call to stop. It is a warning to all those who were about to be overcome by that 'progress' so alluringly painted by those philosophers who fraudulently flattered their despotic patrons.

If both utopias are cries of alarm, neither pretends to solve the deepest agonies of man's unfortunate condition. The civil state, even at its best in Sparta, has a vast number of inconveniences, far worse than those of nature.[2] The Golden Age is not so riddled with

---

[1] *Emile*, 157.   [2] Vaughan, II, 97 (*Contrat Social*).

difficulties, but men are too volatile to bear its peace. There is, in short, no perfection, because there is no suitable abode for men. Utopia is therefore a protest against history and a challenge to its madness, not in the name of eternity, but in response to the spectacle of unremitting human suffering. And because that suffering is so limitless Rousseau was forced to accept the harsh lesson taught by classical philosophy: that wisdom is in resignation—even when one contemplates utopia.

SPARTA AND THE AGE OF GOLD

The Spartan model was, in time at least, the first one. It made its appearance in the very first of Rousseau's major writings, the *Discourse on the Arts and Sciences*, in which the ancient virtues and the modern decline of citizenship were eloquently proclaimed. The origin of the Spartan image, like all his works, whether pedagogic, political, or fictional, was, according to his own testimony, in his daydreams. He read his Plutarch in early childhood and had indulged in heroic fantasies ever since. He claimed that he became addicted to daydreaming as an apprentice, to escape from his misery, and that he had never overcome the habit because he had never made the normal transition from apprentice to master craftsman.[1] Like many timid and frail people, Rousseau was probably given to compensating for a sense of his own failings by dreaming of being a heroic figure. In this there was surely a good deal of self-hatred as well. His contemporaries were not wrong in ascribing his 'lacédémonisme aigu' to an overheated imagination.[2] For there was an element of personal identification with the ancient ideal here that was lacking among those many pupils of the Jesuits or Jansenists who also admired antiquity.[3] It was as a 'citizen of Geneva', a republican, especially, that Rousseau felt exceptionally close in

---

[1] *Confessions*, I, 9, 32. 'De là se forma ... ce gout heroique et romanesque qui n'a fait qu'augmenter jusqu'à present, et qui acheva de me degouter de tout, hors ce qui ressembloit à mes folies.' *Lettres à Malesherbes*, II, *O.C.*, I, 1134. For his heroic fancies see *ibid.* III, 1140, and I, 1131; *Ebauches des Confessions*, *O.C.*, I, 1157; *Confessions*, VI, 256; Vaughan, 314–15 (*Fragment*).

[2] Pire, '*Du Bon Plutarque au Citoyen de Genève*', 515.

[3] It is, nevertheless, important to remember their existence and influence, if one wishes to understand Rousseau. See Peter Gay, *The Party of Humanity* (New York, 1964), 9–10, 242–4.

spirit and in social experience to the ancient heroes. This feeling did not usually survive any direct contact with Geneva, but it did sustain Rousseau's spirits in his bruising encounters with the great world of Paris and its class system.[1]

Sparta and Rome were, however, not merely private daydreams for Rousseau. They had social functions. Negatively they served as swords with which to smite his contemporaries. Positively he drew from them an image of the perfectly socialized man, the citizen whose entire life is absorbed by his social role. In its turn, this picture of an integrated existence could not but illuminate the distress of actual men, who had never known the patriotic life.

The structure of argument in the *First Discourse* is a series of contrasts. The Spartan model is deliberately contrived to be the polar opposite of modern actuality. It mattered far less to Rousseau whether the heroes of Sparta and Rome had ever really existed, than that such men could *not* be found at all in modern times.[2] The vision of classical heroism is always followed by an example of modern corruption. It is an itemized account of ancient virtue and modern delinquency. Any serious criticism that could be raised against the Spartan-Rome idol was immediately met with the reply that matters were even worse now.[3] A random glance at any of Rousseau's

[1] Thus in the *Epitre à M. Bordes* of 1741, *O.C.*, II, 1130.
> Mais mois, qui connois peu les usages de France,
> Moi, fier républicain que blesse l'arrogance.
And the no less bitterly class conscious *Epitre à M. Parisot* of 1742, *ibid.* 1137–8:
> Tout petit que j'etois, foible, obscur Cytoien
> Je fesois cependant membre du souverain,
> Qu'il faloit soutenir un si noble avantage
> Par le cœur d'un Heros, par les vertus d'un sage.

> Nous n'y connoissons point la superbe arrogance.
Years later Rousseau could still let one of his heroines exclaim after a visit to Geneva that had she been born there she would have had 'l'âme toute Romaine'. *N.H.*, Part VI, Letter V. For other identifications of Sparta and Geneva, see Vaughan, I, 133–4 (*Inégalité*).
[2] *Réponse au Roi de Pologne* (Hachette), I, 35–6; Vaughan, I, 314 (*Fragment*); *Rousseau Juge de Jean-Jacques*, II, 819. Saint-Preux tells Julie to read only ancient and Swiss history, for only there can men of valor and character be found. *N.H.*, Part I, Letter XII. See also '*Préface*' à *Narcisse*, 971–2; *Letter to d'Alembert*, 19, 77–9; *N.H.*, Part II, Letter XVII; Vaughan, I, 260 (*Economie Politique*); Vaughan, II, 427–30 (*Poland*); *Emile*, 7–8, 308, 418.
[3] For example, see Vaughan, II, 97, 124–5 (*Contrat Social*); *Emile*, 7; *Réponse à M. Bordes*, 62.

later works, moreover, reveals that he consistently clung to these images. Sparta was a mirror that could always be raised to reveal modern man at his worst. To the self-satisfied, to men proud of their civilized ways and confident of the future, it was a devastating challenge.

Not the least striking aspect of Rousseau's classical model is that it is so overwhelmingly military in character. Throughout the *First Discourse* there is little discussion of any virtues other than military valor and endurance, and success in battle.[1] Nor was this a passing fancy. Admiration for the soldierly spirit was a recurrent theme in all of Rousseau's work. Geneva itself, when admired, was praised for its *ésprit guerrier*, happily divorced from the furious spirit of conquest.[2] Even Emile, who certainly would never go to war, is trained to be ready for a military expedition.[3] Rousseau knew that there were significant differences between Sparta and Rome, but their common military-civic ethos was what mattered to him. He treated them, therefore, as a single image of perfected civic mores and his Spartan utopia is an amalgam of both.[4] And martial valor was a primary feature of that utopia. So late a work as his *Considerations on the Government of Poland* shows no discernible abatement of the military enthusiasm with which Rousseau's career as a writer had begun. It is here, in fact, that the quality of the soldierly ideal is most completely revealed. It has almost nothing to do with war of any sort, and certainly nothing with the warfare of Rousseau's own age. To be sure, he recognized that Poland's problems were primarily military, and even assured the Poles that they could count on military success if they followed his plans. However, he did not show the slightest interest in, or understanding of, eighteenth-century warfare. He certainly did not offer any discussion of the military policies of Poland's mighty neighbors, nor did he present a single reason for believing that Poland, with a classical militia, would overcome their organized mercenaries. Indeed, the pseudo-realism of his Polish plan, with its endless descriptions of the details of organization and ritual, make it the

[1] *Discours: Si le Rétablissement des Sciences et des Arts a Contribué à Epurer les Mœurs* (Hachette), I, 5-6, 12-15.   [2] Vaughan, I, 127 (*Inégalité*).
[3] *Emile*, 84, 102.   [4] Vaughan, I, 314-20 (*Fragment*).

most visionary, pejoratively utopian, of his works. What does emerge, however, is the degree to which Rousseau's military schemes were instruments of political education, even if their success depended on Poland's being divided into thirty-two small republics.[1]

In Poland the choice between man and citizen is to be clearcut. A young Polish adult is not a man, he is a Pole. He may dislike and shun all foreigners as long as he is at one with his fellow-citizens. What is needed is a national soul. For, sensibly enough, Rousseau knew that Polish survival would be salvaged in the minds of the Poles, not on the battlefield.[2] The soldierly ideal finds its justification here. For the military life is the most perfect model of public service. Here, as in no other form of social endeavor, the individual loses his personal identity and becomes a part of a purposive social unit. Here alone the group absorbs all his resources, emotional as well as physical. For this, among other aspects, is an exclusively masculine society, a point not lost upon Rousseau. The one Spartan custom that he really disliked was the military training and equality of women. Secluded and excluded Roman matrons suited him far better.[3] In the citizen-army, the *moi humain* really is crushed by the *moi commun*. And this is the very essence of the psychological transformation of man into a citizen.[4]

Rousseau's admiration for the physical and ethical life of the ancient soldier did not extend to the obvious ends of classical military policy: territorial expansion and conquest. Indeed, he rejected them completely. In this he was not terribly 'realistic'. Perpetual military alertness, for defensive purposes only, has never been a convincing policy. Rousseau, however, was not concerned with policy. He hated mercenaries, not because they were impolitic, but because they served no moral ends.[5] Military activity was valuable only when it was exercised in a Spartan social order. For it was only in this setting that, what might now, perhaps vaguely, be called a 'meaningful' life, was possible. By completely internalizing

---

[1] Vaughan, II, 431, 438 (*Poland*). See Chap. 3, *infra*, for the reasons for this strange scheme. [2] *Ibid.* 432, 434, 438, 486, 491.
[3] *Emile*, 326, 329–30; *Letter to d'Alembert*, 82–92.
[4] Vaughan, I, 248 (*Economie Politique*).
[5] *Réponse à M. Bordes*, 55; Vaughan, I, 264 (*Economie Politique*); *Emile*, 420.

public ends the soldier-citizen can justify and explain his every action in terms of values that are external, shared by those around him and more general in scope than any that his purely private self could offer. He has an undivided moral self-assurance and an inner poise that are unknown to the victims of a half-socialized system; for he is not helplessly driven by a private *amour-propre*. His vanity has not been destroyed, but reoriented toward communal, public ends.[1] As such, it may make him a xenophobe, but he lives at peace with himself and with his immediate neighbors.[2] It is, thus, when he appears to be most collectivist, in his military-patriotic pose, that Rousseau's concern with the psychological condition of individual men is really at its most intense. In the case of the Polish plan there is at least the semblance of a collective aim: national survival. In most of his descriptions of the Spartan-Roman model even this is lacking. It is a picture of the public education of perfectly socialized men—who do not suffer the miseries of actual men.

Because citizenship is a matter of *self*-repression, Spartan man is also free, in at least one of the senses that Rousseau attached to that word. Not only is he secure from the hostility of his fellow citizens, he is not subject to *external* coercive pressures, because by the time he reaches maturity his education has made him completely self-disciplined.[3] It may be a morality of a lower order than that of the pure voice of conscience.[4] However, it remains self-directing. For although society supports and encourages the individual, making it relatively easy for him to do his duty, it does not go so far as to impair his independence and moral responsibility. The good of the whole never existed for Rousseau apart from the well-being of its members. Indeed, it was one of his most telling arguments against the belief in human progress and any sort of cosmic optimism that the gains made by the race as a whole in no way compensated individuals for their immediate personal sufferings.[5] In his most rigorously Spartan utopia, that of *Economie Politique*, he also insisted most on the rights of the individual, whose person and property

---

[1] Vaughan, I, 251 (*Economie Politique*); *ibid.* II, 344–5 (*Projet de Consitution pour la Corse*, hereafter cited as *Corsica*).   [2] *Ibid.* I, 242, 250–1 (*Economie Politique*).
[3] *Ibid.* 246–8 (*Economie Politique*).   [4] *N.H.*, Part III, Letter XVIII.
[5] Vaughan, I, 203 (*Inégalité*); 224 (*Letter to M. Philopolis*).

must receive complete respect.[1] That was not all. Rousseau did not think it either right or possible to ignore personal moral consciousness once it had been awakened.[2] Not even actual society which mutilates moral man can totally obliterate conscience. Spartan society, to be sure, does not allow that 'divine instinct' the scope that a purely personal morality would give it. There is not much room for choice in a system where education engraves the law upon the hearts of its children, and public opinion is always watchfully at work. Within these civic limits, however, the individual is free, needs to fear no one, and can give his moral consent to the society in which he lives because it is just. What he utterly lacks is any opportunity for self-expression. Moreover, it emerges clearly in the *Social Contract* that there are other moral and political costs. For no society of men can be perfect.

Not the least remarkable aspect of Rousseau's Spartan reveries was that out of this 'tissue of fables' he was able to draw a system of political principles.[3] For the *Social Contract* was not meant to be a plan for any future society, but a standard for judging existing institutions. It was a yardstick, not a program. 'Principles of political law' must be 'a scale' to which the laws of every polity are compared by Emile and his master when they come to apply the doctrines of the *Social Contract* to the study and judgment of actual governments.[4] Even as a scale the *Social Contract* does not present a picture of a model of a flawless political order, but of one to which men *might* aspire. Above all, that means that some degree of inequality

---

[1] *Ibid.* I, 253–4 (*Economie Politique*).

[2] *Ibid.* I, 449 (*Première Version*); II, 36 (*Contrat Social*).

[3] Rousseau wrote the *Social Contract* in part to warn the Genevans against their magistrates. *Confessions*, IX, 404–5. To that extent he was quite truthful when he said that his book was based on Genevan experience. *Lettres Ecrites de la Montagne*, VI, 204–5. As he admitted to a friend he had not, however, studied Genevan history or institutions seriously until his books were burned and his person proscribed there 'Lettre à M. J-F. De Luc', 25 octobre 1763, *C.G.*, X, 188–90. Even on those occasions when he praised Geneva as the place he loved best, he held up Rome as the model of all free peoples; for example, see Vaughan, I, 126–7 (*Inégalité*). Thus though a flowery dedication to Geneva opens the *Social Contract*, its institutions and history are scarcely ever mentioned again. Sparta and Rome are the models, and it is the institutions of the latter that receive an exhaustive discussion. Vaughan, II, 23, 91, 109–23.

[4] *Emile*, 422. 'Je cherche le droit et la raison, et ne dispute pas des faits. Cherchons sur ces règles quels jugements on doit porter des autres voies d'association civiles...', Vaughan, I, 462 (*Première Version*).

in wealth and power must be endured. For this, the heaviest cross that social life imposes upon us, is ineradicable, once we leave nature behind us.[1] That is why civil society might be made morally justifiable, but cannot be perfected. The recognition that political society is bound to involve some form of inequality explains why Rousseau was able to be relatively complacent about Spartan slavery and Polish serfdom, even though he knew them to be so utterly wrong.[2] The just civic order is not based on extremes of inequality, but it cannot expect to be either fully egalitarian or democratic. Civil life even at its conceivable best is full of inconveniences, as are all men's contrivances. Not even Sparta is a perfect abode for men.

Given these assumptions, it is not always perfectly clear what Rousseau meant when he insisted that the liberty and equality of the citizens are the only legitimate ends of civil association. In what forms of behavior do freedom and equality manifest themselves? As in so many other cases, Rousseau was most explicit in showing what they were not, what he wished to avoid. The political participation that liberty and equality demand is not a matter of self-expression. The citizens are not meant to bring their private interests, hopes, and opinions to bear upon public affairs. On the contrary, political participation is a potent form of civil education. Its importance is not in what the citizen contributes to the polity, but in what it does for him. Everything that threatens his *moi commun* is bad. All that supports it is good. Rousseau's entire case against Christianity is based on its incompatibility with the civic ethos.[3] Political participation, on the other hand, is the best and most necessary way of maintaining the civic sense. That also determines its quality.

Civic pride and devotion, however deeply felt and however gratifying, are not the same thing as social equality. And indeed Rousseau was concerned with eliminating inequality in all its

[1] Vaughan, I, 167, 190–2 (*Inégalité*); 497 (*Première Version*); II, 61 (*Contrat Social*).
[2] *Ibid.* II, 27–9, 97–8 (*Contrat Social*); 445–6, 499 (*Poland*). There was thus nothing particularly 'realistic' in his acceptance of Polish serfdom and of a very slow process of enfranchisement. He was only repeating the principles of the *Social Contract* as he, indeed, announced quite explicitly; *ibid.* II, 448, 449, 504 (*Poland*).
[3] *Ibid.* I, 503–5 (*Première Version*); II, 128–31 (*Contrat Social*); *Lettres Ecrites de la Montagne*, Part I, Letter I, 130–2; 'Lettre à Voltaire', 18 août 1756, *C.G.*, III, 303–24; 'Lettre à M. Marcet de Mézières', 24 juillet 1762, *ibid.* VIII, 35–8; 'Lettre à Usteri', 30 avril 1763, *ibid.* IX, 264–6; 'Lettre à Usteri', 18 juillet 1763, *ibid.* X, 36–40.

emotional and social manifestations, rather than with establishing an egalitarian order. Inequality for him was always an intensely personal experience, a display of cruelty and power on one side and corresponding servility and fear on the other. Above all he wanted to eliminate those opinions which bind the strong in their pride and the weak in their aspirations together into a single relationship of mutual destruction. The civic ethos does just that. It redirects *amour-propre* from pursuing personal exploitation to positive public enterprises. The whole political structure of Sparta has no other end. That is why it can absorb both competitive and inegalitarian behavior without damage to its citizens or even to their sense of sovereignty.

Rousseau complained bitterly, and with some justice, that the readers of the *Social Contract* refused to keep apart what he had been so careful to separate: sovereignty and government. The principles of the *Social Contract*, he insisted, were reducible to two: that sovereignty must rest in the hands of the people and that aristocratic government is the best of all.[1] His readers cannot be blamed entirely for their difficulties, for Rousseau made many remarks favorable to democracy and his discussion of sovereignty is not always lucid. Nevertheless, the limits of democratic government are clearly stated in the *Social Contract* and should surprise no one. Democracy may be the form of government most natural to mankind, as equality in general is natural. Civil government, however, is not natural. On the contrary, the more perfect it is, the more denatured it must be.[2] Tendencies toward self-government in republican orders such as Athens and Rome were entirely deplorable. They were lapses in civic discipline.[3] For purposes of day-to-day government frequent assemblies are not advisable. And the glory of republican citizens is in obeying their legitimate magistrates.[4]

---

[1] Vaughan, I, 241, 274-5 (*Economie Politique*); II, 40-1, 69 (*Contrat Social*); *Lettres Ecrites de la Montagne*, VIII, 224; 'Lettre à M. Marcet de Mézières', 24 juillet 1762, C.G., VIII, 35-8.

[2] Vaughan, I, 189 (*Inégalité*); 312 (*Fragment*); 449-54, 477-83 (*Première Version*); II, 51-2, 91 (*Contrat Social*).

[3] *Ibid.* II, 45, 73 (*Contrat Social*); *Lettres Ecrites de la Montagne*, Part II, Letter IX, 255; 'Lettre à Coindet', 9 fevrier 1768, C.G., XVIII, 98-105.

[4] 'Lettre à M. d'Ivernois', 9 fevrier 1768, *C.G.*, XVIII, 114-15; to same, 24 mars 1768, *ibid.* 175-8.

The proper sphere of popular action is in the exercise of sovereignty, not in that of government, and the scope of governmental power is very wide, including matters of such importance as war and peace.[1]

What, then, is sovereignty, the realm of popular civic action? That it is popular and that it is limited to the framing of general laws is clear. Beyond that, however, there is much doubt as to what sorts of activity are involved. Its ends are, however, much more certain. The fixed periodic assemblies of the people, at which they express their sovereignty, are primarily preventive in purpose. Their chief political aim is to halt the all but irresistible tendency of any government to become arbitrary and despotic. Their positive function is symbolic and ritualistic. They actually *do* very little. The 'Great Legislator' must initially give a people its fundamental institutions and put men in a condition fit for civic life. Their consent to his laws and to the forms and personnel of government is, to be sure, essential.[2] They are, however, passive even in this. Their will, the character of their consent, is created for them by an outside agent and maintained by a variety of educative pressures.[3] The very occasion of consenting, the assembly, is a device for keeping their country before their eyes, and their public selves intact.[4] Like the endless ceremonies and festivals that Rousseau urged upon the Poles, the assemblies exist to remind men of their public role.[5] Even if in just republics there is no need for public ceremonies to alleviate the stress of inequality that prevails in places like Poland, the pull of the *moi humain*, the natural self, is so great, that the artificial civic self needs constant reinforcement. The sense of citizenship cannot be left to take care of itself.

The social contract, the creation of a rightful bond of association, is not only an act and an agreement. It is a continuing process. To keep a man in a psychological state in which 'he was neither Caius nor Lucius, he was a Roman' is a perpetual affront to his nature, and one that cannot be relaxed. The social contract is a constant transformation. For justice to replace instinct, and the idea of

---

[1] Vaughan, II, 41 (*Contrat Social*).
[2] *Ibid.* II, 39–46, 101–2 (*Contrat Social*); 447 (*Poland*); 98–100 (*Contrat Social*).
[3] *Ibid.* II, 51–4 (*Contrat Social*); I, 322, 328, 336 (*Fragment*); 248–50 (*Economie Politique*); II, 427, 440 (*Poland*); *Letter to d'Alembert*, 22, 67, 74.
[4] Vaughan, II, 95–6 (*Contrat Social*).   [5] *Ibid.* II, 434–5 (*Poland*).

duty that of appetite, requires an unceasing effort. Self-love and distaste for the sight of sufferings, man's uncertain and impulsive natural equipment, must be superseded at every turn, if patriotism and the morality of general rules, impersonally applied, are to dominate his behavior. That is why government is a matter of education in the truly civic order. Its benefits are not negligible. The citizen is a man without inner conflicts and he finds it easy to do his duty.[1] His *amour-propre* is socialized and does not fill him with insatiable personal ambitions and frustrations. And an active soldierly life leaves him no idle hours in which he might indulge in reflection and regret. In every way he is free from the miseries that haunt the inhabitants of modern cities. Fortunately for Rousseau and his readers this is not the only model of a better life open to mankind.

The full cost of Spartan life can hardly be estimated until civic man is compared to a member of a happy family, living in the Golden Age. For Rousseau's other model, that of the quiet village, is in every respect the very opposite of the ancient city. The happiness of men in the Golden Age, the paradigm of the utopia of innocence, springs from one source only, unspoiled family love. And the Spartan city is explicitly built on the destruction of the family and of all its emotional and social gratifications.[2] The perfect Spartan mother is indifferent to the death of her sons as she gives thanks for victory on the battlefield. Brutus kills his sons to preserve the republic. These conquests over natural feeling are not easy, but they are the very essence of citizenship.[3] If citizens are to be denatured so as to identify wholly with the republic, then their loyalties must not be shared with a family. That is why paternal authority, which is a mere expression of natural solicitude, cannot be a model for republican magistrates who need 'more sublime virtues'. Indeed,

---

[1] *Emile*, 7; Vaughan, II, 88–9, 36–7, 40, 69–70 (*Contrat Social*). He may not be happy, but he is at one with himself and others. Vaughan, II, 326–7 (*Fragment*).
[2] Vaughan, I, 237–40, 280 (*Economie Politique*); 462–6 (*Première Version*). In the *Social Contract* Rousseau was later to say that the family was the model of political society because it was the oldest and most natural. The only meaning this could have, given the principles developed later in that work, is that the family is the proof of man's capacity for association in general. Vaughan, II, 24 (*Contrat Social*). Only once, in *Emile*, did he really wonder if the family would or should be destroyed; 326.
[3] *Réponse à M. Bordes*, 59–60; *Emile*, 8; Vaughan, I, 337 (*Fragment*).

within the city the family cannot even play an educative role. The rearing of young citizens must be left to distinguished magistrates and soldiers, not to the personal inclinations of parents.[1]

Although it is more spontaneously gratifying than the civic order, the family household is also a social institution, and not the natural state of man.[2] As such it is, in its perfect form, quite as unattainable as any other social model. This, too, is a utopia, not a plausible plan of action. To be sure, its realization would not depend on a great leader and collective conditions, as the setting up of a republican order does. Anyone *can* simply leave civilization behind him and set up an isolated family. But the fantastic care with which Emile is educated in order to be able to do just that shows how difficult such a choice would be. Indeed, it is a duty, for 'one of the examples which the good should give to others is that of a patriarchal, rural life, the earliest life of man, the most peaceful, the most natural, and the most attractive to the uncorrupted heart'.[3] Unhappily there are no good men and no uncorrupted hearts left in a world in which inequality has destroyed simplicity. And inequality is not just the lot of modern man. It is the fundamental condition of all historic life, ever since 'grain and iron' were introduced to end the prehistoric age.[4] 'Neufchatel perhaps unique on earth,' and an occasional village in the Alps, remind us of what we might have been.[5] However, these outposts of uncivilized happiness are doomed by history.[6] Even Rousseau's two imaginary accounts of isolated family bliss end in failure. Emile, brought up so carefully to be a man, leaves his rural abode, and he and his wife destroy their marriage in Paris.[7] Julie recognizes as she dies that her perfect family life had not made her happy, since she could not bear to renounce Saint-Preux's love.[8] Torn between sexual inclination and

---

[1] Vaughan, I, 255–8; 278–9 (*Economie Politique*).
[2] A. O. Lovejoy, 'The Supposed Primitivism of Rousseau's Discourse on Inequality', *Essays in the History of Ideas* (New York, 1960), 14–37; H. V. S. Ogden, 'The Antithesis of Nature and Art and Rousseau's Rejection of the Theory of Natural Rights', *American Political Science Review*, XXXII (1936), 643–54; *Emile*, 368–9.
[3] *Emile*, 438.   [4] Vaughan, I, 176 (*Inégalité*).
[5] *Letter to d'Alembert*, 60.
[6] 'Lettre à M. Jacob Vernet', 29 novembre 1760, *C.G.*, V, 270–2; *Réponse au Roi de Pologne* (Hachette), I, 46.   [7] *Emile et Sophie*, Hachette, I, 1–22. See Appendix.
[8] *N.H.*, Part VI, Letter XII. See Appendix.

moral duty she can find happiness in neither. Sooner or later her effort to live in isolated rural bliss must fail, because it is psychologically impossible to overcome the effects of social life: inner conflict.[1] The model of simplicity is no more available to actual men than the civic one. Both should be contemplated and sought, but neither can be attained.

Although the Golden Age is one of villages, the only social life that matters is within each household. This, moreover, shelters not a clan, but only a primary family, parents and their children. Self-sufficient and self-contained, they need no one but each other. Theirs is the only relationship free from *amour-propre*. Only within the family is perfect uncompetitive affection possible. Here alone self-love and love for others are one. Only here are goodness and happiness inseparable, as *égalité d'âme*, instead of inner tension, is the common state of man.[2] And this is as true of the family of a Swiss peasant as of the Wolmars at Clarens, as long as they do not step outside their intimate circle. For the individual households ought not to meet frequently and must in no way depend on one another. In Neufchatel during the long winter the weather keeps each family confined to its own house.[3] In the Haut Valais the rarity of strangers of any sort has reduced suspicion and self-consciousness so much that its families are the most generous and hospitable people on earth. The adjacent Bas Valais, in contrast, is much frequented by travelers and merchants. Its inhabitants are inevitably hostile and mean.[4] The peasantry of France, of course, oppressed by tax collectors, is reduced to a state of constant fear and mistrust.[5] It is not peasant life as such, but the absence of social contacts other than family relationships, that creates ease and happiness.

Once the autonomy of the family is established it can remain happy in a variety of ways. The men of the Golden Age were ignorant boors, whose only intellectual attainment was the acquisition of language.[6] The mountaineers of Neufchatel, however, are

[1] *Emile*, 9.   [2] *N.H.*, Part V, Letter II; Part I, Letter XXIII.
[3] *Letter to d'Alembert*, 60–3; *Emile*, 26.   [4] *N.H.*, Part I, Letter XXIII.
[5] *Confessions*, IV, 163–4. For the importance of Rousseau's encounter with an oppressed peasant see C. J. Friedrich, *Inevitable Peace* (Cambridge, Mass., 1948), 161–3.
[6] Vaughan, I, 153–4 (*Inégalité*); *Essai sur l'Origine des Langues* (Hachette), I, 384–5.

not badly educated.[1] Emile is not illiterate, even though his intellectual equipment is not very complex. Rousseau did not favor a brutish ignorance, but he thought that knowledge should not exceed the faculties of ordinary people, that it should limit itself to a human scale.[2] Above all it should not become an instrument of *amour-propre*, a weapon in social combat. When opportunities for mischief are few, and when man's natural laziness has been overcome without reaching the perpetual activity of the civilized, then the arts and crafts and books are not at all harmful. They are neither means for self-disguisement, nor manifestations of luxury, but innocent and useful entertainments.[3] As long as families stay away from each other, there is no reason why they should long for the pure state of nature, which is one of fear and suspicion, fed by ignorance.[4]

The real joys of the Golden Age, in all its versions, arise from the relations of the members of the family to each other. It is the *absence* of strangers that allows one to say exactly what one thinks, to express all one's feelings in perfect confidence, and simply to be whatever one is. It is the very paradise of unrestrained self-expression, but it is not an idle one. The family has a purpose, and an overwhelmingly important one: the education of the children. This is the Wolmars' chief occupation.[5] The child-centered family was undeniably born on the pages of *Emile* and *La Nouvelle Héloïse*. Rousseau thought that the creating of new men has its gratifications for parents also; it is their final self-fulfillment, the completion of their own education. That is why complete solitude cannot be an ideal condition. It is not good for man to live alone. Emile must marry and raise a family.[6] Solitude is, at best, the last resort of those who have lost all hope of friendship. The ultimate end of man, the condition that makes a Wolmar god-like, is to be a father and the head of a household.[7] A man is complete only when he is ready to become a father. That is the last act of the drama of Emile's education—of man, that is.

[1] *Letter to d'Alembert*, 60–3.
[2] *Emile*, 82–3, 147, 151, 161; *Réponse au Roi de Pologne*, 31, 33, 44.
[3] Vaughan, I, 172–3, 175 (*Inégalité*); *Essai sur l'Origine des Langues*, 388; *Préface à Narcisse*, 969–70.
[4] *Essai sur l'Origine des Langues*, 384; Vaughan, I, 293–4 (*L'état de guerre*).
[5] *N.H.*, Part IV, Letter XI; Part V, Letter II; Part V, Letter III.
[6] *Emile*, 321. [7] *N.H.*, Part IV, Letter X; Part III, Letter XX.

Within the happy family there is no inequality, according to Rousseau. In fact, however, he was a firm believer in paternal supremacy. This was the one form of inequality that he did not even recognize as such, because he did not think that it created any of the emotional miseries that every other sort of inequality brought with it. In any case, paternal authority, at its best, is limited. Children who have reached the age of reason ought to become the equals of their parents as in the Haut Valais.[1] Women, however, are always meant to be the obedient inferiors of their husbands, in principle at least. When Rousseau came to draw a picture of the perfect family, he made the mother fully the equal of the father. It is she, in fact, who is the dominating spirit of the family. The only real form of inequality that exists as part of domestic society arises when servants and laborers are employed. It is only when there are human relationships other than those between members of the primary family and, perhaps, their dearest friends, that inequality appears. A wise, patriarchal employer can do much to diminish its injustice and its impersonal cruelty, but he cannot erase it. The family is the one and only society that is not subject to the evils of inequality. That is why it is the essence of the Golden Age.

The equality of the Golden Age throws a harsh light upon all other forms of society, for it reveals the psychological destructiveness that rendered inequality so odious in Rousseau's eyes. It is, indeed, the absence of inequality, rather than equality as a positive benefit, that, in his usual negative mode of thought, concerned him most. When inequality and *amour-propre* do not exist, as they do not among people who enjoy a perfect intimacy, then each one can express fully his undisguised self and recognize others as they really are, not as assumed *personae*.[2] In the letter about his visit to the Swiss peasant family, Saint-Preux is even allowed to dwell freely on the sexual attractions of the women. The tone is quite unlike the prudish circumlocution in which he and his mistress generally engage. In the Swiss village the constraints imposed by civilization and inequality are so relaxed that there is even no tension between

---

[1] *Ibid.* Part I, Letter XXIII; Vaughan, II, 24 (*Contrat Social*).
[2] *Rousseau Juge de Jean-Jacques*, II, 812–13; *N.H.*, 'Séconde Préface'; Part IV, Letter XI.

masters and domestic servants. Consider the contrast presented by Paris, where Saint-Preux sees 'many masks but no human faces!'[1] Here master and servant live in a state of mutual hostility and common corruption; 'neither belongs to a family, but only to a class'.[2] Above all, how could one ever forget Mme de Vercellis, who would never see a person, but only her footman, in Rousseau?[3] For it was less the injustice than the coldness of wealth that infuriated Rousseau. The sympathies of the rich simply atrophy as they cut themselves off from the poor.[4] However, just because inequality is so much a matter of attitude, much can be done to alleviate its effects, if not its actuality. The rich have a duty 'never to make people conscious of inequalities of wealth'. They also must work, shun luxury, and remain open to pity.[5] If this does not bring about perfection, it at least allows people to accept their positions.[6] Recognize the dignity of physical labor, remain on the land, and preserve the peace of society.[7] It is the least painful condition.

Rural society is not, of course, necessarily moral, just as not all families would flourish simply by leaving the city. It is worth the effort, if only because the family living in the midst of polite society, which allows conventional public values to intrude into every corner of its life, can offer no moral or psychological support to its members.[8] The family which withdraws both physically and spiritually from the city at least provides a setting within which self-communion and self-expression might flourish. But it is not isolation as such that has a universal value; it is the mental ability to escape into oneself that matters. Men must learn to enter into their own hearts to find again the sources of virtue that society has stifled. This is a form of self-healing, a recovery of one's true self which can always be attempted.[9] The good family encourages it, the bad prevents it. In these reflections Rousseau surely had a profound intuition of one of the functions that the primary family would

---

[1] *N.H.*, Part I, Letter XXIII; Part II, Letter XIV.
[2] *Emile*, 369; *N.H.*, Part IV, Letter X. [3] *Confessions*, II, 82.
[4] *Ibid.* IV, 147; *Emile*, 182–7, 190. [5] *Emile*, 314.
[6] *N.H.*, Part IV, Letter X; Part V, Letters II, VII.
[7] *Emile*, 158; Vaughan, II, 310–11, 317, 346–7 (*Corsica*).
[8] *N.H.*, 'Séconde Préface'; Part II, Letter XVII.
[9] *Rousseau Juge de Jean-Jacques*, 687; 'Lettre à Vernes', 25 mars 1758, *C.G.*, II, 314–15; 'Lettres Morales', VI, 369–70; Starobinski, *op. cit.*, 50, 126.

fulfill in modern civilization: to shut out the public world and to protect its members against its pressures. Even when the social prerequisites of rural self-sufficiency have been destroyed, the family remains as the last refuge from a hostile external world, and also from those competitive and aggressive urges within each person which create and sustain organized oppression and which drive him back into it. The family might preserve at least a semblance of those gratifications which the progress of inequality has so systematically undermined.

Given the negative, defensive social purpose of the autonomous family group, it is not altogether surprising that Rousseau found it quite difficult to envision any communal ties among the separate households. The Golden Age is less pre-political than anti-political. 'The entire universe is nothing to its inhabitants.' After arranging marriages, neighbors do not have to meet often, and, indeed, prefer not to. There are no nations, no public units at all.[1] Nevertheless, Rousseau did suggest that these families might overcome their indifference to each other sufficiently to form some sort of political society. The Swiss canton is the replica of such families, and the peasant in a 'free state' is said to be the happiest of men.[2] This notion also guided Rousseau in his plan for Corsica. However, it is precisely this attempt that also reveals the political limitations of familial society. For it becomes plain that as long as it flourishes there is no real need for public organization and for the human dispositions that this involves. The first part of the Corsican project holds up rural Switzerland as the model to be imitated. Even the *Social Contract*, which is so much a distillation of the Spartan dream, contains a hint of this village model. The pure democracy of the Swiss canton shows the possibility of men who are as happy as they are equal and wise in their collective behavior. The Corsicans, afflicted by a general poverty, might learn to live as democratically, if they made equality the fundamental law of all their institutions. This, the true *système rustique*, would give each family no object beyond keeping itself comfortable and perpetuating the existing state of affairs. Above all, no cities! There

[1] *Essai sur l'Origine des Langues*, 385, 392; Vaughan, II, 320 (*Corsica*).
[2] *N.H.*, Part I, Letter XXIII; Part V, Letter II.

would be no conflicts of interest, since a shared poverty would give rise to no resentments; it is inequality that generates hostility. Under such circumstances a few magistrates chosen at frequent elections would provide all that was needed in the way of imposed government. Direct self-determination, as in the Swiss cantons, would take care of all other common needs.[1]

Idyllic as this prospect must have seemed to Rousseau, he was not able to believe that the 'true rustic system' could endure. Sooner or later *amour-propre* would emerge to do its destructive worst. Moreover, he had been asked to provide a plan of government for the whole island of Corsica, not only for its individual villages. Both of these considerations forced him to abandon the Swiss canton and to return to Sparta for a model. After all, had he not, in the *Social Contract*, declared Corsica to be the last remaining place fit for civic legislation? With the discussion of public finances, the need for which is never made clear, Swiss imagery suddenly disappears from the Corsican project and is replaced by Spartan-Roman tones. The socialization of *amour-propre* through civic integration replaces the calm of family life. Public pride, patriotism, and the whole program of denaturation are brought out again, implicitly demonstrating the fragility of the Golden Age.[2] This split in the Corsican project only mirrors that of the *Social Contract*. Its conditions of legitimacy are compatible only with 'rustic democracy', but that is impossible, so men must settle for Spartan-Roman government, which may not be legitimate. However, his main concern was not legitimacy. The Corsicans are to remain underdeveloped, at any cost. Whatever they chose to become, men or citizens, Swiss or Romans, they were to avoid material progress, and with it, the implacable advances of inequality. Rousseau never wavered in this denial.

In advising the Corsicans to remain primitive Rousseau was not only protecting them against the evils of civilization, but against change as such. Change was the proof of the imperfection of all human life. For it is imagination and memory, the sense of a lost past and of future possibilities, that prevent men from enjoying the present and from prolonging it by remaining

[1] Vaughan, II, 102–3 (*Contrat Social*); 309–34 (*Corsica*).
[2] *Ibid.* 61 (*Contrat Social*); 336–8, 343–7 (*Corsica*).

28

inactive.[1] The Golden Age is dull and men are restless. That is its great defect.[2] It cannot last. It is a fault that also afflicts civic society.[3] Rousseau went well beyond the obvious utopian consideration that a perfected model can suffer only changes for the worse, that here alteration and deterioration must be synonymous. He thought that any experience of change was always psychologically debilitating. Change meant uncertainty and upheaval for those who lived through it and as such it was at all times a source of suffering. Hope itself was psychologically disruptive, because it disturbed one's inner repose. Nothing set Rousseau more drastically apart from the prophets of progress than these psychological considerations. They also led him to regard social immobility as the best possible policy under all conditions, even iniquitous ones. Thus ancient Egypt, surely not his ideal, could be praised because sons had been forced to follow the occupations of their fathers.[4] The laws regulating inheritance of property and taxation should always aim at stabilizing the prospects of families.[5] Wolmar does his best to persuade his peasant neighbors to accept their social positions and to stay in their native village.[6] The purpose of these policies is always the same: to avoid ambition and frustration and to foster resignation.

Not only change, but social complexity also is disturbing. In fact, the two go together. The division of labor is the source of both these related evils. Village society is not only uneventful, its social structure is elemental. In this it is the non-city, rather than any actual place. It is the sum of all that Rousseau missed in Paris. It is not a complex web of relationships, it is not based on specialization of functions, and, above all, it is not riven by the inequalities that necessarily mark urban life.[7] The division of labor, the vehicle of progress, was evidently nothing but an infernal engine in Rousseau's eyes. It is part of that process by which men have become the victims of a system they have themselves created.[8] Not only does it make

[1] See, for example, *Rêveries*, v, 1046.   [2] *Essai sur l'Origine des Langues*, 392–3.
[3] Vaughan, II, 91 (*Contrat Social*).
[4] *Emile*, 9; *Lettre à Christophe de Beaumont, Archevêque de Paris*, Hachette, III, 96.
[5] Vaughan, I, 259–60 (*Economie Politique*); II, 479–81 (*Poland*).
[6] *N.H.*, Part IV, Letter X; Part V, Letter II.   [7] Vaughan, I, 176–9 (*Inégalité*).
[8] *Rousseau Juge de Jean-Jacques*, II, 828.

for hostility between men forced to depend upon each other, but it deforms each one. Even in the unlikely event that there should be a society in which talents and employments were perfectly matched, and each person were to occupy the position for which he was suited, the division of labor would still impose hardships. For the cultivation of specialized talents does not fulfill any basic human need, while living a quiet self-sufficient life does. Whatever the 'objective' needs of society, the cost to its individual members was too high.[1]

The combination of a psychology and a moral outlook exclusively concerned with the needs of the individual, an extreme hatred for inequality, and an intense dislike for change make it particularly useless to impose the conventional classifications of later political theory upon Rousseau. He was neither a traditionalist nor a revolutionary of any sort. So deep a hatred of inequality is a perpetual challenge to any known society. The demand that the psychological and moral integrity of individuals must be served before all else is always radical. Before such uncompromising standards all history stands condemned.[2] Nothing could be more radical than this criticism. It is just as clear that Rousseau's preference for peace, stability, and resignation is incompatible with any sort of social activism or programmatic politics. And, in fact, Rousseau was intent upon only one thing: judgment. To reveal the failures of actuality and to condemn the unpardonable was enough. It was an exercise in indignation. To this end his two models were admirably suited. Together they showed what men had lost by failing to make their choice between humanity and citizenship, and how they had forever denied themselves both inner and social peace.

Although both models are remote from history and although men are never likely to be capable of making the necessary choice between them, they did represent the psychological poles between which the generations since Rousseau have oscillated. Whether to

---

[1] *N.H.*, Part V, Letter II.

[2] Indeed, it is only by slighting this element in Rousseau's thought that it is possible to call him a 'reactionary utopist', for example, Alfred Cobban, *Rousseau and the Modern State* (London, 1934), 198. No less misleading are efforts to reduce him to a respectable conservative moralist; for example, Iring Fetscher, *Rousseaus Politische Philosophie* (Neuwied-Rhein, 1960), 259–62 and Bertrand de Jouvenel, 'Essai sur la Politique de Rousseau', *Du Contrat Social* (Geneva, 1947), 18–20, 35–6, 131.

lose oneself in the service of the public cause or to cultivate the private joys was to be a choice that was to confront men continually, and which defined the possible forms of behavior open to them. It was not the least of Rousseau's merits that he was perfectly clear about the costs of either choice. The denial of one's *moi humain* and the rejection of a *moi commun* are both losses. The Spartan city excludes all private affections and associations, not only the family. It precludes contemplative and universal religiosity, as all inclinations are bent before xenophobia, communal isolation and pride, and a virtue that is sustained by the pressure of public opinion rather than by benevolence or love.[1] Village life would seem infinitely more attractive by comparison. Self-love here leads effortlessly to a love of humanity. A Christianity designed to comfort and console can flourish here.[2] Education is made to support the more amiable aspects of man's endowment, and to suit him to society without destroying these. The lazy and stupid animal is socialized without being denatured.[3] Nevertheless, this is not a faultless state either. It is stultifying in its dullness. The peasant or man of the Golden Age is brutish and stupid. He is quite capable of irrational violence when he confronts anyone other than his family.[4] Happily he rarely does see anyone else. Rousseau was not blind to the coarseness of village life. Only the artificially created village, the cultivated family withdrawing to the land really seemed idyllic. This, too, has its flaws; the impact of civilization cannot be shaken off by mere physical escape. Its psychological imprint is indelible and warps or destroys these efforts to retreat into rustic life. To live like a peasant one must be a real peasant, and that is a condition which, although it is golden, is not lacking in blemishes. The wish to play a public role, to develop one's civic capacities, to belong to a purposeful order, to

---

[1] Vaughan, I, 242–3 (*Economie Politique*); II, 42–3, 103–4 (*Contrat Social*).

[2] *N.H.*, 'Séconde Préface', 16–17; *Rousseau Juge de Jean-Jacques*, I, 669–72; II, 864–5.

[3] *N.H.*, Part V, Letter VIII; *Emile*, 57–8.

[4] Vaughan, I, 174–5 (*Inégalité*). In writing to his patron, M de Luxembourg, Rousseau gave delightful and humorous accounts of Swiss peasant life which were not free from malice and certainly did not ignore the crudities of rustic man. Whether Rousseau was simply trying to amuse a great nobleman at the expense of his folk-heroes or whether he was, for once, describing actuality as he knew it to be, is hard to say. In any case, it does point to the function of his model, which was less to idealize the simple life than to show up the evils of contemporary society. 'Lettre à M. le Maréchal de Luxembourg', 20 janvier 1763, *C.G.*, IX, 61–8.

take part in an organized drama, is as much a part of a morally adult life as the desire to be a self-sufficient whole, united only with those whom one loves and independent of all that interferes with one's real needs. Choose, however, one must, or rather ought, even though one never does. To recognize the choice, at the very least, is to escape from the unthinking misery of actuality. Even if nothing is gained thereby in inner peace or social unity, one has been forced into an act of awareness which can never be undone. It was Rousseau's purpose to disturb the unconcerned, and he succeeded simply by drawing a map of the worlds that might be, but that never were or would be. 'He felt obliged to speak the truth without disguise,' he wrote, 'he had seen evil and had tried to find its causes.'[1] Others, more brave or more insane, might choose to do something about it, but not he. He was on a voyage of discovery, not on a military expedition.

[1] *Réponse à M. Bordes*, 65.

2

MORAL PSYCHOLOGY

THE BIOGRAPHY OF EVERYMAN

The road away from nature might have led man to Spartan virtue or to domestic bliss. In actuality he chose civilization, a condition in which neither duty nor felicity is possible. How did it come about? To answer this question required an exploration into that 'history of the human heart' which was also 'the genealogy' of the vices.[1] For Rousseau saw the history of the species, not as a succession of events, but as the moral and psychological biography of 'man in general'.[2] Introspective psychology, which served him so well in writing his autobiography, was also applied to his review of the process by which 'man in general' had enslaved himself. 'I write less the history of these events [of my life] in themselves than that of the state of my soul, as they occurred', he proclaimed.[3] That also was how the sorry biography of mankind was written.

Rousseau's profound debt to Lockean sensationalist psychology was evident in all these endeavors, whether autobiographical or impersonal, but he added to that theory a new kind of introspection and a moral sensibility which were transforming. The psychology of learning became in his hands a psychology of feeling and suffering and an indictment of civilization so extensive that it touched every aspect of individual and collective experience. It was from Locke directly, or indirectly through Condillac, that Rousseau learned 'this historical, plain method'.[4] His account of man's drift into civilization was a genetic one. It was not, however, the history of political or sociological actualities. Rousseau left that to Montesquieu whom he did not wish to repeat or follow, but to augment.[5] Like Locke he was too deeply individualist to forget for long the experiences of the human soul as a discrete, personal entity.

[1] *Lettre à Christophe de Beaumont*, 64.
[2] It was to 'man in general' also that this history was addressed; that is, to that which is common to the species at all times and in all places. Vaughan, I, 141 (*Inégalité*).
[3] *Ébauches des Confessions*, 1150. See also *Confessions*, VII, 278.
[4] John Locke, *An Essay Concerning Human Understanding*, *Works* (London, 1823), I–III, Bk. I, Ch. I, s. 2.　　　　　[5] *Emile*, 432.

33

Moreover, the moral drama was, for him, the interplay between social situations created by men and the experiences individuals endure in them. And if society had been man's undoing in actuality, it might also be his salvation.[1] This drama was not an historical one. It did not use facts to illuminate other facts. It was to replace 'the truth of facts' with 'moral truth'. And it rested in the depth of the human heart.[2] Rousseau can scarcely be said to have written either history or a philosophy of history. He did offer a reconstruction of the psychic growth of immorality and oppression and with them the emergence of their opposites, morality and freedom, as possibilities ever-present to man. The events of history are mere stage settings, the action is that of the soul's response and aspirations. And the soul is that of Everyman, as Rousseau had come to know it in himself.

The first experience of any human being is the feeling of helplessness. It is also the source of all our miseries and wickedness. The first cry of the baby is a call for help. The second is an effort to tyrannize over his mother.[3] Dependence and the desire to dominate are born simultaneously. As soon as men become aware of others they develop an artificial self that is a response to imagined, rather than to real needs. The original natural self answers only to the call of the senses for satisfaction and comfort, and these should be met. If a child develops the habit of ordering people around he is doomed to dependence on others. He should, rather, be taught 'to confine [his] wishes within the limits of [his] powers'.[4] Real strength comes from realistic desires.[5] To have no others is the only way men can avoid abusing their own and each other's powers. A good mother, like Julie, discourages the despotic urges of her children. She protects them and provides for all their physical and emotional needs, but she makes them completely aware of the laws of necessity. To that, and that alone, they learn to submit without a murmur. Their imagination is controlled, they develop no habits and no concern for past or future.[6] They are the masters of their inner life, as is Emile, victims of neither memory nor anticipation. Their independence and self-reliance is complete. They see other men

---

[1] Vaughan, I, 323 (*Fragment*); 454 (*Première Version*).   [2] *Rêveries*, IV, 1033.
[3] *Emile*, 33.   [4] *Ibid.* 35, 128.   [5] *Ibid.* 45.
[6] *N.H.*, Part V, Letter III; *Emile*, 46–9, 125–6; *Pensées*, XLIX, 1309.

'not as tools to be used', but as beings like themselves, subject to the same necessities, sensations and pains. Compassion and independence combine to stifle any malevolence.[1]

Health and happiness depend entirely on independence and on the ability to be and feel self-sufficient. The most solid basis of happiness is to desire nothing that is not within one's reach. The free man alone finds his happiness because he 'desires what he is able to perform and [to do] what he desires'.[2] The tyrant is only a spoiled child, feeble precisely because he depends on other men to gratify his wishes. Cruelty is a response to fear and weakness.[3] Society moreover is a system of dependence. Artifical needs lead men together, but their feebleness is not overcome by association.[4] On the contrary the growth of social awareness weakens men and out of weakness comes the desire for domination. The biography of 'man in general' is the movement from illusion to enslavement.

To Rousseau the two most fundamental and pervasive realities of civilized life were inequality and oppression. From the first stirrings of that *amour-propre*, which is the desire for inequality, to an ever-widening web of constraints, mankind has devised its own psychological and physical chains. 'The first source of evil is inequality', he wrote in an early pamphlet.[5] It is a phrase that could have appeared in any one of his writings. Nor was there ever any doubt in his mind about the outcome. 'Civilized man is born and dies a slave. The infant is bound up in swaddling clothes, the corpse is nailed down in his coffin. All his life man is imprisoned by our institutions.'[6] To understand the ways in which this had come about was the chief end of Rousseau's moral psychology.

Rousseau was very much aware that 'the genius of men in groups is very different from the character of the individual man and that we have a very imperfect knowledge of the human heart if we do not also examine it in crowds'. He was to engage in some very fascinating explorations of the effects of opinion and association in creating group wills. Nevertheless, as he goes on to say, 'to judge of men we must study the individual man, and that he who has a perfect

[1] *Emile*, 34, 174-5, 183-4.   [2] *Ibid.* 47-9; *Pensées*, XXXI, 1305.
[3] *Essai sur l'Origine des Langues*, 384.
[4] Vaughan, I, 167, 203 (*Inégalité*); 447-8 (*Première Version*).
[5] *Réponse au Roi de Pologne*, 41.   [6] *Emile*, 19.

35

knowledge of the inclinations of each individual' might foresee what a nation, for instance, would be like.[1] The *Discourse on Inequality* being the biography of 'man in general' and *Emile* that of an imaginary child have the same structure, both are individual life-histories. The differences, to be sure, are striking. *Emile* is brought up *not* to repeat the errors of the species, he is a well-born 'victim snatched from prejudice'.[2] Each new-born child is a new opportunity and a new hope. The tragic tone of the early pages of *Emile* arises from the knowledge that the promise will not be fulfilled and that the swaddling clothes will inevitably strangle each new child's intelligence and goodness. 'Man in general' is an imaginary creature in that he is an unknown man, denuded of all acquired character-istics. The child, however, is naturally at birth in a state of pure potentiality.[3] 'We are born capable of learning, but knowing nothing, receiving nothing.'[4] However, Rousseau never was so simple as to confuse philogenesis and ontogenesis or to regard the savage as any sort of child. The child is stupid because he is immature. The peasant is stupid because his faculties have been stunted by oppression. But the savage is neither undeveloped nor dull. He is merely uncivilized.[5] *Emile* is not to emulate him. However, in order to keep a child unspoiled the genesis of degener-ation must be fully understood and in the *Second Discourse* its high-points are exposed, one by one. To show how 'anyman' became miserable, and how 'anychild' might yet be made healthy, meant that their common psychology had to be traced. Above all, it meant that the danger that faces each child so overwhelmingly must never be forgotten. Natural man, savage man and growing boy must at every turn be confronted with actuality: the miserable image of civilized man, swaddled and coffined. The two biographies are therefore also studies in the contrast between potential man and actual man.

The life-history of our species, in Rousseau's view, begins not with any known, but with a hypothetical man, the man of pure sensation, a being shorn of every attribute that might conceivably be social in its origin. Beyond a sense of his own existence and self-love,

---

[1] *Emile*, 202.   [2] *Ibid.* 20.   [3] Vaughan, I, 134 (*Inégalité*); *Emile*, 28–31.
[4] *Emile*, 28.   [5] *Ibid.* 82–3.

expressed in the instinct for survival, he has nothing within him except his potentialities.[1] He is the pure man of sensationalist psychology. Self-awareness is a matter of intuition, the ability to feel pain and pleasure are innate, and everything else is acquired through psychic processes set in motion by contact with the external world. He is Locke's blank slate to all intents and purposes.[2] Rousseau's interest in this approach to human development was more than passing. He had indeed planned to compose a treatise on the psychology of learning which he meant to call *la morale sensitive* or *le matérialisme du sage*. It was to describe all the environmental forces which act upon 'our machine and consequently upon our soul'. The force of climate, of sound, of repose, in fact everything impinging upon man, was to be examined in its effects on him, in order that his present vices might be prevented by 'forcing the animal economy to favour the moral order within us'.[3] No such book was ever written, but both *Emile* and *La Nouvelle Héloïse* fulfill its intentions. Above all, in the *Lettres Morales*, addressed to Mme d'Houdetot, Rousseau gave a perfect account of his moral psychology.

In one respect Rousseau's ideas remained always closer to those of Locke than to the more radical sensationalism of the later Condillac and of Helvétius. Like Locke he always believed that there were at least some latent potentialities natural to man, which were only aroused by external stimuli, but which were not *created* directly by these experiences. It is, moreover, just these powers that most distinguish men from other animals. Locke, concerned with man's understanding, pointed to intellectual possibilities, most notably that of combining simple ideas into complex ones. For our moral understanding, he saw, moreover, the 'candle of the Lord,' in us to

---

[1] Vaughan, I, 153 (*Inégalité*).

[2] On the intuitive nature of one's knowledge of one's existence and the innateness of nothing but pain and pleasure, see Locke, *Essay*, Bk. IV, Ch. 9, s. 3 and Bk. I, Ch. 3, s. 3. Rousseau's debt to Locke's and Condillac's psychological theories was enormous. For their bearing on Emile see Peter D. Jimack, 'La Genèse et la Rédaction de l'*Emile* de J.-J. Rousseau', *Studies on Voltaire and the Eighteenth Century*, XIII, 1960, 318–44; and on the *Second Discourse* see Jean Morel, 'Récherches sur les sources du *Discours de L'Inégalité*', *Annales de la Société Jean-Jacques Rousseau*, V, 1909, 143–60 and 179–98.

[3] *Confessions*, IX, 409.

help us grow, if we would only try.[1] Rousseau saw different capacities, but he also took several to be inherent. First of all he noted the ability to make choices. Secondly, there are the imagination, memory, and capacity for self-perfection. Most important of all, there is an ability to feel pity at the sight of suffering.[2] To be sure, an impetus from the external world must awaken them within men, but these powers are there nevertheless. When he came to write the *Lettres Morales* and *Emile* Rousseau added a sense of obligation, of justice, to these potentialities. Conscience is an instinct and we feel it, like any other, as a form of pain or pleasure. Pleasure attends benevolence, and remorse is, along with physical pain, the only natural woe men suffer.[3] The universality of justice was thus, for Rousseau, not deduced from any metaphysically grounded theory of human nature or any form of Stoic natural law. It was drawn solely from the evidence of introspective psychology. The laws of human nature were the laws of psychology. They are the sum of predictable human responses. That does not exhaust all that men in their indefiniteness might be and do, but it suffices to explain the moral life of 'man in general'. Conscience is just like a physical pain, *not* because moral and physical experiences are identical, far from it, but because both are specific human reactions to identifiable external pressures. Remorse is a necessary spiritual response to the memory of a bad action, just as pain is a physical reaction to bodily harm. Both are the known consequence of injury to the self, both are 'passions', and both preserve us from destruction.

The primacy of passion over reason was something that he simply accepted along with the other main principles of the new science of the mind. Certainly that was not one of his original contributions to it.[4] Rousseau's uniqueness was in his reactions to Lockean psychology. Unlike his contemporaries he did not feel liberated by it. It was not for him a weapon against traditional dogmatism and clerical authority. On the contrary, it only confirmed his deepest anxieties and his sense of victimhood. As the creature of

[1] *Essay*, Bk. I, Ch. I, 55; Bk. II, Ch. XII, ss. 1 and 2, Bk. IV, Ch. III, s. 20.
[2] Vaughan, I, 149-50, 160-1 (*Inégalité*).
[3] *Lettres Morales*, C.G., III, 360, 364-6; *Emile*, 45, 64-5, 253-4.
[4] E. Cassirer, *The Philosophy of the Enlightenment*, trans. by F. C. A. Koellin and J. P. Pettegrove (Boston, 1955), 108.

sensations, as the product of the environment, man is a passive being, the plaything of external circumstances, weak, defenseless, helpless and dependent. The fact that 'man is made for felicity' did not for Rousseau open the door to a garden of libertine delights. Far from it. It only revealed man's actual failure to find happiness. It heightened his awareness of the extent and depth of human suffering. 'Victims of the blind inconsistency of our hearts' and unable to know how to live, 'we die without having lived'.[1]

Sensationalist psychology in Rousseau's hands became the science of feeling and of suffering. It made him indifferent to epistemology, but it fed his powers as a great novelist. For Locke and his followers psychology was the study of human knowledge, an answer to the questions, 'what can we and what do we know?' Rousseau's scepticism in the face of these queries was bottomless. We know nothing and we can know nothing about this world or the next. We are sightlessly wandering about a vast universe of which each one of us has only some fantastic notion of his own. The talk of philosophers, their quarrels and succeeding systems, only show how useless and ignorant they are. Far from helping mankind, all the accumulated knowledge of the centuries has rendered us no happier and has not taught us to understand the one thing we really need to know: ourselves.[2] The only thing, in fact, that we *can* know is ourselves, and the path to self-knowledge is not the one mapped out by Locke's psychology of intellectual growth. Only a new kind of introspection, the deepest analysis of one's own feelings, can bring insight. However, even here we are not likely to achieve even a semblance of objectivity, because our fellow-men remain hidden from us, and we thus have no 'intellectual mirror' in which to see ourselves.[3]

Introspection serves, in turn, only to augment one's sense of insignificance and weakness.[4] It brings us up again against the elemental fact of our lives, our suffering. No amount of collective progress, of civilization, in the least attenuates the agonies of each individual life. On the contrary, man's creations only add to them. Rousseau saw them as only a burden, a source of self-created pain.

[1] *Lettres Morales*, 349–50.
[2] *Ibid.* 351–4.
[3] *Ibid.* 354.
[4] *Ibid.* 359.

If 'man is born to suffer, pain [being] the means to his preservation', this bodily pain is but a small part of his misery. '[It] is not the twinges of gout which make a man kill himself, it is mental suffering that leads to despair.'[1] And these ills are all of our own making. Nature teaches resignation but we refuse to heed her lessons. Even if we cannot expect to achieve a happiness that is more than 'a negative state', an absence of acute pain, we need not enhance our ills as in our weakness we have actually done.[2] Had we never learned at all, we might have suffered less. In the full history of the human heart that part which deals with our social and personal acquisitions is a tale of pure self-inflicted suffering.

Lockean psychology also began with introspection, but one looked for the growth of knowledge and judgment in oneself. Rousseau looked into his soul to find out how it felt to be gradually torn from nature and moulded into a civilizee. Where Locke, for example, saw an agent growing to independence, Rousseau saw a suffering patient subjected to deformation. With no ideas innate in us, Locke saw each one of us free at last to answer whatever question one set himself, in whatever way seemed most reasonable. No one could now use the notion of intellectual necessity to prevent men from questioning accepted belief. Knowing oneself to be self-made there would be an end to accepting too much from others on trust.[3] Autonomous man would now build, out of his own experience, principles conformable to his own understanding and so become truly rational at last. For it is precisely in the personal origin of one's beliefs that their strength should lie. 'For the floating of other men's opinions in our brains makes us not one jot the more knowing, though they happen to be true.'[4] Unfettered by received opinions men are now ready for a self-oriented education. The only worry is to protect one's intellectual 'own' from inappropriate interferences. Certainly there is no need to assist such a being. Man is morally quite strong enough to control himself. Even a child has a mind to show that he is free, that his good actions come from himself, as the result of rational calculations of hope and fear. No need for 'slavish discipline,' it only makes 'slavish men'. Argue and persuade, set

---

[1] *Emile*, 15.
[2] *Ibid.* 44.
[3] *Essay*, Bk. I, Ch. IV, s. 25 and Ch. III, ss. 21–5.
[4] *Ibid.* Bk. I, Ch. IV, s. 24.

examples, but remember, men at an early age can and should answer for themselves.[1] Let no one say 'he cannot govern his passions . . . for what he can do before a prince or a great man, he can do alone or in the presence of God, if he will'.[2] This was just what Rousseau did say. He did not doubt the need for tolerance and independence and freedom of belief. His concern was, no less than Locke's, with individual man and personal potentialities. What he did not believe was that man could govern himself, that his will was strong or that his moral weakness could ever be overcome. Locke's was the individualism of the strong, Rousseau's the individualism of the weak.

The discovery of human weakness was in himself. When Rousseau opened his *Confessions* with the ringing announcement that this was a completely unique enterprise he was not mistaken. It was written, as he proclaimed, out of a justified sense of his own difference from other men and it was meant to reveal 'a man in all the truth of nature'.[3] However much one may doubt Rousseau's impartiality in this self-defensive work, it does succeed in revealing, as he meant it to, how he had felt. Moreover, while this exercise certainly expressed Rousseau's personal need for self-justification and for exposing all his sufferings and deformities of character, it had another, impersonal, public end as well, and one that his great novel also pursued. It was meant to be a strike for sincerity and a service to others. In a world where men hide their inner selves no one can know himself or another. By presenting the history of his own soul to other men he hoped to liberate them from their self-deceptions and to bring them to that self-knowledge which alone is worthy of the name of wisdom.[4] Psychological realism had both a private and a social sphere, in the *Confessions* as well as in the *Nouvelle Héloise*.

By looking into himself to uncover those first traits which have now disappeared in most men, he was able, he felt, to paint the picture of primitive man. In him, and perhaps in him alone, natural man

---

[1] *Some Thoughts Concerning Education, Works*, IX, ss. 41, 50, 52, 54, 73, 76 and 81.
[2] *Essay*, Bk. II, Ch. XXI, s. 53.   [3] *Confessions*, I, 5.
[4] *Lettres Morales*, 369–70; Ronald Grimsley, *Jean-Jacques Rousseau* (Cardiff, 1961), 228, 260–1. See also Ian Watt, *The Rise of the Novel* (Berkeley, 1967), 9–34, for the relation between the Lockean psychology and the formally realistic novel of personality.

still survived.[1] To bring this basic man into the open was his first service to his fellow men. The second was simply to show them a true picture of another man. For even those who think they know mankind, in fact only know themselves. No one but oneself can write one's life. To fully understand oneself, however, one must know more than that. One must know at least one other man in order to have some basis for comparison. Only because he was not like other men, Rousseau felt that he was peculiarly qualified to paint that true picture of his soul, in all its gradual transformations and deformations.[2] Not only was he a being apart, because nature still spoke through him and he was willing to reveal it to others, but his experiences also had enriched his vision beyond that of other men. With no settled station in society he had been able to feel and see what others in this 'learned and philosophic century' had overlooked. He alone had been able 'to experience and observe' the entire social hierarchy. 'Let no one say that because I am only a man of the people I have nothing to say that merits the attention of the reader. . . If I have thought more and better than kings, the history of my soul is more interesting than theirs.'[3] A soul still natural, the will to look into himself and to display what he saw and unusually rich social experiences, all combined to make him the perfect historian of the human heart and the ideal novelist. Now, at last, other men could look at his soul's history and contemplate their own with a greater understanding of what was permanently human and what transient experiences had impressed upon them.

It was a difficult project, Rousseau admitted. To know mankind by looking into oneself tests all one's faculties. We are prompted by vanity to misjudge ourselves and each other at every turn. We impute our own worst motives to others and at the same time we are far from willing to face ourselves impartially. That is why a full picture of at least one other man is so necessary for everyone. Because he was unlike other men, moreover, he could offer a picture of himself that could serve as a mirror for them to see and judge themselves and others.[4] 'I conceived of a new service to mankind. That is to offer them a faithful picture of one among them

---

[1] *Rousseau Juge de Jean-Jacques*, III, 936, 939.　　[2] *Ébauche des Confessions*, 1148–9.
[3] *Ibid.* 1150.　　[4] *Ibid.* 1158–9.

so that they might learn to know themselves.'[1] To be sure the picture of himself was to prove to the world that no one could now show him 'a man better than myself'.[2] It was not, in spite of that, the portrait of a saint. Rather it was an account of the weakness that he shared with all other human beings, and which had made his and their degeneration all but inevitable. It thus revealed something common to all. He was by no means the only man who was better than he seemed. By tearing off the disguises that all men wear, one might discover that 'their faces are fairer than the mask that conceals them'.[3] If he was unlike other men, it was in his candor and lack of vanity which made it easier for him to recognize and show his inner self, but he was not morally stronger than his fellows. His vices had been caused by his situation, not by himself.[4] That was their general 'genealogy'.

All men begin with weak souls that are vulnerable and subject to the shocks inflicted upon them from without.[5] All are victims. Rousseau, however, meant to go beyond this generalized oppression to its specific social forms. Again he felt well qualified. Not only had he experienced greater hardships, but he felt these more intensely than other men. He adored liberty and could endure no constraint, no discomfort and no subjugation whatever.[6] Moreover, all society was a form of enslavement for him, since it inevitably forced him to do something he did not feel like doing. At all times it afflicted and discomfited him.[7]

Rousseau traced these emotions back to his childhood. Until adolescence he had lived in perfect equality and affection with his elders. Apprenticeship had been a terrifying shock. It gave him an intense sense of the difference between 'filial dependence and servile slavery'. He could now only see the privileges and freedom of the master, and the deprivation and enslavement that he himself had to endure. Envy began to consume him, and from then on he knew why all valets and apprentices are, and must be, scoundrels. Impotence and resentment can make them nothing else. He found

---

[1] *Mon Portrait*, 1120.
[2] *Lettres à Malesherbes*, I, 1132; *Confessions*, I, 5.   [3] *Emile*, 198.
[4] E.g. *Mon Portrait*, 1124; *Rousseau Juge de Jean-Jacques*, II, 774; *Rêveries*, VIII, 1079; *Lettres à Malesherbes*, II, 1136.   [5] *Rousseau Juge de Jean-Jacques*, I, 669.
[6] *Confessions*, I, 38.   [7] *Rêveries*, VI, 1051.

escape from this intolerable condition by fleeing into a world of fantasy and he never outgrew this bad habit. It became a permanent affliction.[1] The sense of injury also survived and was reinforced over and over again. As a valet and as a secretary his sense of subjugation was bound to flourish. He soon discovered that 'what is called good order' demanded that the weak should never obtain justice in their conflicts with the strong and 'that all unequal association is always disadvantageous to the weaker party'.[2] The Opéra had robbed him of his royalties—that was the right of the stronger.[3] No one, certainly, was in a better position to appreciate the feelings of peasants whose fields were destroyed by the hunting parties of their landlords.[4] Inclination and experience fed an overwhelming sense of social oppression until he felt surrounded by an organized conspiracy that was ubiquitous and sinister.[5] However, long before he reached that point, Rousseau had made himself the chronicler of the sufferings of victimized 'man in general'.

The life-history of our species is a record of the suffering that every human *tabula rasa* undergoes in the course of becoming civilized and in enduring that condition. That was Rousseau's personal experience, as it was now the lot of every child born within civilization. How had all this come about? How had men created a system of inequality which constrained all and kept most of them in a state of abject subjugation to the will of a few of their own kind? Certainly nature had decreed no such state. Natural man, socially naked man, is also undifferentiated man. That is the equality of sameness, and identity was always Rousseau's model of genuine human equality. To be sure there have always been natural inequalities of size, strength, age, health and intelligence. These are of no importance as long as the conditions of life are the same for all, 'simple, uniform and solitary'.[6] Without any awareness of each other and with no differentiating educative pressures to develop them, these inequalities are of no concern at all to man in nature.[7]

The existence of innately unequal *potentialities* was, however, a

[1] *Confessions*, I, 31–2.   [2] *Ibid.* VII, 325; X, 514.   [3] *Ibid.* VIII, 386.
[4] *Ibid.* XI, 574–5.   [5] E.g. *Rousseau Juge de Jean-Jacques*, I, 729, 736–40, 756–9.
[6] Vaughan, I, 140, 146 (*Inégalité*).   [7] *Ibid.* 166–8 (*Inégalité*).

matter of utmost importance to Rousseau. Without them the progress of inequality would be impossible. As soon as the process of 'perfectibility' begins, the hitherto dormant differences between men's talents become manifest and they form the basis of all subsequent inequality.[1] That is why inequality is not just man's curse. It is his fate. Rousseau was not dogmatic in his rejection of Helvétius' assertion that men at birth are identical in their powers. Like d'Alembert and Diderot he was far too sceptical, however, to accept this notion without evidence. In the *Nouvelle Héloise*, his *alter ego*, Saint-Preux, presents a very fair argument in favor of Helvétius' proposition that all differences between men are acquired through educative experiences. To be sure, since from our earliest days we are exposed to different environmental pressures, we begin very soon to develop individual personalities. Wolmar, however, demonstrates that even animals are not alike at birth. Both men agree that in raising children the existence of a distinct personality must be taken for granted, whether it be innate or acquired at an early age.[2]

Helvétius was quick to realize what Rousseau meant. His reply to Rousseau was concentrated in his most radical slogan: '*l'éducation peut tout*'.[3] That was certainly the necessary psychological foundation for political radicalism and egalitarianism. It was not Rousseau's view. Education might do much to avert our present miseries, but it was infinitely difficult and far from omnipotent. To forget that would be both to hide the distance between natural and civilized man and the extent of man's actual difficulties.

As far as natural men are concerned, it does not matter at all that their endowments differ, since they are not aware of them and do not develop them. Their laziness is so extreme that it prevents any exertion beyond the absolutely necessary. Reacting passively to the same stimuli they remain much alike. Their likeness extends to their utter indifference to each other, which is interrupted only during their brief and entirely casual sexual encounters.[4] In such a state men cannot be said to be either equal or unequal, since they are so unaware of each other as to have no relationships at all. No mutual

---

[1] *Ibid.* 178, 192 (*Inégalité*).
[2] *N.H.*, Part V, Letter III; *Emile*, 58; Helvétius, *De l'Esprit* (*Œuvres*, Paris, 1793), I, 344–6. See *infra*, Chap. 3.
[3] Helvétius, *De l'Homme*, *Œuvres*, v, 125.   [4] Vaughan, I, 163–5 (*Inégalité*).

acts of appreciation are imaginable as long as men are so 'alone and lazy'.[1] The combination of laziness and indifference to other men was something Rousseau had found in himself, as part of his peculiarly natural personality. He could use so strong a word as subjugation to describe all social life, because he felt that his spirit wanted to move at its own pace without ever having to submit to that of another.[2] His laziness was his substitute for virtue, he wrote. Since he did nothing, he did no harm.[3] This extreme love of liberty he, moreover, knew to be the fruit of pure laziness. Laziness, Rousseau assumed, was part of everyone's nature, just as labor was the characteristic pain of civilization.[4] The happiness of independence is greater than that of a great station, precisely because it is more natural. And the greatest happiness that Rousseau had ever experienced was that of a vagabond.[5] Never had he 'thought so much, existed so much, lived so much, or been so much himself' as when he wandered about aimlessly and alone.[6] It is as a vagrant that Emile eventually discovers freedom as his creator had experienced it in his own youth.[7] Vagrancy thus became the model of natural freedom, the condition of natural man as he aimlessly wanders about the uncultivated earth.

In this condition of separateness and likeness, it is clear, no distinctions of any kind can be made between men. No moral relations, conceptions or judgments are even thinkable.[8] Pre-moral man is, however, capable of one active response that has an immediate social relevance, the feeling of pity.[9] Aversion for the sight of suffering, as an extension of self-love to the sufferer, is an instinctive reaction. It is also the psychic source of all possible goodness in human relations. It arises in human beings at the most crucial period of their development, during adolescence, when it accompanies mature sexuality. It is then that it will either become a permanent disposition, or be forever crushed in the young adult.[10] Natural man

---

[1] Vaughan, I, 148 (*Inégalité*).   [2] *Confessions*, III, 115, 119.

[3] 'Lettre à Vernet', 29 novembre 1760, C.G., v, 270–2; See also Prierre Burgelin, *La Philosophie de l'Existence de J.-J. Rousseau* (Paris, 1952), 57–8, 131–2.

[4] *Confessions*, I, 38; VII, 281; XII, 640; *Rousseau Juge de Jean-Jacques*, II, 809, 811, 820–4, 845, 855, 857; *Lettres à Malesherbes*, I, 1132–3; *Essai sur l'Origine des Langues*, 388–9.

[5] 'Lettre au Prince de Wurtemberg', 15 avril 1764, C.G., XI, 13–15.

[6] *Confessions*, IV, 162; II, 58–9; III, 102–3.   [7] *Emile et Sophie*, 22–4.

[8] Vaughan, I, 159 (*Inégalité*).   [9] *Ibid.* 138, 160–3 (*Inégalité*).   [10] *Emile*, 182.

never loses the faculty, though he may not really need it much. It prevents his being cruel, but since he 'does not need his fellow men', he has little occasion to be either brutal or kind.[1] However, he is not like a child so wrapped up in its own ego as to be immune to other men's feelings and above all, he is not, like the socialized man, systematically pitiless. For social man, who really needs to feel pity, is generally not compassionate. Inequality damages the ability to feel for others and to identify with their suffering more immediately and directly than it does any other human faculty. Without pity man is a monster, so compassion has not been entirely destroyed even in civilized men. Indeed among simple people it still survives. Among the rich and reasonable it has been largely repressed as they no longer recognize themselves in their inferiors. The rich are so callous because they have convinced themselves very conveniently that 'the poor are too stupid to feel'. Kings feel no pity for their subjects because they do not expect to become ordinary men.[2]

If he were rich, Emile's tutor feels, he also would become a 'scornful spectator of the suffering of the lower classes'.[3] Such also is Philinte, the 'decent member of high society' in Molière's *Misanthrope*, 'endowed with a most meritorious gentleness with which [he is] able to support the misfortunes of others'.[4] Wealth and power alone would not suffice to stifle nature so utterly in us. It takes intelligence and reasoning as well. Indeed it is education and reflection that isolate us by creating and sustaining the deepest sense of inequality among us. When there is a street brawl the poor people rush to the scene and try to separate the fighters. The unmoved philosopher prudently walks away or closes his window.[5] That is how indifference, born of inequality, makes men radically cruel. In a state of natural isolation men need only rarely feel pity or anything else for each other. In society where they really need to respond to each other's sufferings they are no longer capable of it. That is how both the demands of our situation and our psychological deformation combine to make our life doubly difficult.

The extinction of compassion is only one of the consequences of

---

[1] *Ibid.* 185–6.   [2] Vaughan, I, 165–6 (*Inégalité*).   [3] *Emile*, 310.
[4] *Letter to d'Alembert*, 39.
[5] Vaughan, I, 162 (*Inégalité*); '*Préface*' à *Narcisse*, 965–7.

that pursuit of inequality that is the obsession of our 'deformed self-love'. Because this spirit of competition arises before morality comes to human consciousness, man's moral development is thwarted from its very beginning. Morality is born only with an awareness of others. The isolation and self-sufficient egoism of natural man are radically amoral. It is only when men associate enough to evaluate each other that the very possibility of moral judgment emerges. However, the first comparisons men make are not moral ones. They do not start with good, better and best and their opposites. The primitive hunter begins by measuring himself against his prey. It is then that such relative terms as strong, weak, large and small come to him. His reasoning powers and his pride are aroused together in measuring himself against beings other than himself.[1] With this comes the realization that he and other men are members of the same species, even if, as yet, there are no enduring, binding ties between them beyond occasional common action. However, man has awoken and the family, the homestead and the Age of Gold are not distant. Dependence on things and true inequality set in, as each man wants to be appreciated and admired by others. The desire for inequality and competition have been born, but the situation of man in the Golden Age is such as to inhibit their growth.[2] However, the roots of eternal hostility are there, and they suffice to make the Golden Age unstable.

As soon as self-contained self-love degenerates into a comparative, competitive self-appreciation a 'negative sensibility' is born. 'The sentiment of inferiority in one respect poisons that of superiority in a thousand others and one forgets all that one has in occupying oneself entirely with the one thing one lacks'.[3] Given the force of such feelings, it was inevitable that the spirit of inequality would destroy the Golden Age, and men drift into a far worse condition.

The yoke of dependence upon material objects also presently becomes heavier, as men cease to live 'in' and 'for' themselves. They learn to cooperate, to increase their goods, to accumulate them and to quarrel about them. To settle disputes one needs rules and judgments. It is thus that the most important of social values,

[1] Vaughan, I, 170 (*Inégalité*).   [2] *Ibid.* 172–5 (*Inégalité*).
[3] *Rousseau Juge de Jean-Jacques*, II, 806.

justice, becomes active in human life.[1] It does not come to men in an instantaneous flash. Innate it may be, as a capacity, but to respond to it fully man must undergo a slow and painful psychological growth. Emile first must be deprived of the fruit of his work in the garden to understand what it means to have a right to something and see that others have claims on his respect and forebearance as well.[2] The sense of obligation, of right and duty, of justice in sum, is born with property. However, as Rousseau emphasized in a letter to a friend, Emile's lesson was meant to show that it is work, and only work, that transforms mere possession into property.[3] The mixing of one's labor with the gifts of nature defines rightful ownership and gives rise to the feeling of having an inviolable claim to things. In all this Rousseau was clearly very close to Locke. The moral importance of personal work was, to be sure, more serious for him especially, perhaps, since he recognized its painfulness for creatures as naturally lazy as he believed men to be. In any case, when Locke came to teach children justice he did not deprive them of the products of their labor, but merely of some cherished gift.[4] However, both Locke and Rousseau agreed on the psychological necessity of a painful experience of injury, of a sense of injustice, in making children aware of their just rights and duties. Emile crying over his uprooted beans and Locke's young gentleman robbed of his present are both learning the hard way, which is indeed the only way, what justice and injustice mean and feel like.

Rousseau did not doubt any more than Locke did that men had a right to their property and that rightful ownership was the origin of all justice. That there could be no liberty and no true security of obligations without the sacred rights of property was perfectly clear to Rousseau also.[5] Again, their respective accounts of moral learning, of how the sense of justice and injustice is originally acquired and then takes such deep roots in the human mind and heart, are not very different. Rousseau's great departure from

[1] Vaughan, I, 185 (*Inégalité*).   [2] *Emile*, 61–4.
[3] 'Lettre à Usteri', 13 septembre 1761, *C.G.*, VI, 211–12.
[4] John Locke, *The Second Treatise of Government* (ed. Peter Laslett, Cambridge, 1960), Ch. V, 26–8; *Some Thoughts Concerning Education*, s. 110.
[5] Vaughan, I, 259 (*Économie Politique*). For a somewhat different interpretation, to which I am, however, indebted, see Mario Einaudi, *The Early Rousseau* (Ithaca, 1967), 139–42, 197–201.

Lockean thought was in his belief that a deep damage is done to men by work, property and obligation under conditions of radical inequality. It is inequality that deforms all three and renders them occasions for vice and oppression. All are experienced as burdens by men, even by those among them who benefit materially from their effects. Our emotional response to work and property is debilitating because we so easily come to depend on objects. And this dependence only stokes the fires of the desire for inequality. Nor is that all. In a state of weakness and inequality moral awareness itself is immediately accompanied by wickedness. 'We are now', he says of Emile as soon as the latter's sense of justice is born, 'in a world of morals, the door to vice is open.'[1] For while natural man and young children are too isolated to recognize or assert claims, social man is too weak to honor them. Self-interest among socialized men is not the egoism of nature which aims only at self-preservation. Now it is competitive and comparative and as such it militates against the newly acquired and far from powerful sense of duty. Men may have an innate feeling for the obligations imposed by promises, but the interest that leads them to make promises will also make them break their word. Duty and inclination have been torn asunder.

Work, when it is socially divided and property when it is unequally distributed, can only lead to exploitation and violence. For now natural differences begin to count. Power and wealth are the rewards of strength and wit.[2] Ambition and ingenuity are stimulated accordingly, and technical advancements, beginning with the discovery of the uses of iron and grain, increase the burdens of work and of inequality. For every advance in technique now promotes the interests of those who enjoy an initial advantage. Fear of inferiority, moreover, keeps everyone locked within this race, from which indeed a whole new set of needs are bred. Deception becomes a way of life, a necessary protective device in the struggle. Being and seeming cease to resemble each other.[3] Hostility grows apace, as the rich depend on the poor for services and the poor on the rich for help. The motives and means for a full-scale state of war are now at

---

[1] *Emile*, 65. [2] Vaughan, I, 178 (*Inégalité*).
[3] *Ibid.* 178–9 (*Inégalité*). *Lettre à Christophe de Beaumont*, 86. For the importance of the distance between 'being' and 'seeming' in Rousseau's thought, see Jean Starobinski, *Jean-Jacques Rousseau: la Transparence et l'Obstacle, passim.*

hand. Work and property thus work to increase human suffering, but
it is inequality that reduces them to such an instrument of oppression. It enhances dependence which breeds hostility, so that the more
necessary men become to each other the greater are the occasions
for mutual hatred. 'Such are the first effects of property and the
inevitable consequences of inequality.'[1]

It is not the last chapter in the history of inequality—a chapter
that may never be written. In the state of war in which men find
themselves when their social career begins, the poor can still
challenge the rich. How, after all, are the latter to justify their
accumulated possessions when so many men starve? And justification is needed now that men have opened the door to vice
and virtue. In this predicament the thought of government comes
to the rich as the best means of legitimizing and so of securing their
wealth. The poor are duped into accepting a quasi-contract which
deprives them of the remnants of their liberty, and the rich get
exactly what they want, law and order in which they can enjoy their
possessions untroubled by the poor. The weak are enfeebled, the
strong gain new powers. That is our present political order.[2] Rotten
to the core, it is certainly not capable of being reformed. What makes
it so utterly intolerable, however, is that at the moment of its birth a
great opportunity was lost, as great as that offered by the Golden
Age. The state of war might have been used, as it was by Lycurgus,
to build 'a good edifice'.[3] Instead, on the foundation of inequality
and enslavement, a semi-legitimate prison, half-natural and half-
civic was put together. The great moment was wasted. And the
stupid and limited animal did not become 'an intelligent being and a
man' by choosing the civil liberty of the citizen, by entering into a
true contract and by giving himself laws.[4] Instead, duped by the
rich and driven by ambition, the vast majority accepted their present
condition. They assented to inequality and everything followed from
that folly. Soon magistrates and laws were added to their burdens
and were usually succeeded by the even worse rule of lawless power.
For the very conditions that make social institutions necessary
'render their abuse inevitable'.[5]

[1] Vaughan, I, 179 (*Inégalité*).   [2] *Ibid.* I, 181–3 (*Inégalité*); 268 (*Économie Politique*).
[3] *Ibid.* I, 183 (*Inégalité*).   [4] *Ibid.* II, 36–7 (*Contrat Social*).
[5] *Ibid.* I, 190–1 (*Inégalité*).

External pressure set mankind on the path to society, but its disasters are all of men's own making. It was and remains their work. As long as they are driven by a passion for inequality and as long as their competitive urges sustain the present system, men will neither be educated for civic virtue nor return to the Golden Age. That is, to be sure, not inevitable. Since men make their social world, they might in principle at least, remake it. However, Rousseau had certainly taken pains to show how deeply rooted inequality and its evils are and how great a part they play in the development of every man. Inequality, unlike other social burdens, cannot be traced back to *any* physical need. Its origin no less than its present prevalence rests on psychological proclivities. Wealth and poverty do not describe relationships between men and things, but between men only. For the rich wealth is important because they have more than other men. Indeed they would not enjoy their wealth if the poor did not suffer. It is in order to be admired and to be able to look down upon the less fortunate that men desire power and possessions.[1] Inequality is the whole object of their striving, not the fulfillment of any immediate needs. That is why luxury is so odious. It is valued solely because it is scarce, because its enjoyment is denied to most men. Luxury is meant to feed only the pride of the rich and the envy of the poor.[2] Both alike are expressions of the desire for inequality which is the dynamic force that keeps society going.

The moral direction and design of Rousseau's history of man in general is now clear. It is, above all, an account of how our feeble will reacts to external pressures and to our passions. This weakness was one that Rousseau had fully recognized in himself. 'A healthy but weak soul, who adores virtue without practising it', he said of his own moral character.[3] As in the individual soul, so in social history, the good but feeble will allows evil and suffering to arise in the first place and then misses every opportunity to extirpate them. If this fires one's indignation it is above all because it is all so unnecessary. The miseries men have inflicted on themselves could be relieved and prevented by men. Emile's education shows that. It is designed to

---

[1] Vaughan, I, 192 (*Inégalité*); 333–4, 346 (*Fragment*).

[2] E.g. *Réponse au Roi de Pologne*, 42; *Réponse à M. Bordes*, 53; Vaughan, II, 73 (*Contrat Social*); *ibid.* 436 (*Pologne*); 'Lettre à M. Moultou', 29 janvier 1760, *C.G.*, V, 31.

[3] *Rousseau Juge de Jean-Jacques*, II, 774, 817, 824–5; *Confessions*, VIII, 368.

give him a strong will and in this it succeeds. Even though Emile finds neither happiness nor a privately created Golden Age possible, his independence and will power, unlike Rousseau's, remain unimpaired. This again shows that Rousseau's self-examination was not meant to produce a glorified picture of himself which others ought to copy. On the contrary, he was deeply aware that he was no hero of the moral life. He also knew that he had always been an oddity and that this had been the cause of much of his unhappiness. Certainly he did not want anyone to follow him into solitude.[1] It was only his willingness to expose his own weakness, and thereby to encourage others to recognize theirs and to overcome it, that was both unique and commendable. In bringing this weak creature into the open, moreover, the whole long travail of primitive man was revealed.

The moral purpose of this exercise in self analysis, no less than the individualizing character of Lockean psychology, contributed to the biographical style of thought. Artistic considerations may well have played their part. Rousseau excelled in drawing fictitious moral portraits. One need only recall the skill which made the characters of *La Nouvelle Héloise* both living individuals and moral types. It was, however, his moral intentions which consciously determined his method. He distrusted the veracity of historians at all times. But even those whom, like Thucydides, he did not accuse of lying, could not tell him what he wanted to know, because they dealt with general social events and complex circumstances. The causes of these could never be known and their moral significance could, therefore, never be assessed. We can judge only individuals. Only individual actions can reveal the effect of those 'external causes which turn our inclinations into vices'.[2] That is why Plutarch, the biographer, was his best guide to the historic past. The knowledge of man in the crowd is indeed necessary, but just as one more means of demonstrating the vast difference between men with and men without social masks. The object of interest remains the individual, in this case deformed by crowding.[3] 'The history of the human heart'

---

[1] E.g. *Confessions*, I, 5; II, 62; *Rousseau Juge de Jean-Jacques*, II, 774; *Mon Portrait*, 1125; 'Lettre à un jeune homme', 1758, *C.G.*, III, 328-9; 'Lettre à M. Moultou', 15 juin 1762, *C.G.*, VII, 297-8; 'Lettre à M. Moultou', 7 janvier 1765, *C.G.*, XII, 203-4.
[2] *Emile*, 199.　　　　　　　　　　　[3] *Ibid.* 200-3.

could only be written as a biography of an individual. That person, however, is neither Emile, nor Julie, nor Rousseau. It is Everyman.

With Everyman as his deepest concern, Rousseau remained closer to Locke's individualism than to that later liberalism which shared the romantic passion for individuality.[1] Rousseau was not in the least interested in the unique personality crushed by mediocrity, nor in the creative imagination stifled by common sense, nor again in the artist-hero persecuted by the philistines. The quite undistinguished universal man, who only wants felicity and who only experiences suffering claimed all his sympathy. Suffering is, in any case, the most universal human experience and Rousseau's identification of active consciousness with suffering was the very essence of his egalitarian vision. If all men have, as Locke believed, some understanding, it is yet true that intelligence and knowledge are acquired to very different degrees. Intellectual and practical competence of every kind separates men in feeling and opinion. Locke, of course, rejoiced in this spectacle of variety. Rousseau, however, considered its costs in suffering. That view, in itself, expressed an egalitarian feeling, which it also enhanced. For suffering is a great equalizer. All men feel it and in much the same way. To illuminate it is to recognize the most common of human experiences and the most binding. That is why pity can hold us together, while every skill tends to separate us from each other.[2]

If this egalitarian view of man's victimhood is remote from Locke, it is even further removed from the romantic notion of Promethean suffering as a dramatic, poetic and creative state. As far as Rousseau was concerned suffering was an unmitigated evil that ought to be reduced in every possible way. The function of morality and of the properly trained will was to protect men, if not from all misery, at least from that great part that they have created for themselves.

Far from glorifying the 'creative imagination', Rousseau saw in this vehicle of 'perfectibility' the deepest source of human misery. What men need most is that sense of reality which forces them to resign themselves to necessity. Fantasy is precisely what destroys them.

---

[1] For a longer discussion of Rousseau's relation to romanticism see the author's *After Utopia* (Princeton, 1957), 26–64, and Starobinski, *Jean-Jacques Rousseau: la Transparence et l'Obstacle*, 50 ff. [2] *Essai sur l'Origine des Langues*, 384–5.

Rousseau knew that he had personally derived more pleasure from his daydreams than from anything else, but that was only because his situation was so intolerable and so insuperable.[1] It had made him an artist, but art itself was a dubious pain-killer, made agreeable by the advances of corruption. Health and happiness, which are the real needs of men, are in no way advanced by a 'creative imagination' and Rousseau's own experiences were a warning, not an example to be followed.

What was wrong with society was not that it lacked creative, artistic grandeur. Society had failed because it was the sum of our self-inflicted pains. These are due not to repressed individuality and stunted yearnings for self-expression, but to the unsatisfied needs of common men for peace, security and inner balance. Not genius, but the primitive man repressed in each of us cries out for help. And primitive man's needs are very simple, arising from the longing to survive without too much effort. They have nothing to do with the needs of the aesthetic soul. What keeps primitive man down, moreover, is fear and ambition and the habitual dissimulation they breed. The displacement and deformation of the instinct for survival, not the paralysis of creativity, matter. To be sure, Rousseau deeply deplored the uniformity of Europeans and cherished peculiarity of character in individuals and in groups. Character was for him the open expression of one's own experiences and needs. This was part of unmasked life in isolated self-sufficiency. As such it could flourish best in the countryside.[2] The conformity that ruled the populations of large cities was the best proof of their oppressiveness, and of the terrible inequality that engendered such chains.

Given Rousseau's belief that each person had specific tendencies so deeply rooted that they created an individual character at an early age, he was bound to recognize that differences in personality were one of the fruits of freedom. However, the qualities that he takes into account all bear upon men's moral disposition and opinions. It is freedom, not originality that is prized, freedom to survive in one's own manner. That manner is different for each man, as his genetic or acquired endowment is peculiarly his own. However,

[1] *Confessions*, IX, 435–6; *Lettres à Malesherbes*, III, 1138–9.
[2] *N.H.* Part II, Letters XIV and XVII; *Emile*, 431–2.

these differences are given and not objects of striving. Left to ourselves we would, each one of us, be unlike anyone else, but there is
no hint in Rousseau of that romantic quest for originality, for the
creation of *new* artifacts or *new* personalities as an end in itself. The
nature that is repressed in us is one that yearns for ease, not for
creation. The nature that is hidden and crushed by conformity, and
deformed by ambition, is not released by outbursts of either violence
or great deeds of any sort.

If the life of civilized uniformity is burdensome, the domestic
bliss of the Golden Age is scarcely an eventful one. The simple
household is composed of domesticated mediocrities and not of
'beautiful' souls and things. Simplicity, not originality, felicity, not
aesthetic striving mark its daily life. As for Spartan man, he is
denatured, but not repressed. If he no longer cares even for his
personal name, he has received something even more valuable,
psychologically, a communal will that expresses a social consciousness which is his very own, even though it be shared by his fellow-
citizens. In both cases, the deceptions forced upon men by inequality
are ended, and in neither case is a romantic daemon released. In one
case the circumstances of the individual are altered so as to impose
no great burdens upon his weak will, in the other his will has been
fortified and buffeted by social discipline. The great problem of
freedom is to avoid personal oppression by other men and dependence on things. It is not to be found in social or artistic inventive-
ness.

The biography of Everyman is a study in social pathology
because all his ills are caused by damaging forms of association. Our
ancestors were not better than men are today, but their social
situation was less intolerable.[1] That need not be taken as an
encouraging thought. The gravity of our condition is rooted in the
profound impact that social experience has on each of us. Our evils
are so radical because they are all internalized to mold each
personality. The utopianism that confronts actual man with his
possible self is not cheering. It is, however, very remote from that
formless *Weltschmerz* of romanticism. It is an altogether objective
and impersonal recognition of human limitations as they reveal

[1] *Discours sur les Sciences et les Arts*, 4; '*Préface*' à *Narcisse*, 964.

56

themselves in the past, the present and within each man. The great challenge of this utopia is aimed at our feeble powers of choice. It is choose that we must, between manhood and citizenship, if we are to recover. The infirmity of the will, however, the inability to be resolute is just what caused our troubles in the first place. It is not likely that we will overcome it.

MORAL STRATEGIES

The capacity to choose is the most fundamental human trait, the one that most clearly separates man from the rest of the animal world. Yet it is just the lack of strength to make and follow necessary choices that allows Everyman to drift into victimhood and civilization, and to remain there. It was always clear to Rousseau that this was not the inevitable fate of mankind. Several better ways of living, both in and out of society, were available. These alternatives presented themselves to him as moral strategies. Their object is to recreate our natural freedom and inner peace by bringing our emotional resources and our external situation into alignment. The intensity of our will power, our general psychic structure and the social environments which we can find or must accept, are all to be taken into account when we plan to become content and healthy again. It is, above all, a matter of emotional manipulation, of repressing all those tendencies which, as experience has by now amply taught us, cause our worst conflicts. Among these, ambition, cupidity, dependence on others, competitiveness are the most in need of extirpation. If this can be done, our conscience will be liberated to assert itself and make goodness relatively easy. This method demands much will power, but less than that perfect independence of spirit for which Emile has been trained and which raises him entirely above his circumstances. Most men must find supporting environments, in the Golden Age where ambition and its destructive progeny did not arise, or in Sparta where nature is crushed. In Sparta indeed the human will finds its most perfect setting, because there society is organized to train and assist it throughout one's life. In less supportive political circumstances one is wise to seek undemanding situations, of which family and village life are the most satisfying. However, while these are certainly appealing, they do not permit us to resolve the conflict between social duty and natural inclination. The tension is eased, but it is not abolished. That is why the Golden Age is, by definition, unstable and fleeting. Sparta is the social cure for the diseases that society has engendered. It is not, however, the only way in which we can escape from victimization. Emile also triumphs over fate, by escaping into himself.

As always, introspection guided Rousseau in his reflections on moral psychology. In examining his own disordered life he discovered that the discord between his inclinations and his situation was at the root of all his troubles.[1] For a person of his penchants and his weaknesses solitude was the least abrasive environment. It was not, however, an appropriate situation for most people.[2] Rousseau did not devise general maxims of conduct out of his personal needs. He only extracted generally shared psychic proclivities from the complex substance of his own experience and emotions. Solitude was a very radical solution. Isolation from other men was not now feasible for most people. It is not even possible to withdraw from the physical presence of others for some part of one's life. Psychologically it is too great an effort. Emile must marry and become a father. Only the benefits of self-understanding and contemplation that solitude permitted were worth gaining.[3] And these could be achieved by spiritual exercises undertaken anywhere, even in Paris, if anyone there should be interested in moral health.

The isolation of natural man cannot be imitated at all. Our inner selves, whether we live alone or not, are social now and we cannot even imagine ourselves back in a presocial state.[4] Our natural equipment for survival, our instincts, are not sufficient now, unaided by education, to guide us through life.[5] Emile is, to say the least, trained. The will, above all, must be steeled by incessant self-culture. The aim of education is, thus, not to release primitive

---

[1] *Confessions*, VII, 277; *Lettres à Malesherbes*, II, 1136.
[2] *Confessions*, III, 115–17, V, 188, IX, 455; *Rousseau Juge de Jean-Jacques*, I, 676, 727–8, II, 792–4; *Mon Portrait*, 1124; *Lettres à Malesherbes*, I, 1132; 'Lettre à M. le comte de Turpin', 12 mai 1754, *C.G.*, II, 63–4.
[3] *N.H.*, Part II, Letter XVII; 'Lettres Morales', IV, 361–2; VI, 370–4.
[4] *Rousseau Juge de Jean-Jacques*, III, 935–6.   [5] *Emile*, 5–6.

Moral strategies

nature in us, but to recapture artfully some of its joys, the feeling of independence and the inner peace that comes in the silence of ambition.[1] To this end, not only our selves, but our situations, must be altered. Emile is the unique work of the pedagogue's art. Most men are, and must be, formed by a social environment. They must flee to a facsimile of the Golden Age or contemplate the remote possibility of Sparta. Between them these two models exhaust the collective satisfaction of human needs.

If Rousseau in his various discussions of moral psychology again concentrated on individual experiences, he did so with a social aim. He could attack contemporary society best by picturing it as a moral prison behind whose bars every moral action was an enormous personal effort. If this leads to a highly egocentric morality, it is one made so by the weight of the world. Indeed it is only when one has followed him in his accounts of the crushing obstacles that society now puts in the way of our feeble moral capacities, that one can understand why the Spartan model seemed so liberating to him. The origin of the burden of immorality is social, its effects are best seen in examples of individual misery. For since evil is pain, just as pleasure is goodness, morality must be seen solely in terms of these feelings. And these very basic emotions are experienced individually and directly, and can be described only in terms of personal experiences and reactions.

Emile was Rousseau's Galatea. He was trained to be a completed man, one who could emotionally survive anything. He is therefore prepared to face victimhood as part of the natural order of things, as a necessity. The social dangers amid which he lives do not upset his inner balance. For he has been taught to accept necessity. He *wills* what is and has to be, and does not have a single desire that he cannot satisfy by his own unaided efforts.[2] It is not enough to make him capable of remaining in the Golden Age or of coping with life in Paris. That is, in many respects, more of a comment on these situations than on Emile. His will, however, has been sufficiently strengthened to make him indifferent to suffering. When he believes himself to have been betrayed by his wife, he simply runs away from his family. Not perhaps the conduct of a responsible man, but

[1] *Ibid.* 157-9. [2] *Ibid.* 48-9, 320; *Emile et Sophie*, 2.

59

it is just what one would expect an independent egoist to do. In due course Emile is sold into slavery and it is then that the real quality of his will is displayed. For it is then that he discovers that he can be dispossessed of everything, even of his body, without loosing his sense of self-possession. 'My will, my understanding, my being were still my own', he writes his old tutor. Without anything except his inner life to command, he felt more his own master than ever before.[1]

Like another slave, Epictetus, he discovers freedom in a total indifference to oppression. The highest moral fortitude is to resign oneself to necessity so perfectly that its burden is not even felt anymore. It is also the lesson of nature which teaches 'the law of resignation'.[2] One is free because one refuses to experience, to react to, the external world. It is shut out. The victory of the victim is in his refusal to accept that definition of himself. He can *feel* free, if he knows how it is done. To confine his desires to the narrowest limits and to reject the environment as irrelevant to himself, is the best strategy for the victim. The spiritual victory of a slave, the most totally victimized of men, is achieved by a supreme effort of the will, by a complete re-creation of the self. It is far from natural. Indeed it is the victory of the moral art, but it is a replica of our natural state: an absence of mental pain and a feeling of perfect independence.[3]

The second moral strategy, far less heroic, is to evade wrong-doing. Since physical pain and the feeling of remorse are our only natural woes, it is very much in one's own interest not to harm others, lest one suffer the pangs of an accusing conscience.[4] The Savoyard Vicar, no less than Emile, is bent upon inner peace. He finds it by pursuing goodness in a life of utter simplicity and regularity in a remote village.[5] There he finds the peace of an untroubled conscience. He is, in this, just as self-centered as Emile is, but he finds felicity in retreat from pain, rather than in self-mastery. His is not the victory of virtue, but a recovery of instinct. He believes in God, since it is reasonable and comforting to do so. Beyond that he need not go in order to function. He is resolutely

---

[1] *Emile et Sophie*, 26–7. [2] *Emile*, 46. [3] *Ibid.* 436–7.
[4] *Ibid.* 45. [5] *Ibid.* 244–6, 257–8.

anti-metaphysical.[1] The instinct to which he listens is conscience, which is self-love, extended through identification to other men. Conscience is a spontaneous 'natural impulsion', which our self-love generates when we do not restrict or quell it.[2] We have a moral and active sensibility which, like a magnet, draws us toward each other.[3] It is what makes us capable of loving other men, not just ourselves. Indeed, no one is totally without it. Moral insensibility is as abnormal as is madness.[4] This erotic force, the only really positive psychic result of human association, is our best hope for personal morality. Indeed, even civic virtue is not possible without a capacity for identifying ourselves with our kind. The strongest bond in a truly civic order is the ability to accept the demand: *que ton frère soi à toi comme tu même*.[5] At all times and under all circumstances it is possible for us to listen to the voice of conscience. For it is a profound source of pleasure to us.

Nothing is more gratifying than to be sure of one's own goodness.[6] That is the Vicar's aim. It is not quite a matter of simply following natural instincts, to be sure. Conscience, as one of these, is independent of reason and judgment, and it is also more powerful, being capable of inspiring feeling and action. But feeble as they are, reason and judgment must guide conscience. They must even fortify it. For in actual society conscience is timid and fearful. It raises its voice only when it is protected against the forces of social opinion and our own ambition. Instincts cannot be left to their own devices in society as we know it. The consequences of impulsive benevolence may be far from pleasant and we must learn to moderate even our kindest inclinations.[7] Julie can afford to follow her kindly impulses at Clarens, only because Wolmar supplies all that is needed of reason and judgment.[8] In the actual world we must think cautiously. 'Distrust instinct as soon as you cease to rely altogether upon it.'[9] In the actual world we must consider our emotional responses to our own behavior very carefully. This is not the prudent calculation of those who defer present pleasures for future ones. Rousseau thought that a very

[1] *Ibid.* 236, 253. [2] 'Lettres Morales', 366–7; *Emile*, 254–5.
[3] *Rousseau Juge de Jean-Jacques*, II, 805. [4] *Ibid.* III, 972.
[5] Vaughan, I, 495 (*Première Version*). [6] 'Lettres Morales', 369–70.
[7] *Rêveries*, 1052. [8] *N.H.*, Part IV, Letter X. [9] *Emile*, 299.

foolish preference for an imagined possibility of pleasure rather than for its reality.[1] 'Pain has little power over those who, having thought little, look neither before nor after', the Vicar claims.[2] It is a matter of psychological insight, rather than a fantasy of foresight. What makes such caution necessary is the semi-socialized state in which we find ourselves, which makes it so difficult for us to master our passions, now that their natural expression has been rendered impossible. For the passions are neither good nor evil in themselves, as long as we master them, and that is up to our will power.[3] In the retreat and resignation that the Vicar has found for himself no terrible demands are made on him and he finds the moral peace that he lost in his more assertive youth.

The story of Julie is in many respects analogous to the Vicar's. Indeed the central theme of Rousseau's novel is the conflict between inclination and duty and the practically hopeless struggle to end it. When Lord Eduard offers the lovers an opportunity to elope and settle on his estate in England, Julie refuses. Torn asunder by her love for Saint-Preux and her loving duty as an only child of elderly parents, she chooses the latter. Felicity would not flourish in York. Remorse would immediately torment her and she would find no inner peace there.[4] Her decision is based entirely on psychological considerations. She knows herself, and takes the less painful path. It is, of course, outrageous to impose such a burden upon a young girl, but that is precisely what our society does to us day in, day out. Given these conditions, however, she follows the proper strategy, not for happiness, which is impossible without Saint-Preux, but for such peace and goodness as is feasible. Once we are socialized our conscience cannot be ignored safely, and it is to our advantage to recognize its insistent demands, even when it contradicts the most powerful of competing instincts. It is our guide to private goodness and a source of positive enjoyment. It is the mark of Julie's strength of character that she is capable of such an act, for she lives in a world where mores do nothing to help her. She has nothing to aid her except her own instincts and will. That is why she is so grateful to Wolmar, when he eventually gives her rational and judicious

---

[1] *Rousseau Juge de Jean-Jacques*, ii, 818. [2] *Emile*, 245.
[3] *Ibid.* 409. [4] *N.H.*, Part II, Letters III and IV.

support. For what would have sustained her in her weakness, especially as she had already demonstrated her inability to resist Saint-Preux's attractions?

The Golden Age to which the Wolmars return is also a moral strategy. It is an escape from those complexities that reduce us to immorality in competitive society. If we want to avoid a bad conscience we must never put ourselves in a situation where our personal interests depend upon the disadvantage of others.[1] The first step toward goodness is to avoid evil, as the first step toward happiness is not to suffer.[2] Our noblest efforts are merely negative: to hurt nobody.[3] That is the real moral end of independence. If we need no one, we misuse no one. Emile found that in spiritual autarchy, Rousseau in solitude, the Vicar in obscurity and Julie, to a far less perfect degree, in Clarens. The morally advantageous situation is one in which we can express our natural self-love without conflict, either within ourselves or with others. In such a situation our malevolence is less likely to grow. Simple peasants are less moved by ill will than are civilized men simply because there is less occasion to feel hostile and aggressive. This does not prevent crimes on their part, but then even real virtue is incapable of preventing that altogether.[4] Here the object of moral strategy is not self-control, but, more simply, escape from moral tasks too great for feeble wills. It is not virtue, to be sure, but it is the peace and quiet of the soul in its Golden Age.

Virtue is more than the easy extension of self-love. It is the silencing of nature by the power of the will through strenuous *travail et combat.*[5] It is not generosity, goodness, pity, the emanations of erotic instinct, but the austere adherence to the law of duty. As such it is so difficult to achieve that there was only one man left to exemplify it, George Keith, Rousseau's protector.[6] He was the last Roman, an ancient patriot without a country, an isolated moral soldier without either an army or a civic cause to serve. So defiant a triumph of the personal will was not likely to endure. The path of inclination was safer, if less spectacular. In antiquity, of course,

---

[1] *Confessions*, I, 56; *Lettres à Malesherbes*, II, 1137.   [2] *N.H.*, Part V, Letter II.
[3] *Emile*, 60.   [4] *Rousseau Juge de Jean-Jacques*, I, 670–1.
[5] *Ibid.* II, 823–4.   [6] *Ibid.* II, 863–4.

virtue was common, but it was nurtured by a Spartan order. Only such an order, not the law of nature, can enlist virtue in its cause. Virtue is a response to social rules only. No law at all presents itself to natural man, since he has no need of rules. That is why Rousseau was entirely consistent in denying that there was any innate knowledge of any such law, least of all of an obscure law that calls upon us to love mankind as a whole. The capacity for learning to be just and faithful is innate. That is why Emile *can* be taught these virtues. They are, however, always learned in society and only society can make them effective. Indeed, it is because they are acquired through social training that they remain artificial and in conflict with our natural urges.[1]

The reconciliation of duty and inclination is what moral strategy tries to achieve, in whatever measure is possible. A wise man, by definition, needs no politically sanctioned laws to help him, and certainly he does not require the constraints imposed by the actual laws of existing states to act well. Reason can tell him what is socially necessary.[2] For reason itself is the creation of social experience. That is indeed why reason is a feeble force and why so few of us are wise. It can tell us what is right and wrong, but we need powerful drives to make us act upon its counsel.[3] Conscience is one such instinct. With some willed repression of competing instincts it can be liberated to push us to goodness. For virtue more is needed than that. One needs a perfected will. That is why Emile's tutor no less than the magistrates of Spartan republics concentrate their efforts upon it.[4] Without such a perfected education and in the absence of supporting mores we cannot hope for moral heroism, but we can always try to be benevolent at least. A moral prodigy is even more uncommon than a giant of the intellect. Just as his criticism of intellectuality explicitly did not apply to a Bacon, a Descartes or a Newton, but to the rest of mankind, so Rousseau recognized that lonely virtue could always arise as an exceptional event.[5] George

[1] Vaughan, I, 322 (*Fragment*); 451–4 (*Première Version*); II, 48 (*Social Contract*). At times Rousseau was a thorough cultural relativist. Occasionally he thought that justice and good faith were admired in all societies, but that is not a *natural* law notion.
[2] *Emile*, 437.   [3] *Ibid.* 34, 146.
[4] *Ibid.* 84–5; Vaughan, I, 240 (*Économie Politique*).
[5] *Discours sur les Sciences et les Arts*, 19.

Moral strategies

Keith, the last and only virtuous man left in Europe, could only cast light on the general degradation around him. He could scarcely encourage one to believe in the likelihood of self-created virtue amid our social ruins. Emile's education, in all its difficulty, only proves the same thing. Heroic, lonely virtue is not impossible, perhaps, but there are psychological limits to what is open to most men. How many of us are George Keith or Newton? They are so exceptional as to bear no message, to set no example, for ordinary men.

It is admirable to try to be virtuous, but it is too difficult and does not yield the serenity that all morality seeks. Julie tries, but she does not become a Spartan matron, nor can she turn herself into a mindless peasant woman. She does her duty at great cost to herself and with much help from Wolmar, but she is never anything but miserable. 'My will', she admits in the end, 'was all for virtue, but my heart was all for love. That was my torment.'[1] Reason told her what to do, conscience moved her, but it was all too late. For her virtue could not achieve its end, to make her whole. Only peasants and Spartans avoid such blighted lives. Only an education as complex and careful as Emile's can teach us to escape such torment. The voice of conscience, rooted in nature and feeling is certainly true and moving.[2] But it is not the force within us that rules the passions. That is the task of the will. Might we not be more gratified by the experience of a good conscience than by a virtue imposed upon us by a will built up by incessant public scrutiny and educative pressure? Julie certainly thinks so when she marries Wolmar.[3] Does she still believe it when she dies? Certainly she has every intention of saving her children from her own conflicts. They are to be educated exactly like Emile, and by his tutor.

There are thus two psychological possibilities for us in our search for inner recovery, benevolence and virtue.[4] Each has its place in a different social setting, each has a different psychological career. The Golden Age and Sparta are, respectively, their collective analogues. These are also the social situations within which they can develop. No

---

[1] *N.H.*, Part VI, Letter XII.
[2] *Emile*, 173–5; *Rêveries*, 1028; *N.H.*, Part III, Letter XVIII.
[3] *N.H.*, Part III, Letter XVIII.
[4] Robert Derathé, *Le Rationalisme de Jean-Jacques Rousseau* (Paris, 1948), 112–24, makes the same distinction, but he has a too rationalist interpretation of 'virtue'.

more than Montesquieu did Rousseau for a moment believe that personal virtue *caused* republican societies. According to Montesquieu virtue is a 'principle', the spirit that animates a republican social structure. It is that 'by which it is made to act', the sum of those 'human passions which set it in motion'. These passions are by no means spontaneously generated. 'In order to love equality and frugality in a republic, these virtues must have been previously established by law'.[1] Virtue is created by following law, by accepting an external standard and making it one's sole guide. To Rousseau also it was clear that republican virtue was the outcome of an interaction between a social situation and predictable human responses to its stimuli. Its core is the triumph of the will over all other inclinations, a victory made possible by social education. Montesquieu saw this virtue as love of the republic. In this, again, Rousseau was at one with him. The psychic energy that the will molds into virtue is always erotic. Virtue is self-love utterly transformed. As such it is an abandonment of spontaneity far more radical than goodness. It is a highly constricting form of love that can thrive only when all the other affections have been erased. That is the work of denaturation that Sparta demands and that is so heroically and unnaturally illustrated by the Spartan mother and by Brutus. Such virtue is not meaningful or attainable in any other setting than the Spartan. It needs a public object. And in modern Europe there were no public causes left, Rousseau felt.

In our world Spartan virtue can serve only to arouse shame. That is the limit of its effective power over our lives. At most, examples of ancient virtue can act as a personal inspiration and even then only to a very slight degree. As in the plays of Racine the heroes of antiquity illustrate universal moral conflicts, struggles between courage, fidelity, perseverance and their opposites. The ancients can, in this way, appeal to Everyman's moral instincts, but they have no public message for men who have no public duties. That is why their admonitions are cold and remote in actuality. There can be no question of becoming a Romulus or a Cato for Saint-Preux, Julie admits, but their memory can awaken his sense of duty to his

[1] *The Spirit of the Laws*, trans. by T. Nugent (New York, 1949), I, III, 19, V, 42; Vaughan, I, 331–2 (*Fragment*).

countrymen, such as they are.[1] In any consideration of our duties we ought to call upon their memory, but it cannot have much bearing upon conduct in our actual situation. Whatever they thought wrong in public behavior is undoubtedly to be avoided at all times, but then we have few occasions for public action. In any case we live in a world of victims and the weakness of even good young men and women is far too great for ancient virtue.[2] Every moral act must be based on accurate psychological insight and on a true appreciation of one's forces and situation. Being no Spartans in Sparta we are best when we listen to conscience and evade situations that stimulate ill will in us.

Julie advising Saint-Preux when he is miserable and adrift in the world begs him to look into the bottom of his soul to find the sacred flame of conscience always burning. Then she does call upon the memory of those noble lives of sacrifice, of Brutus, Cato and Socrates. Finally she reminds him of the real pleasures that a self-satisfied conscience will bring him.[3] It is the same advice that Rousseau gave his friend Mme d'Houdetot.[4] Look into yourself, into the depth of your own being. There alone can be found that instinctive force of self-love of which conscience is the expression. To reject conscience is to suffer the most painful of all the frustrations that repressed instinct can inflict, remorse. Its fulfillment, like that of all other instinctual satisfactions, brings peace, rest, the absence of need and pain. The example of antiquity can here serve only as a reminder. It is not a guide to specific action. Saint-Preux is not asked to sacrifice himself for a great cause. He is only entreated to pursue his own best interests. It is, therefore, not fair to say that Rousseau extolled moral repression for its own sake as a pointless psychic exercise.[5] He saw it as a means to inner peace. After all, when Saint-Preux finally does end up in a whore-house he is afflicted with the pangs of shame and self-disgust.[6]

In cases where social customs are involved the example of antiquity may have a greater part to play. When Saint-Preux is

---

[1] *N.H.*, Part II, Letter XI. [2] *Ibid.* Part I, Letters I and II.
[3] *Ibid.* Part II, Letter XI. [4] 'Lettres Morales', 364–9.
[5] E.g. Albert Schinz, *La Pensée de Jean-Jacques Rousseau*, 172–3.
[6] *N.H.*, Part III, Letter XXVI. Also *Emile*, 354. Even in pursuit of silly notions, self-mastery is a great good—it is a power man must possess.

about to fight a duel, he is reminded that duelling was not practiced by the ancients. It cannot, therefore, be an honorable custom. In such matters their example is conclusive. Nevertheless, this is not enough. Julie again summons the voice of conscience to remind him that it is wrong to kill and to be killed in this way. The remorse he would suffer if his opponent were to die would be altogether frightful. Indeed, the original instinctive spring of all our feelings, our natural desire to survive, cries out against so wanton a risk of life.[1] As always, moral argument is strategic insight into oneself.

This structure of reasoning is again repeated in the great debate between Saint-Preux and Lord Eduard about suicide.[2] Saint-Preux defends his right to take his own life by pointing to the example of the ancients, to his commendable indifference to worldly things and to his right to please himself by ending his own suffering without causing pain to others. He is neither a father, nor a citizen, so there are, for him, no overriding duties. It is the voice of pure egocentricity. If life has become a useless burden, why not shed it? To this rather persuasive argument Lord Eduard replies scornfully. Saint-Preux is suffering from a feeble will. His suicide would bear no resemblance to that of the Romans, since theirs was a public act designed to demonstrate some civic principle, while his could only be an escape from private misery. Their suicide was a sacrifice, his would be an act of self-indulgence. In any case the sorrow of Saint-Preux's friends and the loss of his talents to his fellow men were not to be treated as negligible considerations. Saint-Preux finally does not answer these fairly feeble arguments. He decides to go on living out of friendship for Lord Eduard, which presumably offers enough to make his life tolerable.

The fact is that on Rousseau's own terms there are no grounds for this choice. After all, neither remorse, nor any other pain can follow Saint-Preux to the grave. God does not punish. In the end Julie, even if her suicide is presented as only part of an act of maternal solicitude, is more than happy to die. Perhaps Lord Eduard, who is said to have a life of public duty to fulfill in England, cannot grasp Saint-Preux's sense of futility. The actual state of affairs is exactly as Saint-Preux describes it. He lives in a society in which he has no

[1] *N.H.*, Part I Letter LVII. [2] *Ibid.* Part III, Letters XXI-XXIII.

functions to fulfill. Its prejudices prevent him from marrying Julie and becoming a father and a full man, and its politics exclude him from public affairs. He has no duties worthy of his talents and not the slightest hope of achieving personal happiness. That is precisely why, as Lord Eduard says, even his suicide cannot be an imitation of classical valor. Here the ancients are no longer a guide to us. They were citizens, Saint-Preux is not. He is, like Rousseau, a mere vagabond. Like Rousseau, also, he is sustained by the dream of friendship. There is, however, no reason why he should not please himself by dying, rather than by living. On the contrary, as Julie dies she explains that her chances of felicity in the next world are greater than on earth, because she will eventually be united there forever with Saint-Preux.[1] The society in which both must live can offer them nothing comparable. Death also is a path to peace.[2]

Saint-Preux's suicide might very well, as Lord Eduard claimed, have sprung more from a feeble will than from a realistic self-appraisal. Psychologically he was probably quite right, especially as Saint-Preux does choose to live as soon as a glimmer of purpose is offered him. His suicide *is* a strategy of evasion. However, is not most of our moral life just that? It is all a matter of avoiding painful responses. We are meant to escape from situations in which we are pushed into performing acts which will cause painful regrets. The great distinction for Rousseau between various kinds of strategy is not in the overt actions that they produce, but in the states of mind that they represent. For goodness we need only some will power. For virtue we need a great deal, since it is the total victory of the social self. To float into contentment is, to be sure, very desirable, but even when it is feasible, which it rarely is, it is still mere passivity. It is not an escape from victimhood. Lord Eduard thus has a real point when he accuses Saint-Preux of drifting into suicide rather than really willing it as the ancients did. That is why his argument is directed less against suicide as such, than against the

---

[1] *Ibid.* Part VI, Letter XII. On Julie's suicide see Schinz, *op. cit.* 313, and generally Ronald Grimsley, 'The Human Problem in "La Nouvelle Héloise" ', *Modern Language Review*, LIII (1958), 171–84.

[2] For a similar interpretation to which I am, in spite of some difference, much indebted see Lionel Gossman, 'The Worlds of *La Nouvelle Héloise*', *Studies on Voltaire and the Eighteenth Century*, XLI (1966), 235–76.

state of mind that is leading Saint-Preux to it. The love-sick youth who kills himself is not comparable to the patriot who suffers a self-inflicted death in order to maintain a public principle. The consequences for the two are, of course, identical, but one has escaped from living, while the other has completed the purpose of his life. The former is a collapse of the will, the latter its triumph.

In every one of these dramas of the moral life the will plays a leading part. It is clear that in Rousseau's anatomy of moral man it is the vital member. It is the very principle of moral life. To recognize the importance, and indeed the character, of this psychic force one must again look at Lockean psychology. For both in its closeness to and remoteness from Locke, Rousseau's moral psychology reveals itself most completely. As might be expected Locke had little patience with metaphysical speculations about the will and its freedom or lack thereof. Willing is a strictly psychological function. The will is 'the power of the mind to determine its thought to the producing, continuing or stopping any action, as far as it depends on us'.[1] Volition is 'an act of the mind directing its thought to the production of any action and thereby exerting its power to produce it'.[2] As long as we are not physically disabled, or under external constraint, we are free and our acts are voluntary. The way to find out about all this is simple introspection. One learns by 'reflecting on his own mind and observing what it does when it wills'.[3] What we discover then is that the will is determined by the desire to escape some present pain or 'uneasiness' as part of our general pursuit of happiness. For good is what gives pleasure and evil is pain. If we ask what determines desire, 'I answer, Happiness and that alone'.[4] That alone is what 'one consistently pursues'.[5]

If happiness is our sole aim, it is evidently a great puzzle why we, in fact, make ourselves so miserable. How is it that men 'chose that which by their own confession has made them miserable?'[6] The fault is in the 'weak and narrow constitution of our minds'.[7] We are not moved to desire our 'true and solid happiness' because we respond only to 'the present uneasiness we are under'.[8] It is our lack

[1] *Essay*, Bk. II, Ch. 21, s. 15.   [2] *Ibid.* s. 28.   [3] *Ibid.* s. 30.
[4] *Ibid.* s. 41.   [5] *Ibid.* s. 43.   [6] *Ibid.* s. 56.
[7] *Ibid.* s. 64.   [8] *Ibid.* ss. 51, 35, 36.

of foresight, our inability to give up any immediate gratification for a remote good, however great or certain, that leads us to our misery.[1] To be sure, we have many strong passions, but they are not the source of our self-inflicted unhappiness. They can always be controlled. The mind, 'as is evident in experience', can always 'suspend the execution and satisfaction of any of its desires'.[2] We are not driven by unmanagable impulses, but we are simply too stupid to recognize and follow our genuine interests in preference to our most immediate urges. Moreover, ignorance, inadvertence, habit, poor education, fashion and common opinion all combine to deform and diminish our intelligence.[3] Nevertheless, if we would only be more realistic, more objective, we could at any time make ourselves happy. If the drunk were to have his hangover just before taking a drink rather than a few hours later, he would never lift his glass.[4] And in the last analysis it is entirely his own want of good sense that leads him to succumb to this desire to end his present uneasiness, for there is nothing that impedes his will.

With much of this Rousseau agreed perfectly. He also was contemptuous of metaphysics. The will is a power of the mind and it is through self-inspection that we discover its functions. Julie speaks with the voice of Locke when she pushes aside all those clever metaphysical discussions about the unfreedom of the will. They all try to prove too much. God has given us enough lights to know good and to love it. We have a conscience. We all make choices and decisions. Those are the emotional facts of life and we all know them because they are common experiences.[5] Like the Vicar she can manage quite well without 'the jargon of metaphysics'.[6] The will does not put us in touch with, or emanate from, any order other than that of our own minds. Above all, Rousseau was as certain as Locke was that the pursuit of happiness was our sole striving, that it defined good and that evil was pain. That is why his most pressing difficulty was the same as Locke's. Why do we so resolutely pursue unhappiness? Why does felicity escape us so completely? Why do we fail so utterly? And it is here that Rousseau

[1] *Ibid.* ss. 63–5.
[2] *Ibid.* ss. 47, 52.
[3] *Ibid.* ss. 67–9.
[4] *Ibid.* s. 63.
[5] *N.H.*, Part VI, Letter VII.
[6] *Emile*, 236, 253; 'Lettres Morales', 366–7.

again leaves Lockean psychology, to follow his own very different observations.

In looking into himself Rousseau found not a single mind with various capacities, but a fragmented self. Our inner life is a state of war. Compulsion is not only a matter of physical restraint. There is also one's common experience of not doing what one desires to do with some part of one's self, and even of not *being* one's self. And this feeling is experienced exactly like an external restriction. In the words of the Vicar, 'I have always the power to will, but not always the strength to do what I will. When I yield to temptation I surrender myself to the action of *external objects*.'[1] 'Man is not one; I will and I will not, I feel myself at once a slave and a free man.'[2] When one follows reason one is active; when one does wrong one is passive, the object of internal compulsion. Only God always does what he wills.[3] Men are not like that, and therefore they suffer.

It is not want of intelligent foresight that makes us self-destructive. Nor would more prudence help us. We should and would enjoy immediate gratification of our desires, if we were not so torn between competing urges. Rousseau knew that it was not just forgetfulness that keeps a drunk drinking. He does not drink, or suffer, because he is foolish, but because he is helpless. What he needs is not more clarity of understanding, but emotional strength. The name of that power is will.

Once we enter society our self is doomed to suffer from conflicts between our instincts and our socially acquired urges. Of these, ambition is the worst. We are not, however, only assailed by this deformation of our self-love. Inclinations which were wholesome and appropriate in our natural state have now ceased to be so, without losing any of their appeal. Of these, our natural laziness is an obvious example.[4] To overcome all these threats to our happiness requires self-repression. Reason tells us what needs to be done, but without the power to defend oneself against the pressures of our 'foreign' self, of our badly acquired, deformed and destructive impulses, we could never heed it. We need a faculty to protect us

---

[1] *Emile*, 243. (My italics.)   [2] *Ibid.* 241.
[3] *Ibid.* 239, 248; *Lettre à Christophe de Beaumont*, 81.
[4] *Rousseau Juge de Jean-Jacques*, II, 824.

from the inner threats to our own happiness. That is why the will, when in command, makes us feel whole, and gives us a sense of self-possession. For since our vices are acquired and not innate, we feel their power in just the same way as we feel external compulsions: as oppression imposed upon us against our will. The will alone can hold them at bay and so liberate our erotic capacities and impulses. For the Vicar and Julie this suffices. In a republic our emotional drives are reoriented entirely to express themselves in love of the republic. Here, however, the will, which makes this possible, is sustained by perpetual education and support from society. In both cases, whether we seek goodness or civic virtue, the will must engage in defensive war against all those of our desires that would destroy our inner peace. The will has ceased to be the ruler of actions. It is far more the force that orders men's inner life and defends it against compulsion.

Rousseau's will is the servant of health and an instrument of happiness, as our end is to live in felicity. It is, as such, Locke's will and not Kant's. However, in many ways Locke was also a distant figure. If he also noted the social causes of moral stupidity, they did not obsess him as they did Rousseau. That is why he did not propose a social cure for personal misery. The education he offered to his young gentleman was not radically directed against the social influences around him. That is just what is done for Emile, however. He is a victim saved from social prejudice. Locke's young man is prepared for intelligent and competent participation in the life of the upper classes. Of that other, even more radical cure open to us, Locke would not have approved at all. Sparta is the remedy that is extracted from the very source of our present disease: society.[1] In a new form of association, based on sound mores and opinions that are the very opposite of our actual ones, we might recover our inner wholeness.

At present it is false public opinion, as we absorb it and make its poisonous ways our own, that destroys us. It is public opinion that moves Julie's father to prevent her marriage to Saint-Preux. It is opinion that drives friends to duels. It is what pushes people to despair and suicide. It is the knot in our swaddling-clothes and the

[1] Vaughan, I, 322 (*Fragment*).

nail in our coffin. It sustains social oppression and war and it generates inner division and compulsive misery within each of us. To this condition there can be only two alternatives: escape to a private desert or the creation of a new, social counter-will.

3

THE EMPIRE OF OPINION

THE NATURAL HISTORY OF OPINION

'I know of only three instruments with which the morals [manners] of a people can be acted upon: the force of the laws, the empire of opinion and the appeal of pleasure.'[1] It is one of Rousseau's most striking sentences, and one that reveals his entire view of life in society. Pleasure calls us, laws coerce us, but it is opinion that rules. Of the three, law is the weakest, for it only affects men's actions, without touching their wills.[2] Pleasure is an indefinite and diffuse motive. It is opinion alone that directs men's purposes. Among all the peoples of the world, it is not nature, but opinion, which decides their choice of pleasures. That is why the quality of conduct depends solely upon opinion.[3] Whatever society one may live in, it is public opinion that rules.

What then is opinion? How does it come to dominate our lives so completely? At its most simple, it is any notion that is more than a direct and immediate response to a physical sensation. 'In everything that does not depend on the first needs of nature, our opinions rule our actions.'[4] As soon as man becomes aware of anything beyond his own existence he can be said to have opinions.[5] This implies a departure from the state of nature, for those vehicles of perfectibility, memory and imagination, have to be aroused for men to acquire those general ideas which are needed to judge the natural environment and their relations to it.[6] This measuring of the self against the natural world is 'experimental physics for [man's] own preservation' and necessary if he is to know what to fear and not to fear.[7] As such it is still natural, pre-moral opinion. Nevertheless it goes well beyond the intellectual capacity of the man of pure sensation, or of a baby. Emile is not introduced to any complex thought until his memory and imagination are sufficiently developed to give him

[1] *Letter to d'Alembert*, 22.
[2] Vaughan, I, 322 (*Fragment*).
[3] Vaughan, II, 122 (*Contrat Social*).
[4] *Rêveries*, III, 1013.
[5] Vaughan, I, 151 (*Inégalité*).
[6] *Ibid.* 156, 164 (*Inégalité*).
[7] *Emile*, 89–90, 175.

some powers of judgment.[1] These mental developments, important as they are, however, are not what is meant by the dominance of opinion. It is only the opinions that arise out of human association that draw us away from nature and replace its rule over our lives.

As soon as men live continuously together, under each other's eyes, they want to be esteemed and considered.[2] With this new urge, comparison, ambition and dependence on the judgments of others begin. That is what the rule of opinion implies. It is essentially the opinion of others, which we need and, therefore, make our own, that can be said to rule us. Man in society lives outside himself, because he only sees himself through the eyes of other men.[3] Even if this is a voluntary act of submission, it is the end of natural freedom. The moment that sees the birth of *amour-propre* is the instant in which opinion becomes the dominant psychological force in human life. Opinion is to *amour-propre* what instinct is to nature.[4] It also marks the first appearance of deception, born of fear of hostile opinion. Emile is not allowed to acquire moral opinions until he reaches adolescence, when he needs them. By then he has lived so long without feeling the judgment of others that the impulse to lie can never move him.[5]

Dependence, fear, dissimulation are for all their misery spontaneous disasters into which men stumble. With inequality a conspiratorial element enters into the making of opinions. The managing of human fears and hopes becomes an instrument of domination in the hands of the strong and wealthy. The false contract by which these men come to rule over their less fortunate fellows is the first great victory of public deception. From then on, all organized social life is a matter of opinions systematically spread from the top downward. Once settled, opinions are not readily changed, they are the supports as well as the emanations of the inequality that all the powers of political society maintain. Opinion, like everything else, depends on politics. Although *amour-propre* drives men to support this order, as their hopes and fears and judgments depend on it, not all men contribute equally to the structure of public opinions. The powerful and rich and those who serve them, exploit these artificial dispositions

[1] *Emile*, 31, 72, 76.   [2] Vaughan, I, 170, 174 (*Inégalité*).
[3] *Emile*, 195–6.   [4] *Lettre à Christophe de Beaumont*, 64–5.   [5] *Emile*, 67, 196.

for their own ends. Most men allow themselves to be deceived because of their socially acquired weakness and ambition. Each person becomes so obsessed with the possibility of rising in the social scale that he forgets his actual misery. Ambition blinds men to their real situation as their eyes are fixed upon higher spheres. Even the artisans in Paris dress up on Sundays so that people on the street will think that they are employed at court. Nevertheless, if all men in society are self-deceived, there are some who profit from it, and who, far more guilty than the hapless multitude, do the actual misleading.[1] Of these merchants of prejudice the priesthood and the men of letters were, in Rousseau's view, the most objectionable. However, even these opinion-makers are only the servants of the rich and powerful whose interests they promote.

There is in these reflections much that had become commonplace among Rousseau's contemporaries. Pascal's observations on the power of opinion over men's minds were quoted over and over again and Hobbes' many admirers did not forget his remark that 'the world is governed by opinion'.[2] Locke's heirs were all especially interested in the transformation of directly felt sensations into complex trains of thoughts and beliefs of all kinds. Some continued to concern themselves, as Locke had, with the rational validity of opinions, but Rousseau was far too skeptical to care about the truth of men's beliefs. All that mattered was their tendency to promote or retard the miseries of social life. In this he was not alone. For many of the *philosophes* the development of aesthetic taste and of general beliefs of any sort was no longer merely a subject of psychological exploration for its own sake. Social criticism permeated everything. As literary men they had an immediate interest in the way tastes were formed and reputations made and undone.[3] Above all, in their struggles against the Church and its political supporters, they were directly engaged in a war for man's minds which made the analysis and critique of 'prejudice' imperative.

[1] Vaughan, I, 180–3, 190–3 (*Inégalité*); 484 (*Première Version*); *N.H.*, Part III, Letter XVIII.

[2] Paul A. Palmer, 'The Concept of Public Opinion in Political Theory', *Essays in History and Political Theory in Honor of Charles Howard McIlwain* (Cambridge, Mass., 1936), 230–57.

[3] For instance, the articles under the heading 'Taste' in the *Encyclopedie*, conveniently reprinted in Diderot *et al.*, *Encyclopedia* (New York, 1965), 335–73.

The empire of opinion

This conflict eventually brought the reality of opinion as a political force to the notice of many impartial observers also. By 1749, the year in which Rousseau's career as a publicist began, something new had clearly emerged in Paris. It was in that year, a pre-Revolutionary historian already noted, that the Court lost its monopoly over acceptable public views and was confronted with a rival power in Paris, with 'the empire of opinion'. Even that phase seems to have been common. The city jails were so overcrowded with unorthodox prisoners that some, like Diderot, had to be put away in distant fortresses like the one at Vincennes.[1] This new severity in official responses to opposition was itself a recognition of the power of opinions as political weapons. That also was part of the intellectual climate that heated Rousseau's imagination when he visited the imprisoned Diderot and discovered with a jolt that he shared none of the opinions around him, neither those of the jailers, nor those of the jailed. In one respect, however, he was at one with both. He also agreed that opinions mattered because they determine man's actions.[2]

Among the *philosophes*, Helvétius has often, and justly, been credited with being the founder of the modern theory of ideology.[3] What is left of that theory, when it is divorced from the Hegelian vision of history, is the notion that ideas are the direct and necessary expressions of the conflicting interests of individuals or groups. If Helvétius had been the consistent materialist that Rousseau claimed that he was, he would not have arrived at these ideas.[4] Perhaps that is why Rousseau felt relatively well-disposed toward him. Helvétius was a good man who had written a terrible book, was all he said.[5] Even in his worst tempers he did not want to enter into an open dispute with this old acquaintance, whom he claimed to respect.[6] In any case, Rousseau's charge that materialism made it impossible to separate the physical from the moral in human experience could scarcely apply to Helvétius.[7] Indeed, the latter went much further than Rousseau did in making that distinction. He

[1] Arthur M. Wilson, *Diderot : The Testing Years* (New York, 1957), 93–116.
[2] *Rêveries*, III, 1012–13.
[3] Hans Barth, *Wahrheit und Ideologie* (Erlensbach-Zurich, 1961), 46–60.
[4] P.-M. Masson, 'Rousseau contre Helvétius', *Révue d'Histoire littéraire de la France*, 18 (1911), 103–24.   [5] 'Lettre à De Leyre', 5 octobre 1758, *C.G.*, IV, 63–5.
[6] *Rousseau Juge de Jean-Jacques*, II, 888 and note 3, 1706.
[7] *Essai sur l'Origine des Langues*, 401.

utterly rejected Montesquieu's theory of the social effects of climate, precisely because it implied dependence of moral development upon physical influences. For Helvétius moral life was completely independent and self-governing.[1] Opinion, taste, knowledge, mores and passions were all ruled by social conditions, that is, moral causes. This was, of course, a belief quite necessary, not to his materialism, but to his political radicalism. 'The vices and virtues of a people are always the necessary effects of its legislation.'[2] 'The hatred most men feel for virtue is not the effect of the corruption of nature, but of the imperfection of legislation.'[3] For him no less than for Rousseau, evidently, everything depended radically upon politics.[4] However, Helvétius arrived at this conclusion by a very different route. He was, in fact, Hobbes' most ardent disciple. Self-interest is the only thing that moves men, and power is what is most wanted and needed to secure one's ends. 'If the physical universe is subject to the laws of motion, the moral universe is no less subject to those of interest.'[5]

To be able to command others was a necessity if they were to contribute to one's well-being.[6] The pursuit of power was, therefore, the one universal and all-explaining political reality. Just because men responded exclusively to such simple self-regarding impulses, the transformation of the moral climate was an easy matter of political change. To make a beginning, enlightenment, the popularization of knowledge as practiced by his friend Fontenelle, would help people recognize where their real interests were to be found.[7] For ignorance was certainly at the root of most human errors.[8]

Enlightenment would also dispel 'the stupid veneration that people have for old laws and customs'.[9] Knowledge, moreover, was a source of power and a means for reaching one's ends. Its diffusion and success would be inevitable once it began to take hold. For this to be possible, however, the power of those who had a stake in the present would have to be shattered. Helvétius' contribution to the

---

[1] Helvétius, *De L'Esprit, Œuvres* (Paris, 1793), II, 158-60, 168-72, 174-7, 191-3. Compare this to Rousseau's considerably greater respect for the theory of climates, *Essai sur l'Origine des Langues*, 384-94.
[2] *De l'Esprit*, II, 124.   [3] *Ibid.* II, 84-5.
[4] *Confessions*, IX, 404.   [5] *De l'Esprit*, I, 120.   [6] *Ibid.* II, 88-9.
[7] *Ibid.* I, 328-32; II, 251-61.   [8] *Ibid.* I, 77-8.   [9] *Ibid.* I, 249.

theory of opinions went well beyond the discovery that men's tastes and beliefs were the expressions of their interests which, in turn, were determined by the society in which they lived. He went far in that direction, showing, for example, how the writing of history disappears under tyrannies, and is replaced by allegorical and lyrical literature. When public discourse becomes pointless, the literature of purely private delectation takes its place.[1]

Beside his analysis of culture, Helvétius was also one of the first to play the real game of ideology, 'unmasking one's opponents'. It was all but inevitable. The war against the Church, being one of beliefs, made it unavoidable that not only the content and effect of 'superstition', but also the motives of its promoters should be attacked. It was not enough to prove that religion was untrue. The priests must also be shown to have contemptible aims if their 'psychic annihilation' was to be effected.[2] Helvétius pursued such arguments with such crudeness that he managed to antagonize even those who shared his views, but even milder men, like d'Alembert, really agreed with him.[3] The object of the Jesuits, he wrote, was to put religion at the service of their 'desire to expand and dominate' and 'govern the universe'; it was a mere mask for a dark design, 'the wielding of power over the minds and hearts of men'.[4] According to Helvétius all priesthoods were after power, to which end they stirred up the fanaticism and insured the ignorance of the people. Socrates was their earliest victim and they had since then persecuted anyone who might enlighten the people.[5] In this their interests were the same as those of tyrants.[6]

The clergy were not, however, the only group whose self-interest fostered illusions and ignorance. All courtiers live in a condition of delusion because it is in their interest to do so. 'One rarely sees crime where one's utility is to be found.' And power has its fascinations, so that men are always apt to see merit where there is power.[7] Indeed, all cliques and organized groups, especially the aristocratic families,

---

[1] *De l'Esprit*, II, 177–83. Tyranny according to Helvétius is like Milton's chaos, an anarchy of private interests in which each human atom is isolated, though all live under a single sword. *Ibid.* II, 89.   [2] Karl Mannheim, *Ideology and Utopia* (New York, n.d.), 38.
[3] D. W. Smith, *Helvétius: A Study in Persecution* (Oxford, 1965), 157–71.
[4] Ronald Grimsley, *Jean d'Alembert* (Oxford, 1963), 186.
[5] *De l'Esprit*, I, 230–2.   [6] *Ibid.* I, 201–2, 310–17, 320–2.   [7] *Ibid.* I, 148–90.

have interests completely opposed to those of the general public, and in their pride and blindness have no concern for anything but their own advantage and mutual hostilities.[1] A true system of legislation would abolish the lot and would redirect pride to public ends, defined by republican sovereignty and maintained by a scientific morality that would identify private and public interests. Classical republics, with their military mores, so unlike the 'spirit of the century', with its superficial politeness, were the model for all this.[2] Redirect self-interest by legislation and solid opinions would rule the world; for true virtue is the identity of personal passion and public good.[3] Only when legislation has reordered men's interests will a good father of a family also be a good citizen.

Many of these ideas were obviously very congenial to Rousseau. Helvétius was one of the few Parisian thinkers who felt an egalitarian enthusiasm for the Spartan ideal. If he did admire learning and science he was, at least, no friend of modern civilization. He also could see that it was not just the clergy, but the entire social structure of France that was corrupt and immoral. Nevertheless, Rousseau's implicit criticisms of Helvétius are very telling and bring out very clearly how much more deeply he looked into the psychology of opinion. Helvétius' egalitarianism had its roots in the belief that all men were identical at birth. Rousseau saw perfectly clearly that this notion could be separated from both materialism and from the notion of self-interest as the sole and universal moral motive. Wolmar, the atheist and materialist, rejects the ideas of mankind's natural identity and competitiveness because they do not correspond to carefully observed facts. Saint-Preux, who believes in the soul, is made to defend Helvétius' psychology on speculation alone. Wolmar, however, despises 'lazy philosophy'. Wolmar is not imprisoned by class barriers, by confining social experiences, nor is he too vain to look into himself to find moral truth. He is above all the pettiness of the intellectuals. To really understand his fellow-men he lived, for a while, in every social class, even as a peasant. The observations he was thus able to make, no less than his first exper-

[1] *Ibid.* I, 142–6, 160–70.
[2] *Ibid.* I, 151–3, 160–1, 192–4, 202, 256–7, 309–10; II, 123–4, 269–80.
[3] *Ibid.* II, 82.

ience of friendship for Julie's father, made him realize that he, like Helvétius, has been wrong in assuming that self-interest was the sole or even the primary motive of human conduct. It was *amour-propre*, only that second half of our self acquired in society, that moves and is moved by the external pressures of custom, law, rank and fortune, and *toute notre police humaine*.[1] *Amour-propre* is the origin and support of inequality. However, if men were naturally completely alike, inequality could scarcely have arisen. That is why Rousseau emphasized that it was men's natural situation that made for equality in identity, not their uncertain endowment which favors inequality as natural differences are allowed to assert themselves.[2]

Rousseau did not deny that the Hobbesian picture of an ordered jungle corresponded to the actual world he knew; he only rejected the assumption that this was natural.[3] What Helvétius took for granted had to be explained. The psychological history of men in perpetual conflict, and of the opinions that were generated in this war, was far from self-evident. Rousseau's account of the growth of inequality was meant to provide the outlines of that slow growth. Moreover, there was here a real difference in concerns. Unlike Helvétius, Rousseau was less stirred by the hope of equality than by the pains of inequality. It was one of those experiences that the former had been too lazy and too fortunate to know. Nor was that all. Rousseau quickly discovered that he had some unmasking of his own to do. The medicine that the followers of Voltaire had so liberally fed to the clergy was now to be administered to them, as well as to the nobility and the magistracy. Were the men of letters not foremost among those who suffered from and spread 'the illusions which give us a stupid admiration for the instruments of our misery'?[4] Rousseau's view of opinion was, thus, both psychologically more profound and socially more extensive than Helvétius'. Nevertheless, the similarities are important. Out of their common acceptance of Lockean psychology both saw opinion as an inner growth stimulated by external forces.

Moral deformation had its roots not in the individual but in his

---

[1] *N.H.*, Part V, Letter III; Part IV, Letter XII.

[2] Vaughan, I, 166–8, 178 (*Inégalité*).

[3] *Ibid.* 159–60, 180–2, 305–7 (*L'état de guerre*).

[4] *Rousseau Juge de Jean-Jacques*, III, 934.

social circumstances. And only the pressures exerted by a few groups, determined to seek their own advantage at any cost, could explain the persistence of opinions so wholly unfavorable to the real interests of those who held them. If Rousseau did not share Helvétius' hope for reform through enlightenment, he was only more consistent, because Helvétius' theory of self-interest did not really provide adequate grounds for such expectations. Sensationalist psychology, when altered from a scientific analysis of the sources of human understanding, to a method of social criticism, is far more suited to account for error and misery than to offer remedies. For although it can show how external forces impinge destructively upon men's minds, these sources of illusion and pain all come from men also, and derive their energy from the same experiences that they reproduce.

Sensationalism was an all-encompassing psychological theory. In principle it could be applied to an understanding of every conceivable emotional and intellectual experience. Aesthetic feeling, love, family life, no less than every kind of knowledge or belief could be traced from its original source. Rousseau was neither original nor very comprehensive in considering these problems psychologically, but the moral and social conclusions he drew were peculiarly his own. For Rousseau, music, alone among the arts, had an enduring fascination, both in its emotional and technical aspects. One of his main objections to the materialists' 'thinking matter' was its failure to account for the way in which human feelings responded to music and poetry. Although the senses were the sole origin of our aesthetic experiences, our response to sound and color were not physical, but moral. Quite in keeping with his Lockean orthodoxy, he believed that there was a fund of aesthetic energy within us that was awakened by physical sensations. Thus feeling speaks directly to feeling and the ear and eye act only as conveyors. The meaning of music can only be grasped by an innate musical faculty which answers to the sounds that the ear brings to bear upon it.[1]

Like every human faculty, musical sense is subject to corruption. Saint-Preux slowly comes to find the simple airs of peasants

[1] *Essai sur l'Origine des Langues*, 395–9; 'Musique', *Dictionnaire de Musique* (Hachette), VII, 179–87.

deeply moving. They are not exciting, but they are, nevertheless, sad and sweet. Singing together in unison is best. The need for chords only proves that one's tastes have become corrupt.[1] Such also is the effect of reflection. 'The man who meditates is a corrupt animal.'[2] The corrupting effect of thought is felt nowhere more directly than in music. Philosophy in general, not just materialism, extinguishes aesthetic capabilities. Its language is that of precision, not of passion, so that it eventually destroys the musical element in language. Because our aesthetic faculties are, according to Rousseau, moral passions, social pressures can and do affect them directly. Oppression has the same effect as philosphy on music and musical language. Oratory, so great an art in ancient Greece and so dependent on the musical and poetic quality of the Greek language, died out with the appearance of philosophy and the absence of freedom. When there was nothing worth saying in public the art of emotive, musical speech declined. Feeling no longer dares to call to feeling and the passions disappear behind masks of fear.[3] The capacity to feel music is never destroyed, but it remains hidden and unsatisfied except among simple people. As the Greek drama was a ritual in which the entire community participated in unison, so popular art is still a joining of men together in common pleasure. High culture, especially the modern theater, may stir men, but it also isolates and corrupts them. At best it consoles them for their lost happiness.[4] As for music, there are cultures whose languages are so atonal that musical expression becomes wholly impossible in them, as it is among the French.[5]

What the ear is to music, sexuality is to love. Sexuality is instinctive, but love is artificial, the result of association. A feeling for physical beauty is born only after couples live more permanently

---

[1] *N.H.*, Part V, Letter VII.   [2] Vaughan, I, 146 (*Inégalité*).

[3] *Essai sur l'Origine des Langues*, 400-1, 404-8.

[4] Letter to d'Alembert, 33, 78-9, 125-31; '*Préface*' à Narcisse, 971-4.

[5] The *Lettre sur la Musique Françoise* (Hachette), VI, 168-98, had this unkind opinion as its sole theme. Rousseau favored Italian music, but hardly because it was artless. To prefer the Italians was to side against the Court, but it did not prevent Rousseau from using French in his operettas. As a corrupt man he could do nothing else, perhaps. What is not explained is why he and other men should respond so deeply and instinctively to music which, even if Italian, was in theory incapable of moving men's souls. Is there a 'false' aesthetic self, like the artificial moral self? (*Confessions*, VIII, 384-5; *Rousseau Juge de Jean-Jacques*, I, 682-3; *N.H.*, Part I, Letter XLVIII.)

together, and when women have learned the art of attracting men through beauty. Love, like music, is a matter of opinion, not of nature, and in both one must separate physical sensation from moral feeling. In both cases beauty enters only into our moral life, not into direct sensation. Natural man has no tastes and feels no attachments. He can copulate at random. That has its advantages, since neither jealousy nor possessiveness disturb him.[1] If love is a socially acquired taste, family life is even more so. The family, although it is a society and a model of all other enduring associations, is natural to the extent that it exists to rear the young. In that respect it is unique, and the glory of the Golden Age. Marriage is, nevertheless, a highly artificial institution, and is therefore even more subject to opinion, especially to public opinion, than is love. In no relationship is the conflict of nature and opinion more intense, and in none is the damage done by social inequality more disastrous.

Natural feeling is no guide to the solid state of matrimony, for this is not a natural condition. Indeed, sexual passion can be a future source of misery.[2] People do not marry in order to think about each other all day long, Julie notes, but to fulfill the duties of civil life, to run a household prudently and to bring up children properly.[3] Unfortunately, the fulfilling of social obligations is not the end of sexual desire, nor of passionate love. When at all possible, love and duty ought to be combined as they are in the Golden Age and among the peasants of the Valais, where public opinion does not yet exist. Passions are not violent and personal inclinations are easily satisfied. Song and dance, no less than the ability to love, are unfettered and uncomplicated among people who are still happy, not because they have a taste for pleasure, but because they are free from pain. Their placid contentment stands out all the more, when it is compared to the refined and agonized love of Saint-Preux for his mistress.[4]

In the world of inequality happy and enduring marriage becomes impossible, because it is so difficult to find a suitable mate. One may not find anyone to love in one's own social class, and it is very difficult to live in lifelong harmony with someone who has been

---

[1] Vaughan, I, 164–5, 167 (*Inégalité*).   [2] *N.H.*, Part III, Letter LVII.
[3] *Ibid*. Part III, Letter XX.   [4] *Ibid*. Part I, Letter XXIII.

brought up in a different level of society.[1] Even worse is the custom of forced conventional marriages which are arranged by fathers solely to satisfy their social ambitions and prejudices. Here the destruction of natural sentiment is at its worst. For here feeling is completely sacrificed to the idols of public opinion, rank and fortune.[2] The mistaken foresight, avarice and tyranny of fathers make marriage a moral hazard for both sexes.[3] Precisely because marriage is, and must be, a social convention it depends 'radically upon the total social order'.[4] That is why modern marriage is one among many repressive bonds. Nevertheless, the passions are not killed by social arrangements, they are only repressed and changed from a source of joy to one of misery. That is the true work of *amour-propre* when it interferes with sexuality and love.

The novel, and the emotions and situations that it lived on, was from the first concerned with the woes of marriage. Rousseau was neither the first nor the last to lament forced marriages.[5] He was, however, unique in recognizing that a free choice of partners by young loves was also no solution, and that social inequality rendered such choices hazardous. Marriage thus illustrates the whole network of insuperable difficulties that society puts in the way of human contentment. Julie would not have been happy with Saint-Preux, and she was miserable with the excellent Wolmar. She would have been as unhappy, socially and erotically, by following her heart as she was by accepting her father's sensible and suitable choice. Emile and Sophie only choose each other in a very limited sense. Freedom in their case was only the last act of careful parental and tutorial preparation. They are literally made for each other by others. Even this solution, in which Sophie 'chooses' and the parents 'consent', in a reversal of prevailing practices, does not work out well. For in the sequel to *Emile*, the marriage collapses under the impact of Parisian social life. Rousseau's social fatalism made all the difference in the world between his novels and all other sentimental fiction. Clarissa Harlowe also ends in disaster, but there is no sense of universal, necessary social victimhood. Rousseau saw that

---

[1] *Emile*, 369.　　　　　　　　　　　[2] *N.H.*, 'Séconde Préface', Part III, Letter I.
[3] *Emile*, 5; Vaughan, I, 205 (*Inégalité*).　　　　　　　　[4] *Confessions*, IX, 435.
[5] Ian Watt, *The Rise of the Novel*, 135-90. Daniel Mornet, *La Nouvelle Héloïse* (Paris, 1923), I, *passim*.

modern marriage was no less painful than arranged matrimony, because both were equally artificial, equally social and therefore equally unsatisfying. Moreover, because he regarded marriage as the very cornerstone of social decency, its failure was that of society itself.

Private happiness and mutual fidelity become equally difficult, as everyone loses in pursuing false advantages. That is the final outcome of socialization, of never living for oneself, but 'wholly outside oneself', seeing oneself only 'in the opinion of others'.[1] In the Spartan order the family disappears and erotic feeling is diverted. Here *la petite famille est destiné à s'éteindre*.[2] In the actual world of inequality, of oppression and of imperfect social education, marriage is the clearest and most painful example of the effects of social opinions. 'Drawn this way by nature and that way by man, compelled to yield to both forces, we make compromises and reach neither goal. We go through life, struggling and hesitating, and die before we have found peace, useless alike to ourselves and others.'[3] Neither the Spartan matron nor the peasant women of the Valais commit suicide like Julie, who cannot stop loving Saint-Preux even though she knows perfectly well that Wolmar is a far more suitable husband.

Rousseau's declared message in the *Nouvelle Héloise* was to encourage those who were capable of it to flee from the society of fantasies and opinion, and to regain a taste for the real pleasures of a simple rural life.[4] There one might still regain some part of one's real self. For 'our habits in retirement are born of our own sentiments, in society they are born of others' opinions'.[5] However, a mere physical retreat from society cannot free men's minds from the influences to which they have been exposed for so long, and which they have absorbed so deeply. 'Opinion, opinion', Julie cries out in exasperation with herself, 'whatever effort one makes to escape its yoke, it never fails to lead us to injustice.'[6] The flight into oneself,

---

[1] Vaughan, I, 195 (*Inégalité*).

[2] *Ibid.* I, 238 (*Economie Politique*). That is why the family with its limited objective, the raising of the young, cannot be a model for the perfect state which encompasses the entire moral life of its members. Vaughan, I, 185 (*Inégalité*); II, 24 (*Contrat Social*).

[3] *Emile*, 9. [4] *N.H.*, 'Séconde Préface'.

[5] *Letter to d'Alembert*, 67. [6] *N.H.*, Part V, Letter XIII.

the freeing of the timid instinct of conscience, always entails an enormous effort. To fight off opinion demands not only an escape from other people's eyes, but from all the accumulated feelings that a life lived 'outside oneself' has built up within one. The web that vanity spins around our inner life can be torn only by a rigorous self-reform.[1] Only self-knowledge and solitude can undo all that *amour-propre* has built into ourselves. The capacity for pleasure, as for love and music, remains with us, but to liberate it is no easy matter after the birth of *amour-propre* and its compulsive response to every pressure from the social environment. For it is now a second instinct and behaves no differently than other impulses, except in its destructiveness and in its unlimited tendency to breed illusions. Under the sway of *amour-propre* men no longer believe what they see, but see what they believe.[2] That is what gives the empire of prejudice its real power. That is what makes the reign of deception possible.

Thus, though our natural, primordial self is indestructible and suffers in deformation, men in society are the creations of the opinions that prevail in their immediate social circle. The child is made by his family, the man is the product of his class, his profession and his country. One can try to escape these influences, but never quite successfully. And the self-understanding needed for such a step provides only the means for a personal solution. To fully recognize how opinion comes to rule requires an understanding of society, not only of the self, but also of the forces that mould it. To understand music one must know both what the ear receives and what the soul hears. To understand opinion it is not enough to know men's nature, real or deformed by *amour-propre*, one must also know what social circumstances do to men. For the nature of opinion is not just a matter of the personality of him who adheres to public values. The latter are real powers that force themselves on the socialized self as even bad music can move us to tears.

The way in which life under the pseudo-contract and under conditions of radical inequality forms people can best be seen in the person of Julie's father in whom class prejudices kill natural feeling,

---

[1] *Lettres Morales*, 369; 'Lettre à Vernes', 25 mars 1758, *C.G.*, III, 314–15.
[2] *Rousseau Juge de Jean-Jacques*, I, 742.

not because he is a bad man, but because he is a nobleman.[1] He is in fact one of Rousseau's psychological masterpieces. Baron d'Etange is an upright and generous gentleman. Julie dotes on the old boy. He is Wolmar's dearest friend. In his way he is devoted to both of them. Wolmar is, after all, an excellent choice. Papa and Saint-Preux become the best of friends as soon as the latter ceases to be a potential son-in-law. Yet even when he admired Saint-Preux's work as a tutor he insisted upon humiliating the young man by paying him a wage; to be indebted in any way to a commoner was intolerable. To have such a son-in-law was utterly unthinkable. Yet had he followed his self-interest, his own need for peace and happiness, he would have welcomed Saint-Preux. Instead he quarrels with his relations, his friends and his daughter. He loses his temper and is ashamed of himself. He makes himself and everyone around him miserable, all because he will not give up the prejudices of his class. This is not due to a want of feeling or affection. He is a decent and likeable man, but he cannot think of Saint-Preux in other than class terms. The young man is an inferior and that is an insuperable obstacle to everyone's happiness, including the Baron's. It is no bar to friendship and good fellowship. He enjoys Saint-Preux's company. However, marriage is ruled by class conventions, and when these come into play Baron d'Etange's *amour-propre* is at once aroused, and his prejudices reign supreme. This is not only a cause of unhappiness to himself and his family. As a typical nobleman he is the enemy of all his fellowmen. 'What have you ever done for the glory of your country or the happiness of mankind?', his friend, Lord Eduard, asks contemptuously. Nothing, of course, since he has been an officer in the army of the King of France all his adult life.[2]

The *Nouvelle Héloise* is a tragedy, not a melodrama, because it has no villains. All the characters are admirable, or at least agreeable, and all are victims of their common situation. Saint-Preux is a good boy and no Lovelace. Any woman would be proud to marry the wonderful Wolmar. Baron d'Etange is not, like Clarissa Harlowe's

[1] *N.H.*, 'Séconde Préface'.
[2] *Ibid.* Part I, Letters XX-XXII, LXII, LXIII; Part IV, Letter XII; Part V, Letter VII.

father, exceptionally heartless. He is typical and that is why he plays so important a part in creating the tragic situation which engulfs him, no less than those whom he loves. For it is not an extrinsic fate, but man-made, social circumstances which set insuperable boundaries to the aspirations of these simple people. It is a very modern tragedy. If it has a hero at all it is certainly not Saint-Preux who is the most passive of all its personages. Wolmar and Julie do in fact struggle to overcome the obstacles that beset them and which in the end defeat them. Their fate is, however, psychological and social, and as such, a general, even a commonplace one. Rousseau made it very clear that the absence of any startling events and the very unexceptional simplicity of the characters in his novel were of utmost importance to him.[1] Its whole force rests on their normalcy and the typical character of their victimhood.

There are, however, real distinctions between the various sorts of victimhood that these people must endure. Baron d'Etange for all his many good, lovable qualities is not merely the victim, he is also the active promoter of prejudices that are a menace to most other men. That is precisely how all *amour-propre* works; it subjugates the self in response to opinion and creates a second self which in turn subjects other men to these prejudices. That is how men's minds are linked in society in a vicious spiral. That is why 'power' itself is servile when it depends on public opinion, and why 'the master of other men is no less a slave than they are'.[2] Master and slave both bear the chains of opinions. There is, however, an obvious difference between the illusions of those who, like Baron d'Etange, tyrannize others and those who, like Saint-Preux and Julie, are their victims. The powerless, whether within a family or in society at large, do not have such rigid and pitiless opinions, and they can be moved more easily even to goodness. But the oppressive interests of 'public men are always the same'.[3] In this the Baron's family is a micro-state. Only the supra-human Wolmar has risen above all prejudices to a god-like love of order that is reflected in *his* family. However, he is one of those exceptions which serve to illuminate the limitations

[1] *Confessions*, XI, 546–7; N. H., 'Séconde Préface'.
[2] *Emile*, 47; Vaughan, I, 23 (*Contrat Social*).
[3] *Lettre à Christophe de Beaumont*, 88.

of 'man in general'. Everyman-Emile's education has to begin by removing him at birth from his prejudice-ridden upper class family. Otherwise he would become domineering also, since it is so simple to make others obey. Most men are only too easily deceived, too ready to allow themselves to succumb to illusion. The peasant is not forced to go to Paris, he is lured there. Political power does not rest on the sword alone, but on a falsely drawn-up contract. The inner weakness of *amour-propre* puts all men in danger of being misled, of becoming the victims of 'illusions that deceive, rather than constrain us, to make us do things, without our knowing it, other than what we want'.[1]

The duty of an honest man, like Wolmar or Rousseau, is to disabuse his fellowmen. Those who fail to do this, or even worse, induce men to comply with the demands of a competitive order, are conspiring against their fellowmen, probably out of dark self-interest. The conspiratorial element in opinion-making sometimes appeared to Rousseau in very simple black and white colors: victims and blood-thirsty oppressors. Mostly he was well aware that matters were far more complicated, as in the case of Julie's father. Rousseau hated the ruling classes, but he loved Maréchal de Luxembourg dearly.[2] He knew that the individual soldier might be a very decent man, who, nevertheless, feels that it is his duty *without knowing why* to kill and mutilate innocent people.[3] The magistrates of Geneva are personally just and incorruptible, men of the utmost integrity. Nevertheless, as members of a governing body, they will stop at nothing to maintain their power.[4] They do this not as individual persons wholly, but as members of a public association, as part of a public body held together by rules and conventions which they must make their own as long as they are members.[5] Such is the character of not only a state or a government, but also of any organized group. It is the result of the social organizing of our artificial selves into enduring groups.

There are 'professions which seem to change a man's nature; for

---

[1] *N.H.*, Part V, Letter I; Vaughan, I, 191 (*Inégalité*).
[2] *Lettres à Malesherbes*, IV, 1143, 1145–6.
[3] Vaughan, I, 182 (*Inégalité*). (My italics.)
[4] *Lettres Ecrites de la Montagne*, IX, 261–4.
[5] Vaughan, I, 301 (*L'état de guerre*).

it is not only in the army that *ésprit de corps* is acquired and its effects are not always for good'.[1] Simply by filling some official post, Emile's tutor admits, he also could become a monster and a 'foe of every kind of virtue'. If he were to become wealthy, he would soon be just as insolent and unfeeling as other rich men. He might be wise enough to use his wealth to make himself and his friends really happy. He might even remain generous and benevolent.[2] Nevertheless, in a society of radical inequality, not even a wise man can be rich without injuring the poor, if only by turning his eyes away from their suffering. The magistrate is in this respect in exactly the same position as the rich man. His public relations to other men are determined by his situation as a governor, not only by his personal character. As members of a corporate governing group magistrates are capable of actions that they would never undertake to further their purely personal interests, and they do this without the slightest feeling of guilt. For these are moral bodies held together by conventions which act as impersonal standards of judgment for their members. They have their own 'morality', even if it be a false one. Indeed, 'each estate and each profession has its own dictionary' which gives them a language to turn vice into virtue. The corruption of our souls is pictured in an increasing refinement of words, which permit a minister to speak of political 'expediency' when he is really exploiting the people.[3] It is all, however, a matter of his social situation. Every magistrate is bound to have three wills and three sets of duties. There is a personal one, a magistral one, and a civic one.[4] If the last is silenced, as it usually is, then only two remain, and of these the second one will, thanks to *amour-propre*, dominate his conduct.

The conditions that mould officials prevail also within other organized associations. Opinions are made in the same way within all groups especially among those which exist in order to influence public policy. 'Every political society is composed of other societies each one of which has its own interests and maxims.' Some are hidden, some open. Some are temporary and some permanent. To understand the mores of a political society one must study the

---

[1] *Emile*, 310.
[2] *Ibid.* 311–20.
[3] Vaughan, I, 335 (*Fragment*).
[4] *Ibid.* II, 69–70 (*Contrat Social*).

relationships of these groups to each other. For as all try to impinge upon the public, they all tend to clash with each other. Above all the effective will of their members is that of their association, and this is usually injurious to society as a whole. 'A man may be a devout preacher, a brave soldier, a zealous patrician and a bad citizen.'[1] He abides by a social morality, but it is a too limited one. That is why Rousseau had no use for lesser associations. As individuals, members of these groups feel virtuous in their submission to collective ends, but these sacrifices of self to society are of no benefit to anyone but the members of a small body. That is how one can remain personally good and yet become a social menace.

Privilege-seeking private associations are only the results of inequality and competition, not their original cause. Only a tyrant would want to keep people wholly apart from each other. Beneficial small public-spirited associations were quite conceivable. In Sparta and Rome they had been set up to promote cooperation and sociability.[2] In his own day, however, Rousseau could think of only one set of decent clubs, the *cercles* of Geneva. According to him they were the social clubs of simple people with no competitive political aims. Their main purpose was to gossip and to keep a sharp eye on the sexual habits of others. As such they were the best of guardians of popular mores. In this Rousseau was somewhat less than candid. The *cercles* were, in fact, very much concerned with politics. They were the political organizations of the Genevan 'burghers' who opposed the ruling families. Several of Rousseau's Genevan acquaintances hastened to remind him of it, but he evidently did not feel moved to alter his picture of the *cercles*.[3] This was not only, perhaps, because he was in sympathy with their members. To Rousseau, they could not appear as a power group, because they were made up of 'the people' whose whole aim was to maintain a popular tradition that favored equality. As such they were one of the last brakes upon the torrent of civilization and inequality. That is what distinguished them from every other lesser association. All the others had in Rousseau's view only one common end, to

[1] Vaughan, I, 242–3 (*Economie Politique*).   [2] *Ibid.* I, 319 (*Fragment*).
[3] *Letter to d'Alembert*, 98–108; Gaston Valette, *Jean-Jacques Rousseau Genevois* (Paris, 1911), 137.

promote inequality by seeking their own aggrandizement and political power. The members of the *cercles*, however, were simple citizens who, neither individually nor collectively, wanted new wealth or power. They merely wanted to preserve an egalitarian order. Nevertheless, Geneva was only a semi-civic order. The best solution of all was the Spartan, in which no private associations existed. If that should prove impossible, the policy of Solon, Nerva and Servius ought to be pursued, and all private associations should be made equal.[1] This would at least eliminate the competition and strife between groups and neutralize their impact upon politics.

Rousseau did not see such policies as restricting individual freedom in any significant way. On the contrary, the individual is released from opinions prejudicial to himself. There was no danger, in his eyes, in clashes of personal interests. These cancel each other out, and the public good emerges victoriously. It is not so when organized groups compete. Then the strongest must always win, and the will and views of the dominant party must prevail. For groups are not limited physically or psychologically in their expansiveness, as are individual men. The state of war between states is merely the most extreme form of group conflict, because states are under no restraint whatever in their perpetual and deadly competition. The individual is repressed by the collectivity to which he belongs, but organized groups, being artificial conventional persons, have neither physical feebleness nor compassion to restrain them in their pursuit of power.[2]

It is just because the interests of organized groups are experienced as objects of moral obligation by their members, who sacrifice their personal preferences to these bodies that the latter are so free from all restrictions in their relations to each other. The devoted citizen of a perfected polity is the enemy of all foreigners. So the members of political associations within any state are hostile to all their fellow citizens. This is more clearly the case with the first two estates, the nobility and clergy. Rousseau's hostility to representative institutions arose entirely from his contempt for these remnants of feudal 'barbarism'. The parliamentary institutions which he knew were still

[1] Vaughan, II, 42–3 (*Contrat Social*).
[2] *Ibid*. I, 294–5, 300, 305 (*L'état de guerre*).

organized to represent the three estates and he saw, quite rightly, that under such an arrangement the first two were always better served than the third. The people are always most easily ignored.[1] If the Poles had to have representatives, let them at least speak only for their constituents, and not as a group apart from the nation. For the nobility of the robe there was no need at all. This was simply a prime example of a professional group that served its own interests at the expense of all others. Their only concern was to obfuscate the law in order to maintain their own powers. Hereditary political groups, in short, inevitably developed interests of their own which were at odds with those whom they were designed to serve.[2]

The best remedy, perhaps, was to enlarge the organs of government, since the larger the governing body, the weaker the corporate bond uniting its members would become.[3] In that event, each member would act as an individual, and that was far less dangerous. For there was a qualitative difference between personal inequalities and corporate ones, such as those created by feudalism.[4] Not only were individuals limited in their life-span and strength, but their competitive urges, though indestructible, could be directed toward useful public ends. The aspirations of the nobility of Poland ought, for instance, to be turned away from wealth to other marks of distinction. For wealth is the most corrupting of all human objects of desire. It cannot but stifle other urges. Much is gained if the passion for distinction expresses itself in a pursuit of public esteem, rank, honors and places. Let the Polish nobility compete for these, as long as this will divert them from mercenary pursuits.[5] Not political authority, but the ability to buy another man is what creates a ruinous inequality. The original source of inequality, that precedes political organization, remains the root of all social evil: the immense gap between poor and rich.[6]

As he became convinced that he was the victim of a universal and systematic conspiracy, Rousseau came to believe that the making of public opinion had changed in his own day. It was no longer a

---

[1] Vaughan, II, 96 (*Contrat Social*); 445 (*Poland*).
[2] *Ibid.* 450-2, 467, 472-3 (*Poland*).
[3] *Ibid.* 70-1, 73 (*Contrat Social*).   [4] *Ibid.* 325 (*Corsica*).
[5] *Ibid.* 436-7, 477-9 (*Poland*); I, 333-4 (*Fragment*).
[6] *Ibid.* 183, 192 (*Inégalité*).

relatively aimless creation of group conflicts, shifting and changing hither and thither. Now it was an organized scheme. However, even before 'the Frenchman', or the public at large, had been cleverly misled by 'them', as Rousseau so frantically claimed in *Rousseau Juge de Jean-Jacques*, he had assumed public opinion *could* be engineered. He had even attempted to teach the kings how they could turn the nobility from their penchant for duelling, by cleverly managing their feelings.[1] Moreover, even when the experience of constant persecution, combined with his extreme sensitivity, had made him irrational, he could still offer an acute and intelligent analysis of the ways in which public opinion was being formed and dominated—in order to destroy him.

The most fundamental cause of the modern despotism of public opinion was the dissolution of positive social bonds. The spread of commerce, the growth of capital cities, the flourishing of the arts and sciences, all contributed to an erosion of those ties of mutual goodwill and esteem that had once held men together. Now only self-interest kept men together in a state of dependence which was without any positive compensations, since it was a competitive order in which men needed each other solely as means, as instruments of their own advancement. Thus, although men lived more and more under each other's eyes, their personal well being depended upon mutual deception and destruction.[2] The result was a general increase in deception all around and in conspiratorial activity especially. The majority of men, for lack of any positive associations and sources of trust, were exposed to the machinations of the most powerful and adroit among them. Moreover, ambition lures the innocent into crediting the opinions of those to whose level they aspire or upon whom they depend. The result is the rule of dominant parties, of which there were, he believed, only two in France: the court, led by the Duc de Choiseul, and the city of Paris, controlled by the *philosophes*. The French as a whole no longer had a personal existence, acting only in masses. Each one was nothing in himself. And there is never any disinterested love of justice in such collectivities; for nature is imprinted only upon the hearts of individuals, where it is quickly erased by the spirit of party. The result is that the

[1] *Letter to d'Alembert*, 67–74.   [2] *'Préface' à Narcisse*, 968–9.

new age was one of hatred and conspiracy. One of the new features of this age of suspicion was that public opinion was now systematically and methodically made at the top of society and spread downward. Once opinions changed without rhyme or reason. Now opinions no longer flowed from the collisions of these passions in an uncontrolled way. The public was subject to direct and planned campaigns in a war between two otherwise unchallenged parties.[1]

These reflections were, to be sure, inspired directly by Rousseau's contemplation of the ubiquitous 'system' that was destroying him and giving 'the Frenchman' such frightful notions about him. How-ever, in spite of their immediate origins in Rousseau's heated imagin-ation and justifiable unhappiness, they were perfectly in keeping with his most enduring and earliest convictions. The state built on inequality and held together by *amour-propre* could only go in one direction, toward tyranny.[2] Moreover, he was responding to the expressed ambitions of many of Voltaire's disciples, even if not to the actualities of their position and influence. Had not Voltaire in a moment of unjustified pride paraphrased Pascal to claim that 'if opinion is the queen of the world, then the *philosophes* govern that queen'?[3] And his followers did try, however unsuccessfully, to organize themselves into a counter-church in the course of combat against the Church of Rome.[4] Voltaire did egg them on to unite and fight, and even the calm and balanced d'Alembert kept appealing to his friends to stick together in imitation of the Jesuits. If the *philos-ophes* would only 'rally, after the manner of the ancient Romans and the Jesuit Order, at first signal of the common enemy!', he pleaded. For 'if they were united, they could give laws to the universe, and laws more praiseworthy and durable than those which Jesuit ambition wished to lay upon the nations. Its power was based on superstition and intrigue; the power of men of letters should be based on understanding and truth, whose strength is far more effective, since it subdues men's minds without constraining them.'[5] No wonder Rousseau came to regard the struggle between the *philosophes* and the Jesuits as a power struggle just like the war

---

[1] *Rousseau Juge de Jean-Jacques*, II, 890–1, 964–5.   [2] Vaughan, I, 190–4 (*Inégalité*).
[3] Peter Gay, *Voltaire's Politics* (Princeton, 1959), 33–4.
[4] Mario Roustan, *The Pioneers of the French Revolution*, trans. by F. Whyte (Boston, 1926), 262.   [5] Grimsley, *D'Alembert*, 130–1.

97

between Rome and Carthage! It was of no concern to him, since there was no moral difference between these equally intolerant parties.[1]

In fact Rousseau mistook d'Alembert's pleas for unity for a fair account of actuality. Since he felt himself to be as much persecuted by both sides he could perhaps not recognize the differences. There was, thus, both shrewdness and madness in these reflections. Rousseau was very perceptive in recognizing how alike groups locked in combat become, however different the ideas that divide them might be. Nor was he far wrong in thinking that the struggle for power as such had a greater impact upon society than the ideas professed by the parties at war. His madness was in his overwhelming sense of a conspiratorial system. Had he not shown how complex the psychological and social development of opinions really was? The 'spiritual epidemic' which he saw around him had not been manufactured by his enemies. The willingness of most men to allow others to do their thinking for them, especially when it suited their self-interest, was an open invitation to the *philosophes* and Jesuits. Contagious diseases, whether moral or physical, spread only when men live in crowded conditions, as in Paris, where each person infects his neighbor.[2] His real objection to the *philosophes* was that they favored this unhealthy state of affairs. Their faith in progress, benevolent despots, and enlightened self-interest could only worsen conditions. The real duty of a wise man is, however, to prevent change, since change means degeneration. 'All that human wisdom can do is to forestall all changes, to arrest from afar all that brings them on.'[3]

The evils of the age had not been created by the *philosophes* but they exploited the opportunities created by Parisian society to exercise their craft. The chance to practice their wiles was not of their own making. Where there are no bonds save those of dependence and ambition, the path to spiritual tyranny is wide open. When Saint-Preux arrives in Paris the first thing he notices is the general aloneness of its inhabitants. Each one lives fearfully under the eyes of others, but no one really belongs to anyone else. There are no ties

[1] *Rousseau Juge de Jean-Jacques*, III, 967–8.　　[2] *Ibid.* II, 880; *Emile*, 26.
[3] *Letter to d'Alembert*, 74.

of loyalty underneath the general politeness. In order to survive in the crowd each one adopts the opinions of whatever group he finds himself in at any given moment. At the top there is a war between factions. Here a very few people do all the thinking for the rest. To be 'like everyone else' is at all times the supreme law and adaptability is a necessity for survival. This 'is done' or 'is not done' are the rules one must follow. In fact, of course, 'everyone' is very few people indeed—the rich and powerful.

Julie, after reading this account, reminds her lover that surely there are people other than those in Paris, the poor and humble, who are ignored by the great and who neither make nor unmake opinions. Had he not a duty to speak for them, to give voice to the needs of those who cannot speak for themselves? Was that not an end more worthy than haunting the salons of the pace-setters? Why was he not devoting his life to the poor and humble who needed his help?[1] Rousseau was obviously questioning himself also at this point. It was not the first or the last time for him to do so. However, in choosing his life's direction he only rarely weighed the claims of public duty and private ambition. The real choice for him was one between intellectual conformity and a compelling need to be true to his inner self. He could not be a toady, but he was not prepared to silence his genius and remain obscure.[2] He always retained his sense of being a simple man and of being able to share the outlook of humble people in a way that only a man of the people could. When he had finally finished his life's work he was able to take up a simple craft and live very modestly. However, this return to his origins was not the same thing as having devoted his life to the poor by living in their midst. Nevertheless, he saw his work as a service to them, even if an indirect one.

Rousseau's defense of his own conduct shows that 'the fundamental issue was that he felt compelled at all cost to become himself'.[3] Being himself meant that he would have to identify himself consistently and openly with his own past, and so, with the interests of the people against those of the rich and powerful. It did not mean that

---

[1] *N.H.*, Part II, Letters XIV, XVII, XVIII.
[2] Jean Guéhnno, *Jean-Jacques Rousseau*, trans. by John and Doreen Weightman (London, 1966), I, 108–11.　　　[3] *Ibid.* I, 192.

he would have to leave the world of letters. That would, after all, also have been self-betraying. For although Rousseau could be very modest about his literary talents, he was not inclined to excuse himself for his views. When he asked the rhetorical question: 'am I the only wise man in the world?', he decided that, indeed, he was.[1] His message *was* himself, and he had a very high regard for his person. He alone among the writers of his age had spoken for the people. He alone had tried to stop the peasants from rushing to their doom in Paris. He alone had opposed the policies and prejudices that were turning the countryside into a desert in the interests of the cities. Was it not important for the happiness of mankind that this torrent of poisonous maxims be stopped?[2] He could not have been as much use to his fellowmen as a mere Genevan citizen as he had been by living in Paris and speaking the truth.[3] He had fulfilled his obligations to the people, not by joining them, but by protecting them. For the voice of the people might well be that of God, but only as long as it had not been corrupted.[4]

Rousseau was far from believing that it was wrong to mould public opinion from above, if it prevented corruption. In Rome and Sparta where this was done to maintain a cohesive society it was all to the good.[5] His own contribution as an opinion-maker was altogether admirable because he alone had tried to warn men against their attachment to a civilization that was destroying them while other authors were doing their best to promote the decline.[6] Sometimes his self-defense was pure casuistry. He had written plays and operas only because in a corrupt society such entertainments served a useful function. They prevented worse crimes. Corrupting though they were, they were necessary in a vicious society.[7] Only the remaining pure societies, such as Geneva, ought to be protected against the evil consequences of theatrical spectacles.

The fact remains that Rousseau's life as a writer was only incidentally a service to his fellow men, in the sense that his quest for

---

[1] *Lettres à Malesherbes*, II, 1136; *Confessions*, XII, 591, 686–9; *Rêveries*, III, 1020.
[2] *N.H.*, 'Seconde Préface'.   [3] *Lettres à Malesherbes*, IV, 1143–4.
[4] Vaughan, I, 243 (*Economie Politique*); *Lettres Ecrites de la Montagne*, VIII, 242.
[5] *Emile*, 286–7; *Letter to d'Alembert*, 66–7.
[6] *Rousseau Juge de Jean-Jacques*, I, 727–9; '*Préface*' à *Narcisse*, 970–1.
[7] '*Préface*' à *Narcisse*, 971–94.

himself necessarily forced him to take up the cause of the people. His literary life began with a declaration of war against his fellow writers and it is to them that all his subsequent writings on politics and religion were addressed. When one compares his and Diderot's accounts of that famous visit to the prison of Vincennes, it is clear that, for all their later quarrels on the subject, there is no difference between their views of what happened to Rousseau. Rousseau claimed that he decided to write an essay against the arts and sciences quite independently of Diderot's advice. Diderot many years later wrote in an unpublished set of reflections that it was he who had urged Rousseau to answer the question of the Academy negatively in order to seem original and so to win the prize. Then he added that if he, Diderot, had written that essay he would certainly not have spent several months in propping up such a bad paradox with sophisms, nor would he have given them all the color that Rousseau did. Certainly he would not have made a philosophic system out of a *jeu d'ésprit*. Rousseau did what he had to do because he was he.[1] That, of course, was the truth. Rousseau had to write what he wrote because he was Rousseau. In all probability he took Diderot's advice and as he began to think about the question he suddenly realized that this was really what he believed! He did not share the faith in progress and did not think that the arts and sciences contributed to man's well-being. He did not share the opinions of his friends.

At that moment also Rousseau discovered the uses of Sparta. His first essay was not only the first of his hymns to that martial utopia. It was also Rousseau's first attack on 'celebrated Arouet', who had sacrificed so much noble and powerful beauty to mere false delicacy and gallantry. It was very cleverly put. By ignoring his rival's assumed name, Rousseau exposed in one sentence both Voltaire's social pretensions and lack of moral and artistic integrity.[2] The two were completely linked in Rousseau's mind, in any case. Civilized art, of which Voltaire was the greatest creator, served oppression directly and indirectly. Just as surely Sparta in its crudity

---

[1] *Confessions*, VIII, 350–2; *Lettres à Malesherbes*, II, 1135–6. Diderot, *Réfutation de l'Ouvrage d'Helvétius Intitulé 'L'Homme', Œuvres Complètes* (Paris, 1875), II, 285–6.
[2] *Discours sur les Sciences et les Arts*, 13. Rousseau's attacks on Rameau were the musical equivalent of his assault on Voltaire.

met all the real needs of the people. That is why Sparta was so essentially anti-Paris. Thus also the very last of Rousseau's Spartan fantasies, the improbable plan to make Spartans out of the Polish nobility, was written far more against the *philosophes* than for the Poles. For if Diderot and Voltaire flattered Catherine the Great, Rousseau was going to idealize her rebellious subjects. Voltaire had often expressed a low opinion of the Poles. Rousseau had no use for enlightened despots and for the civilized values with which they oppressed their groaning subjects.[1]

From his first public act of self-definition to his very last political statement, Rousseau clung to the Spartan utopia, because it was everything that polite society was not. For if his autobiographical writings had a public purpose, his books on public subjects also served a private end. Once he saw himself as the last citizen, he was

---

[1] The history of how Rousseau came to write the *Considérations sur le Gouvernement de Pologne* is one of endless complexity. In his excellent notes of his edition of the text, M. Jean Fabre has shown that Rousseau did some reading on Polish history, but not very much. He does show, line by line, that every one of Rousseau's proposals was a rejection of the ideas of Mably, who had already written a similar project, also at the request of Count Wielhorski, who gave it to Rousseau to help him in his own work. Now Rousseau had special reasons to hate Mably. After years of friendship the abbé not only plagiarized him on various occasions, but in the hour of his greatest need he had betrayed Rousseau in favor of Voltaire and Voltaire's Genevan disciples. That was not all. In his project Mably had not disguised his contempt for the Poles and for their clergy. In this he also followed Voltaire, who had frequently taken pains to please his friend the Empress by abusing the Poles. In the *Dictionnaire Philosophique*, under the heading '*Philosophie*', he not only praised Catherine the Great for her enlightened spirit, but also scolded the rebellious Poles for their lack of philosophic sense in resisting her rule. Under the heading '*Peter the Great*', he delivered a tasteless and bitter attack on Rousseau, who had made some disparaging remarks in the *Contrat Social* about the czar. It is clear why Voltaire hated Rousseau; it was the latter's firm, and guilt-inspiring, rejection of the despots, whom Voltaire did serve. It is also easy to see why Rousseau should have been so oddly prepared to have a high opinion of the Catholic and politically disoriented Polish nobility. Their enemies were their greatest distinction in his eyes. If they were so remote from Voltaire's spirit, there must surely be some virtue in them and he was willing to forget their religion and feudalism, as he discovered, somehow, traces of ancient vigor in the Polish national soul. To be sure, there were serfs, there was a large territory, there was wealth and poverty. But at least there was no Voltaire. Diderot and Voltaire, finally, might choose to flatter and serve Catherine the Great, but Rousseau would not. At whatever loss of political realism, he preferred to serve her rebellious subjects by reminding them of Sparta. See Jean Fabre, 'Introduction' and 'Notes et Variantes', in *Œuvres Complétes* (Pléiade, Paris, 1964), III, CCXVI-CCXLV, 1733-1804; Gay, *Voltaire's Politics*, 178-9. On Mably and Rousseau, see *Confessions*, XII, 621; 'Lettre à M. l'Abbé de Mably', 6 février 1765, *C.G.*, XII, 317-19; 'Lettre de Mably à Rousseau', le 11 février 1765, *C.G*, XII, 359-60.

bound to return to Geneva, to challenge Voltaire and embark on his career as an opinion-maker, dedicated to exposing the vices of the prevailing empire. In the first moment of self-discovery he found both his opponents and his enduring vocation. To be himself was to be the last Cato, thundering against the intellectual environment and those who had made it.

THE OPINION-MAKERS

Public opinion is made for the benefit of the powerful by their literary servants. What place was Rousseau to occupy among these, if he was to exercise any moral influence? What was to be his method in stemming the tide of corrupting opinion that threatened to destroy the last remnants of social virtue? As an author he addressed the same public as they did: the educated and rich. He spoke to them as an equal, if not as a superior. If he alone was willing and able to protect the innocent people, he was not addressing them. It was not for them that he wrote, but against their enemies. He was perfectly right when he told the Genevan authorities that he had never thought of himself as a popular prophet or dogmatizer and had never been a disturber of the public order.[1] He wrote for the wise and against the powerful. There was nothing contradictory in this position, since Rousseau believed in the need for censorial supervision of public opinion, even under the best civic conditions.[2] He saw himself as the last Roman censor, born into an unhappy age. When he felt that there was something ambiguous about speaking to those whom he rejected so violently, especially when he was entertaining them, he simply fell back upon the corruption of the age, especially the newly organized conspiratorial direction of public opinion. These circumstances offered Rousseau a full justification for his overwhelming interest in the activities of the conspirators at the top of the social pyramid.

There were also less evident reasons for Rousseau's preoccupation with his fellow intellectuals. Because of the highly personal character of his concern with even the most impersonal subjects, the scope of his interests was often limited. He could not bring himself to deal

---

[1] *Lettres Ecrites de la Montagne*, v, 185–6; *Emile*, 274.
[2] Vaughan, II, 122–3 (*Contrat Social*).

with anything that was too remote from himself and his pursuit of his true self. He never wrote about the actual life of either the urban or rural poor. Like Saint-Preux he ignored them. His peasants are prosperous utopian figures designed to shame the degenerate civilizees of Paris. He put his experiences as a footman and a tutor to remarkable literary and polemical use. His brief apprenticeship was, however, only a painful memory. Nothing much was said about other apprentices, journeymen or craftsmen. He never discussed the commercial life of his native city and was uninterested in the merchants and artisans of Paris. The useful crafts were left to Diderot's intellectual care. If he identified with any group it was with the Genevan burghers, in as much as they represented a civic, anti-Parisian ideal. However, as soon as he realized that his own cause in Geneva was lost, he told his friends and defenders among the citizens to give up the common struggle against the ruling families and to seek the help of Voltaire in making peace. In the end the burghers certainly got a lot more support from the old scoffer than they could ever expect from Rousseau.[1]

When the rulers of Geneva rejected him, Rousseau turned his back on his fellow citizens and never worried himself again even about those among them who had come to his support. Geneva had played its part in his voyage of self-discovery. In ranging himself with its burghers against Voltaire, the rich and the theater, he had found himself. That was the limit of his citizenship. To be sure, he had never claimed to have any interest in, or liking for, popular insurrections. He was wholly preoccupied with the structure, legitimacy, durability and decline of governments, especially republican ones. For everything depended on that. Politics was the study of governmental institutions and Rousseau's eyes were set most often upon the magistracy. *The Social Contract* is primarily concerned with ways of inhibiting republican governments from following their self-destructive propensities.[2]

---

[1] Valette, *op. cit.* 340; Gay, *Voltaire's Politics*, 210–38.
[2] On Rousseau's preoccupation with decline in general and with the fall of republics especially and on how this melancholy sense of corruption links him with the Latin authors, most notably Seneca and Tacitus, see Bertrand de Jouvenel's excellent articles, 'Rousseau the Pessimistic Evolutionist', *Yale French Studies* (1961–2), 93–96, and 'Essai sur la politique de Rousseau', *Du Contrat Social* (Geneva, 1947), 18–38.

As always these ideas can be traced to personal experiences. For Rousseau did have direct political experiences of a sort. To be sure he was not a political insider in the way that Montesquieu had been. He had tried and failed. He was very ambitious to succeed when he made an attempt at a diplomatic career, and was very proud of himself while it lasted. Venice was the beginning of his political education in several ways. In his continual dealings with the local officials he could observe at close hand how republican governments rot, a process he was to find of enduring interest. More important, the injuries that he suffered without redress at the hands of the ambassador made him realize that he could never find a fit place in the existing order which was, moreover, unjust through and through.[1] At the bottom of that injustice was the system of inequality. From then on Rousseau knew that politics was something that was being done *to* him, a source of injury. His career as a professional victim of oppression had begun. Posterity is still, perhaps, in M. de Montaigu's debt for having contributed so much to the writing of the *Discourse on Inequality*.[2]

The brush with the French diplomatic service was not the end of Rousseau's relations with the political powers of his day. When he returned to Geneva in 1754, he made some friends among the magistrates there and they welcomed this celebrity quite warmly. Nevertheless, by then Rousseau knew what Voltaire had yet to learn: that talent was not enough to make one a member of any ruling class. Moreover, he knew that his message would not be welcome to any magistrate. No amount of sugar-coating in the 'Dedication' could render the contents of the *Discourse on Inequality* palatable to any government. Rousseau did not, therefore, even try to get the members of the Council to give him permission to dedicate that work to them, as some of his Genevan friends urged him to do. He inscribed it to the Geneva of his dreams instead, not to the real city which he did not really like.[3] His political position was already defined. Even during these years of public success and approbation he was the man at the bottom of the social pyramid,

---

[1] *Confessions*, VII, 297–312, 323–7; IX, 404–6.
[2] Guéhnno, *Jean-Jacques Rousseau*, I, 139.
[3] 'Lettre à M. Perdriau', 28 septembre 1754, *C.G.*, II, 130–6; Valette, *op. cit.* 85–102.

denouncing the men at the top. For victimhood corresponded to his innermost experiences and it already suited his vision of himself. It was not his actual social situation, but a consciously adopted stance.

From this vantage point and with a single-minded devotion to his critical mission, Rousseau did not need to concern himself with anything that seemed uninteresting or irrelevant to his ends. He could not, for instance, be bothered with the details of world politics. Work on the papers of the Abbé de Saint-Pierre was an impossibly tedious chore. There is no character more ridiculous in the *Nouvelle Héloise* than Julie's uncle who is so interested in international affairs that he has no time for his family. This armchair politician spends his days thinking about the Pragmatic Sanction when he should be looking after his daughter's future! Julie and Claire regard him as simply hopeless. Why should she interest herself in such questions, Julie asks? Why should she concern herself with ills that she cannot alter when there are so many people right around her whom she can help effectively?[1] Rousseau only took half of her advice, since he rarely did anything for other people. However, neither high policy nor charity were necessary to his chosen position as a professional victim, nor to his vocation as a public censor.

When he was eventually really and cruelly persecuted it had its liberating effects. It proved in practice what he had always felt, and it gave him occasions for telling the established ecclesiastical and political powers in Paris and Geneva exactly what he had always thought of them. At last he was free to confront the Genevan establishment openly. Like all governing powers the magistrates were the deceivers of a duped people. Ruse, prejudice, interest, fear, hope, vanity, specious colors, a pretence of order, subordination—everything in Geneva was arranged, as it was everywhere, to favor the stratagems of those who are in power. United to rule, trained in the art of abusing people, with funds, clients and dependents at their disposal, their power was always superior to that of anyone who might challenge them, whatever his merits.[2] It is a picture of government seen from the depth of powerlessness. Was there not always a 'natural league of the strong' which made them invincible, while the feebleness of the weak was always certain because they could not

[1] *N.H.*, Part II, Letters V and XXVIII.   [2] *Lettres Ecrites de la Montagne*, VIII, 243.

assert themselves?[1] Conspiratorial omnipotence at the top and utter helplessness at the bottom were inseparable and inevitable in any unequal order, and Geneva was no different in this respect.

Gloomy as these reflections appear, they were not without psychological rewards for Rousseau. It made his victimhood a public badge of his own purity, justified his passivity, and underwrote his utopianism. It also gave his self-liberation an heroic character. He was, after all, not just a simple victim. He alone among his contemporaries had not been taken in by public opinion or been dazzled by the favors of the great. In his way he was thus more his own master than those who remained enslaved by sham and illusion. Thus he hovered between omnipotence and impotence. He was one of the people in his hopeless helplessness, but he was also greater than the mighty, since he was less deluded and less dependent on public opinion than they were.

The sense of an all-powerful conspiracy was not entirely in keeping with Rousseau's more subtle insights into the interplay between *amour-propre* and self-delusion, and between ambition and conformity. He often had far more complex notions about the social interaction of competing groups than this simple picture of a pyramidal order suggests. Conspiracy is, to be sure, easier to denounce, and continual persecution did much to heighten Rousseau's sensitivity to the evils of power. Moreover, he had always seen a conspiratorial element in the politics of inequality. Partly this arose out of his ambiguous feelings about 'the people'. The people alone has remnants of virtue and a capacity for happiness, but that is a hidden potentiality. In actuality the public is so stupid and so readily misled that it is past being instructed.[2] Everything must be done for it, but not directly. To allow the natural goodness of Everyman to emerge again from his actual degradation, he must first of all be liberated from the evil influences that deform him. In practice, therefore, it is the activities of those who mislead that is politically relevant. It is the men who impose opinions, not those who consume them so avidly and idiotically, who make history. Above all, for purposes of moral indignation there is nothing like a conspiracy.

[1] *Ibid.* IX, 263.   [2] 'Lettre à M. l'Abbé de Raynal', juin 1753, *C.G.*, II, 47–50.

Rousseau's defense of himself as the voice and defender of the people was often disingenuous and he knew it. His search for appropriate beliefs was a personal one, in which he looked for what was right for him, for what matched his inner needs. He drifted into authorship to extricate himself from opinions which he could not assimilate. That is why he began and ended with denunciation. Unlike the superficial publicists of his days, he alone had known that self-knowledge had to be gained before one could even begin to teach others, he wrote.[1] To do that he had to distinguish his ideas from those that engulfed him. First of all he had to dispose of all the opinions around him. To that end two groups of opinion-makers were singled out for his special animadversion: the *philosophes* and the clergy. The intellectual grounds for this hostility are easily found in his very first public statement on religion, his letter to Voltaire, refuting the latter's cosmic pessimism. Rousseau was infinitely more skeptical than either the atheists or the orthodox believers. Since God is unknowable, religion was simply a matter of psychological need and social utility.[2]

He was a complete agnostic, but with a difference: although he did not know, he did care. He entirely agreed with the clergy: what men did depended on what they believed and religion with its profound bearing on morality could not be ignored.[3] Emile is not much of a scholar, but his religious education is serious. As soon as he reaches sexual maturity he is treated to a long discourse on natural religion. For 'neglect of religion leads to neglect of one's duties'.[4] No aspect of public opinion was more important than religious belief and unbelief.

Even though religion did not play any direct part in Rousseau's own emotional life and did not move him deeply, he was driven to consider it frequently and contentiously.[5] If social inequality was uppermost in his mind even when he attacked Voltaire, he could not have evaded the religious question in defining his position against this greatest of his intellectual adversaries. If the denial of religiosity

---

[1] *Rêveries*, III, 1012–13.
[2] Lettre à de Voltaire, *C.G.*, II, 316–21.
[3] *Rêveries*, III, 1013–14.   [4] *Emile*, 225.
[5] At most he had a sense of nature mysticism, into which God's name did not even enter directly. *Lettres à Malesherbes*, III, 1141.

was Voltaire's passion, then Rousseau had to begin by affirming its value, especially its civic value. The orthodox for their part could not afford to ignore him. Although in Rousseau's fantasy world it was Voltaire's party that was driving him to his grave, it was in fact the powers of orthodoxy in Paris and in Geneva who did the actual persecuting. As an entrenched part of the social order that he had attacked so passionately they were not likely to favor him. And his version of natural religion was a greater threat in their eyes than the sophisticated deism or atheism of the *philosophes*. When the orthodox had fired the first shot Rousseau felt free to speak his mind to them also, and clearly he had never regarded them as anything but the servants of despotic government.

Nevertheless, from first to last Rousseau was more deeply interested in denouncing the philosophic lights of Paris among whom he had once lived. Not the least interesting aspect of his attack on his fellow writers is that it was not as unique as he claimed it to be. He was far from being the only successful man of letters to deplore the character and conduct of this new breed of intellectuals. D'Alembert, in a sober and profoundly unhappy essay, implored them to show more dignity and a greater loyalty to the genuine ends of the republic of letters. The mathematician and scientist, he noted, is not exposed to social temptations; his subject is pursued because of its intrinsic interest. The artist, however, serves a public and he is out to make a reputation, not only among his peers, but among his patrons. The latter can only corrupt, for they are not really devoted to the arts and to letters. Idle noblemen, reduced by Louis XIV to boredom in Paris, had become patrons of the arts and letters to entertain themselves. It is not, however, in the chambers of the aristocracy that great thoughts and great works of art flourish. Patronage had only brought into being a large new class of generally mediocre scribblers. Lacking genuine standards, they cherished the illusion that the great regarded men of talent as their equals, rather than as their servants. They had failed to choose their proper public: posterity and the republic of letters, rather than the grandees.[1]

In these appeals d'Alembert showed himself to be wiser than

[1] *Essai sur la Société des Gens de Lettres et les Grands, Œuvres Complètes de d'Alembert* (Paris, 1822), II, 337–73.

Voltaire. Indeed, he reproached Voltaire for his unwarranted faith in the friendship of Mme de Pompadour and the dukes of Choiseul and Richelieu.[1] And there was something demeaning in Voltaire's life-long inability to accept the fact that in the class system of the *ancien régime* he could never be accepted as an equal by the highest aristocracy.[2] D'Alembert was not alone in deploring the conditions and character of Parisian literary life. He could not approve any more than Rousseau Diderot's final capitulation to a patroness as unedifying as Catherine the Great. However, Diderot had worn himself out in years of fighting publishers, printers and censors, and he simply gave up in the end.[3] D'Alembert was more upright, but he could, for all his severity, see the complexity of the social situation which was undermining high culture. Rousseau could only see wilful viciousness and a conspiracy to deceive.

To begin with, Rousseau had no respect for high culture, not only because it was morally corrupting, but because it was an integral part of unequal society. Artists and poets merely weave 'garlands of flowers to cover the iron chains' that weigh down people.[4] The very subject matter of art and learning depended on the prevalence of social oppression. What was jurisprudence without injustice, history without war, art without luxury? Who would have time for philosophy if all were occupied with the duties of man and of the citizen?[5] It is not by the pleasures they give, but by the miseries they hide that the arts and sciences ought to be judged. People live by custom; that is their best morality. The sciences only disturb them and destroy them without offering anything of value to ordinary men. Science is not made for 'man in general'. Popular mores are a treasure to be preserved, not small change to be spent on dangerous trifles. The world was made for ordinary men, not for genius.[6] Public opinion is easily shaped by the arts and their message is always dangerous, since it always accelerates the progress of corruption and inequality.[7] Rousseau was no puritan. He did not want to pull down maypoles.

---

[1] Grimsley, *D'Alembert*, 124–5.
[2] Gay, *Voltaire's Politics*, 35–9; *Confessions*, IX, 429–30; 'Lettre de M. le Docteur Tronchin', 1 septembre 1756, *C.G.*, II, 326–8.
[3] Jacques Proust, *Diderot et l'Encyclopédie* (Paris, 1962), 81–116.
[4] *Discours sur les Sciences et les Arts*, 3.   [5] *Ibid.* 10–11.
[6] *'Préface' à Narcisse*, 970–1.   [7] *Letter to d'Alembert*, 22–5, 51, 63–5.

The Golden Age was one of song and dance. This is the art of communal participation, not of professional creation. Like the public festivals of antiquity, they unite men in shared joy and give simple people their rightful pleasures.[1] Luxury was something quite different, a social disease of inequality that sumptuary laws ought to cure.[2] And the arts of a high culture are nothing but forms of luxury. The evil of high culture is its destructive impact on society, and this effect is willed by those who make it and by those for whom it is made, the intellectuals, the artists and their patrons, the rich and powerful.

What made the men of letters so contemptible? What drove them on? To Rousseau they were both the victims and the promoters of social conditions which necessarily caused them to corrupt their fellow men. Of all men they are the most consumed by *amour-propre*. Since they work to gain a reputation, their sole ambition is to be, not just admired, but to be more admired than anyone else.[3] Even he, so pure as a rule, was devoured by ambition and vanity while he pursued a literary career.[4] Driven by the passion for distinction, intellectuals flatter, intrigue and abase themselves and soon become masters in the art of deception. The opinions they support express nothing but their own ambitions and deceits. Their sole function is to enhance inequality in society and with it all the miseries and crimes that it breeds.[5] Yet they are also psychological and social victims of the very order which they so energetically support. A true sense of one's honor comes from deep self-esteem, not from public opinion. Because it is so uncertain, those who pursue their fortune by depending on the opinion of others doom themselves to unhappiness and insecurity.[6]

Nor is that all, for the men of letters have also become the mere domestic servants of the rich, whose favor and good opinion they need. What were they if not mere valets? Essentially they were courtiers. The *corps littéraire* only cheers on princes when they oppress their peoples. After all, it is the princes who give rewards and make reputations. And what is a courtier, literary or otherwise, but a valet? Indeed, the whole nobility is a *corps de valets*. 'Servitude is

---

[1] *Ibid.* 33, 77–9, 126–37; *N.H.*, Part II, Letter XVII; Part V, Letter VII.
[2] Vaughan, II, 434–7 *(Poland)*.   [3] *'Préface' à Narcisse*, 968–9.
[4] *Rousseau Juge de Jean-Jacques*, III, 806; *Rêveries*, VIII, 1079.
[5] *'Préface' à Narcisse*, 968–9.   [6] *N.H.*, Part I, Letter XXIV.

always the same, only the masters differ.'[1] The valet was for Rousseau a symbolic figure. He had been one himself and it was without a doubt the worst thing that had ever happened to him. When he said that all footmen were necessarily scoundrels, he knew what he was talking about. He himself had been a thief and a liar and had betrayed his fellow servants.[2] All valets, he came to feel, shared the same vices: dishonesty, vanity, anger, envy. That is the result of their condition. Indeed, they only imitate their masters.[3] Paris as a whole is a city of valets, 'the most degraded of men'.[4] For ultimately it is impotence that breeds wickedness, in children, in servants, in authors and in noblemen alike.[5] 'Strength and liberty make excellent men. Weakness and slavery have never made anything but evildoers.'[6] It was part of his own superiority to other men that he alone had known, not only that he was not meant to be a valet or a mere author, but that he had managed to escape both conditions.[7] That is why he was so hated and why his solitude and his simple life as a copyist were such a threat to the *amour-propre* of his former friends in the literary world. For their rebellion against the prevailing order was not a liberation. Having accepted slavery once in order to dominate others, they had now turned against their former masters in order to replace them. However, their war against the old powers, especially against the Jesuits, had only forced them into a new subservience to the leaders of their own party and in this condition they were only too happy to persecute and hate anyone who refused to join, who dissociated himself and disagreed with all the dominant opinions, whether old or new.[8] Fanaticism escalates in restrictive organizations because it is an expression of the insecurity of its enslaved members. Rousseau had the outsider's keen eye for the malaise of the conformist and the ex-footman's knowledge of the bitterness of envy, wherever it arose.

Atheism was merely the opinion that corresponded to the interests and situation of the literary world. 'It was a purely

---

[1] Vaughan, II, 303 (*état de guerre*); Vaughan, I, 357 (*Fragment*); N.H., Part III, XXIII; Part IV, Letter XII.   [2] *Confessions*, II, 84–7.
[3] *N.H.*, Part V, Letter III.   [4] *Emile*, 59.
[5] *Ibid.* 33.   [6] *Rêveries*, VI, 1067.
[7] *Confessions*, III, 93, 98–9; *Lettres à Malesherbes*, II, 1136–7.
[8] *Rousseau Juge de Jean-Jacques*, II, 890–1.

offensive morality. . . good only for aggression.'[1] It was an attitude
that has its roots in resentment and flowered in combat. It expressed
the deep inner discontent of the intellectuals with their own lot, and
in the end it served only the rich and powerful. The position to
which ambition had raised even the most successful writers was not
really a satisfying one. Voltaire found the world so intolerable and
believed it to be ruled by an evil providence because of his own
situation. If he had ever spoken to a Swiss peasant he would have
known that not all men were unhappy in their condition.[2] These
remarks were among the first that Rousseau ever made about faith
and unbelief, and every sentence makes it clear that he was moved by
emotional and social concerns, not by theology. The dissatisfactions
felt by Voltaire were the result   of ambition and social mobility.
Intellectuals, not prosperous peasants, found life on earth a burden,
and it was the former who, impelled by their own distress, were
determined to make life unbearable for everyone else.

It was the inner rage of competition and frustration, then, that
drove the followers of Voltaire to encourage the wildest egotism and
to tear asunder the last ties that bound society together. For
atheism was a doctrine designed to achieve no other end. It could
only serve the interests of the rich, who would now be free from
those last constraints on their selfishness which religion was able
to impose upon them.[3] For the rich, religion was a mere inconveni-
ence; with its removal their tyranny would now know no restraints.[4]
This was, moreover, entirely to be expected. For the philosophers
catered to the rich who make literary reputations. Patrons have to be
pleased.[5] The triumph of atheism will bring with it the peace of
tyranny, ultimately worse than the violence of even the worst wars
of fanaticism. 'If atheism does not lead to bloodshed, it is less from
love of peace than from indifference to what is good; as if it mattered
little what happened to others, provided the sage remained undisturbed in his study. . . The indifference of the philosopher is like the
peace in a despotic state, it is the repose of death.'[6]

With these blasts at the motives, the fanaticism and the dangers of

---

[1] *Rêveries*, II, 1022.   [2] 'Lettre à Voltaire', 308–9.
[3] 'Lettre à De Leyre', 5 octobre 1758, *C.G.*, IV, 63–5.
[4] *Rousseau Juge de Jean-Jacques*, III, 971–2.
[5] *Lettre à Christophe de Beaumont*, 87.   [6] *Emile*, 276–7.

atheism Rousseau was not about to throw himself into the arms of the orthodox. He was no more inclined toward the clerical party than toward that of the atheists. Both camps of opinion-makers were in fact alike. The newcomers had learned their lessons from their Jesuit enemies. Thus, although Rousseau's interest in religion was initially stirred by his hostility to Voltaire, it was not possible for him to please the powers of orthodoxy. His contempt for superstition, for clerical ambition and militant intolerance had never been hidden. He had not, however, felt bound to challenge the orthodox as explicitly or as violently as the followers of Voltaire. The orthodox party was simply not emotionally important to Rousseau. They were no threat to his inner self; for he had never been one of them. It was in this respect that Rousseau differed most from his contemporaries in Paris. This inability to feel either religion or its opposite deeply is clearly reflected in everything he wrote. It is never easy to know what any other human being really believes, and Rousseau was perhaps not entirely certain about his own religious state of mind. A man who could write to Voltaire, as Rousseau did, that 'he preferred your kind of Christian to that of the Sorbonne', was evidently no orthodox Christian.[1] Both his clerical and anti-clerical readers recognized that perfectly clearly. There were plenty of good reasons for d'Alembert to claim that the Savoyard Vicar's 'Confession of Faith' was a superfluous bit of 'mummery'.[2] However, it is evident that Emile's tutor is less religious than the Vicar, and Rousseau never went beyond saying that he greatly approved of Julie's and the Vicar's faith. His own was more or less like it, but not the same.[3]

It has been well noted that Rousseau's deepest concern was not to find God, but his own true and complete self.[4] His final account of his religious experiences shows nothing more than the very common drift from a conventional Protestantism to religious indifference which left only a sentimental attachment to Christian morality in its wake. He had never experienced the inner struggles of

[1] 'Lettre à Voltaire', 318.
[2] Grimsley, *D'Alembert*, 156; Samuel S. B. Taylor, 'Rousseau's Contemporary Reputation in France', *Studies on Voltaire and the Eighteenth Century* (1963), 27, 1545–74.
[3] *Emile*, 218–23, 278–9; *Lettres Ecrites de la Montagne*, I, 123; *Rêveries*, III, 1018–23.
[4] Grimsley, *Rousseau*, 242–3, 327–9.

the Frenchmen who rallied to Voltaire's cry '*écrasez l'infame*', and he could not share their passions. There had never been a break with family and friends to assert a radical denial of religion. He had not, like Diderot, been tonsured as a child of ten, had not like d'Alembert spent years under Jansenist teachers. There were no brothers who were abbés, no sisters in convents and no schoolmates and teachers to be rejected. There were no parents to be wounded. When Rousseau slipped out of Geneva he left its religion behind him in the same lighthearted way as he bid farewell to all other constraints of life in his native city. He became a Catholic for reasons that had no connection with religion, and evidently it was not an affecting experience.

When he returned to Geneva to resume his citizenship he rejoined the church of his ancestors as part of a civic act.[1] He did not claim that it was anything else. Neither doubt, nor conversion, nor conformity stirred him in any way comparable to his sudden realization that he did not believe in the benefits of intellectual progress. When he visited Geneva he did make friends with a few congenial pastors. These men had shared some of his experiences as they also had slipped from Calvinism to a simple theism. They felt no need to make any public issue of their beliefs, bound as they were by a multitude of ties to their city.[2] When d'Alembert announced to the public that most Genevan pastors were Socinians, they were thoroughly upset, not because it was false, but because this foreigner was meddling in their affairs and creating all sorts of unnecessary trouble. In his reply to d'Alembert, Rousseau devoted only a few pages to the whole matter and evaded the substance of the problem. Moreover, d'Alembert was just as hostile to Protestantism as he was to Catholicism, an opinion neither Rousseau nor his Genevan friends shared in the least.[3] To be anti-Catholic was to Rousseau the essence of Protestantism and it was something he had simply taken for granted.[4] He was long past getting excited about it.

Rousseau knew that there were limits to religious and intellectual freedom in Geneva. One of his reasons for preferring to live in

---

[1] *Confessions*, VIII, 392.
[2] P.-M. Masson, *La Religion de Jean-Jacques Rousseau* (Paris, 1916), I, 193–213; III, 162–79; François Jost, *Jean-Jacques Rousseau Suisse* (Fribourg, 1961), I, 265–70.
[3] Grimsley, *D'Alembert*, 196.   [4] *Lettres Ecrites de la Montagne*, II, 135–7.

Paris was that he thought he would, as a Protestant, have more freedom there. When he was eventually persecuted he wrote to the Archbishop of Paris, with some justice, that it was a bit late in the day for Catholics to be so disturbed by the writings of a Protestant published in Holland.[1] He had thought that in this age of religious indifference his efforts to present a new rational, natural religion would bring spiritual peace to men who were separated by religious differences which had long since become meaningless.[2] In this he had certainly been mistaken, and his error was due to his inability to enter into the depth of feeling that both orthodox faith and militant atheism expressed. Neither in Geneva nor in Paris was there any inclination to take religion lightly. To be sure, Rousseau came to liken the intolerance of the Voltairean party to that of the Jesuits only when he felt personally persecuted by both.[3] But in one sense at least he was right. Both belonged to an essentially Catholic culture: worldly, hierarchical and intensely intellectual. That is why Rousseau insisted that his essentially Protestant writings need not have been burned in Paris. They were not dangerous in France, where absolutely everyone held equality in contempt.[4] However, he misjudged the spiritual situation in Geneva just as completely. Missionary zeal, whether atheist or orthodox, was too remote from his own feelings about religion to be comprehensible to him.

It is thus quite easy to understand why Rousseau said over and over that he had never been able to feel entirely at ease in the society of Parisian unbelievers. He admitted that this was not a matter of rational objections to their views, but one of emotion. There was no reason why he should have felt close to them. Most of the contributors to Diderot's *Encyclopédie* came from well-established and, occasionally, even affluent families. Almost all owned some property and most had positions that gave them a secure place in the society of the old regime.[5] Rousseau was thus not only an outsider because of his Genevan religious past, but also because of his poverty. Thus, when he looked into himself he found that he simply did not feel as

[1] *Confessions*, IX, 406–7; *Lettre à Christophe de Beaumont*, 60–1.
[2] *Lettres Ecrites de la Montagne*, V, 199–200.
[3] 'Lettre à Duchesne', 28 mai 1764, *C.G.*, XI, 94–6; *Rousseau Juge de Jean-Jacques*, II, 890–1, III, 967–8.
[4] *Lettre à Christophe de Beaumont*, 96.   [5] Proust, *Diderot et l'Encyclopédie*, 9–38.

they did. He discovered in himself strong remnants of affection for a gentle childhood faith that they had never known.[1] These memories were part of his fantasy about a Geneva that was still pure and just, as his own childhood had been. That is why atheism was so completely linked in his mind to the interests and attitudes of the wealthy and powerful. He could see only their rejection of the culture of 'the people', among whom he had grown up. That also made the presence and glory of Voltaire and his brand of irreligion in Geneva so intolerable.

The invasion of Geneva by this epitome of sophisticated urbanity was a challenge to Rousseau's whole vision of himself and of his native city.[2] The fact that he admired Voltaire's genius and, perhaps, knew him to be his only peer, only exacerbated his anger. The *Letter to d'Alembert* was really addressed to Voltaire, who had, in fact, contributed heavily to d'Alembert's challenging article.[3] Nevertheless, Rousseau's sense of himself as the true voice of Geneva, even if only in Paris, was not shared by even the more radical local pastors. For all his flattering remarks about their purity and patriotism, Rousseau's views were far from compatible with those of *any* member of the clergy who still exercised his calling.[4]

To see how far Rousseau was from even the more liberal pastors, one need only recall that he had no use for any sort of organized clergy. Wherever the clergy is organized in a body, it will inevitably be the master of society, even if the political sovereign should be the titular head of an established church as in Russia or England. Institutionalized Christianity is a 'bizarre system', and his outline of the 'civil religion' does not make mention of any sort of clergy at all, except to denounce its political dangers.[5] Marriage is explicitly recognized as a civil contract and the education of the Poles, like that of the Spartans, is to be put into the hands of experienced magistrates and soldiers.[6] In short, he could think of no useful

---

[1] *Letter to d'Alembert*, 11; 'Lettre à Vernes', 18 février 1758, *C.G.*, III, 286–8; *Rêveries*, III, 1013–14.　　　　[2] *Confessions*, VIII, 396–7; *Lettres à Malesherbes*, IV, 1143.
[3] Gay, *Voltaire's Politics*, 72; Grimsley, *D'Alembert*, 53, 110.
[4] Vaughan, I, 132 (*Inégalité*).　　　　　　　　　　[5] *Ibid.* II, 127–9 (*Contrat Social*).
[6] *Ibid.* 133 (*Contrat Social*); 437–41 (*Poland*); I, 256–8 (*Economie Politique*). In a commercial republic such as Geneva the ideal was unattainable, so a mixed system of public and private education was most suitable. 'Lettre à Tronchin', 26 novembre 1758, *C.G.*, IV, 143.

function for a professional clergy. On the contrary, collectively they were precisely the sort of power group that tore society apart and oppressed its weaker members in order to promote their own interests.

Among the many pleasant things that Rousseau said to the Archbishop of Paris was that the latter did not care for God's cause, as long as the interests of the clergy were well protected.[1] Religious fanaticism is a political instrument of which all existing religions make use to intimidate other men.[2] Wars of religion are started by courts and only serve the rulers who pursue them. Peasants and merchants do not foment intrigues and cabals; they are merely aroused by their own governors in the name of God, and led to their own destruction.[3] As for missionaries, they are no better than conquerors.[4] Nor did his final message to his Genevan persecutors differ from his reply to the Archbishop. Desist from making religion an instrument of clerical tyranny! Superstition, whatever its form or origin, is a deadly political danger for the people.[5]

Rousseau's own version of the Protestant message was, in fact, radically anti-clerical. Precisely because religion was a matter of feeling it should not be dogmatized or even debated, and there was therefore no place for a specialized body of theological experts in religious life. In fact, dogmatism and superstition can only drive men to quarrelsome sectarianism and then to atheism.[6] To intellectualize religion was to take men's minds off their real duties and to inspire vain quarrels. How could it be otherwise, since dogma asserted as truth matters which were mere guesses?[7] The clergy, in short, present exactly the same sort of danger to mankind as other intellectuals. They exploit the simplicity of their fellow men to carve out an empire for themselves.

Anti-clericalism was not the sum of Rousseau's objections to Christianity. He thought Christianity in all its manifestations to be a socially harmful religion. The humility of the genuine Christian is an open invitation to oppressors. How can a religion that turns men's minds to another life bind them to their earthly country? It may be

---

[1] *Lettre à Christophe de Beaumont*, 108.   [2] *Ibid.* 89–91.
[3] *Ibid.* 96–7.   [4] *Ibid.* 93.
[5] *Lettres Ecrites de la Montagne*, I, 123, 129.
[6] *Lettre à Christophe de Beaumont*, 98–9; *N.H.*, Part V, Letter V; *Emile*, 277.
[7] *Letter à Christophe de Beaumont*, 90–3, 100–12; *Lettre à Voltaire*, 312–20.

advantageous for mankind as a whole that men be made more loving and gentle, but that is not a blessing in the world as it is. A Christian republic is a contradiction in terms. 'Christianity preaches only servility and dependence. Its spirit is too favorable to tyranny for the latter not to always profit from it. True Christians are made to be slaves.' They are no match, militarily or politically, for Spartans and Romans. A crusader is just not a Christian, especially if he is a good soldier.[1] 'The patriotic spirit is exclusive and makes us look upon all those who are not our fellow citizens as strangers and almost enemies. Such was the Spirit of Sparta and of Rome. The spirit of Christianity, on the contrary, makes us look upon all men, whoever they may be, as our brothers, as children of God. . . It is not good for making republicans or soldiers, only Christians and men.' Could any Christian do what Judith and Mutius Scaevola did?[2] Christian passivity was certainly not what he urged upon the Poles! The Spartan utopia is as radically unchristian an order as it is an unintellectual one.

Could Christianity contribute anything to the Golden Age? What of its personal, non-political merits? Julie is certainly a very pious woman, far too devout to need the advice of a minister, to whom, indeed, she preaches on her death-bed. For her, as for her creator, Christianity is not a matter of truth or error, but a source of personal comfort. She wants to convert the atheist Wolmar not to make him better, since he is already perfect, nor to ensure his eternal salvation, but only to make him happier here and now.[3] She believes that she will find a life after death and be eventually reunited with Saint-Preux. This thought makes her long to die, when she can no longer hide from herself that all her good deeds have not made her happy and that, in any case, happiness bores her. She has within her, she cries out, powers which she simply cannot express or use in the world in which she must live. What remedy is there for 'a disgust with well-being'? She has no interest in mysticism which only takes one away from one's duties, nor for the abyss of metaphysical speculations. Her death releases her from a world which has

---

[1] Vaughan, II, 130-1 (*Contrat Social*); *Lettres Ecrites de la Montagne*, I, 130-1.
[2] 'Lettres à M. Usteri', 30 avril 1763, *C.G.*, IX, 264-6 and 18 juillet 1764, *C.G.*, X, 36-40.
[3] *N.H.*, Part V, Letter V; Part VI, Letter VIII.

no room for her immense capacity to love and which prevents her from expressing it fully.

Are we to believe that Rousseau thought religious belief to be the outcome of sexual frustration? It is certainly implied in Julie's death and her compulsive need for faith. There is, however, more than that here. For Julie's difficulties are not only personal, but also social. The unhappiness which only religious hope can make tolerable is the result of social constraint. Domestic life is not enough for a woman of Julie's emotional energies and the society in which she must live allows her no scope beyond it. That is why she is so bored by domestic bliss.[1] The world refuses to accept all her love. She dies as part of an act of maternal love and on her deathbed she can at last speak frankly of all the kinds and the full extent of love and solicitude that she feels. For she is, among other things, a Christ figure. To bring this point home, Rousseau even added a scene in which a demented servant girl believes that she has seen Julie resurrected after her death.[2] Her cousin often speaks of Julie's gift for loving that is unlike any other, and that makes everyone return her love. That is why she possesses the most powerful of all empires, one that extends over the will of anyone whom she touches. It gives a new being to all the hearts around her.[3]

Great as her power of love is, Julie could achieve nothing without the material order created by the atheist Wolmar. Even here Christianity has only a supplementary function. Their estate, Clarens, is only a recreated Golden Age, and religious faith is needed to cope with the miseries that can never be avoided once men have experienced civilization. The real Golden Age exists without religion. The miseries which we can endure only with the comforts of religion are not the creation of nature, but of men. Religion has its beginnings in society, and the earliest function of the gods is to govern men.[4] The erotic energies of Christianity could find better outlets, and hope and faith are medicines for diseases of the spirit that men should never have suffered at all.

The core of Rousseau's own faith never went beyond his sense of

[1] *N.H.*, Part VI, Letters VIII and XII.   [2] *Ibid.* Part VI, Letter XI.
[3] *Ibid.* Part II, Letter V; Part IV, Letter II.
[4] Vaughan, I, 189 (*Inégalité*); II, 124 (*Contrat Social*).

needing religion emotionally. An 'inner sentiment', he wrote, moves me to see 'a correspondence between my immortal nature and the constitution of this world and the physical order which I see ruling it'. The moral system he had drawn from these observations 'is the support I need to bear the miseries of my life. . . Let us hold to that which is alone sufficient to make me happy in spite of fortune and of men'.[1] That is how Rousseau felt at the close of his life and that is what he had said to Voltaire many years earlier. He and most of suffering mankind need to believe in a benevolent deity, if they are to survive the blows that daily life inflicts upon them. Here as always Rousseau was concerned with his own inner life, the needs of his own self. His vision of this self, however, demanded that he speak and be recognized as a man of the people. That is what made him so certain that his own religious needs, though not his opinions, were those of the people. He alone could know what the people should be taught, what they required both for their emotional fulfillment and social guidance. He could provide what the clerical servants of power refused to offer and the philosophic valets spurned. For the beliefs of the people could be purified, if only men without prejudice taught men without passions![2]

To begin with, one should recognize that no one can know the truth. Only God knows that. The crime of intolerance is to punish men for what they cannot help, their diversity of perception and feeling.[3] Protestantism, properly understood, is essentially tolerance. The whole end of the Reformation, according to Rousseau, was to allow each man to interpret the Bible as he saw fit. The only thing that must be believed is that God exists and is omnipotent.[4] Everything else is a matter of personal preference. He personally wanted to believe in an after-life, but only because he would be miserable without this hope.[5] The belief in God is to be taught to the people who cannot, as wise men can, recognize a supreme being in the structure and order of nature. The perfect man, Wolmar, is an atheist, but he, like Newton, only illuminates the very different needs of 'man in general'. For most men, as for the Vicar, God *must* exist if

---

[1] *Rêveries*, III, 1018–19.   [2] *Lettre à Christophe de Beaumont*, 88.
[3] *Ibid.* 59, 78–81, 98, 100–7.
[4] *Ibid.* 82–3; *Lettres Ecrites de la Montagne*, II, 138; III, 152; IV, 166, 174–5.
[5] *Letter to d'Alembert*, 12–13; *Lettre à Voltaire*, 318–20.

they are not to think that 'the wicked is right and the good man nothing but a fool'.[1] The moral life of Everyman depends on a certain minimal degree of piety. As for Christianity, only the message of fraternity ought to be spread.[2] Not the divinity of Jesus, but his goodness matters. Rousseau regarded himself as a follower of Christ to that extent, but not as a disciple of priests.[3] Religion should nourish our sentiments of sociability.[4] It can do no other good. Nor need the religious variety that would emerge under conditions of tolerance be feared. It is fanaticized multitudes and intolerant minorities that alone cause religious strife.[5] War, here as everywhere, is a contrived political effort. Legislation ought to concern itself with religion only when the latter has specific social consequences. The intolerant only should be curbed. However, human belief is no concern of government; only social conduct may be subject to regulation by public authorities.[6]

When he addressed the religious powers, Rousseau assumed the haughty tone of the tribune of the people. To them he did not speak as one of the humble poor, but as their protector. There was both plebeian resentment and a claim to power in his remarks to the Archbishop. How he could make the world laugh, he wrote, if he were to reveal what petty intrigues had led all the states of Europe to unite against 'the son of a watchmaker'![7] He was perfectly capable of unmasking the designs of the mighty. This was the 'man of the people' who had more to say because he knew more than the kings of the world.[8] This sense of superiority arose also from the fact that Rousseau shared one important belief with the clergy: the common people need spiritual guidance. Natural religion was what they should be taught, but ordinary men are too dull and too over-worked to be able to discover God for themselves; they need instruction.[9] This is possible only for wise men, such as Rousseau himself. His purely personal beliefs were, moreover, not for popular consump-

---

[1] *Emile*, 255.
[2] *Lettres Ecrites de la Montagne*, I, 125-8.
[3] *Lettre à Christophe de Beaumont*, 82.
[4] *Ibid.* 93-4; Vaughan, II, 132 (*Contrat Social*); *Pensées*, X, 1301.
[5] *Lettre à Christophe de Beaumont*, 98.
[6] *Ibid.* 91; *Lettres Ecrites de la Montagne*, I, 129-30, V, 188; Vaughan, II, 132 (*Contrat Social*).   [7] *Ibid.* 62.
[8] 'Lettres Morales', 360.   [9] *Lettre à Christophe de Beaumont*, 75-7.

tion.[1] Even the Vicar's message was for wise readers only. He had no intention of disturbing the faith of simple men or of loosening the existing bonds that tied men together in actual societies.[2]

Precisely because religion has so great a bearing upon conduct, it is important that men should never be deprived of its teachings. Fear of punishment does not restrain men adequately; it only stimulates secret crimes. Religion is necessary to keep men from losing all sense of mutual obligation and nothing ought to disturb the prevailing beliefs if these contribute to socialization.[3] Superstition does nothing of the sort, of course, and must be attacked on political grounds as much as on intellectual ones. That, however, is in itself no excuse for attacking the faith that sustains society.[4] He had seen 'in religion the same falseness as in politics: one preached rites in which one did not believe and which served neither the human heart nor reason'.[5] What was needed to undo this reign of deception was not the abolition of religion, but an understanding of its true uses. A book on 'the utility of religion' was badly needed, but there was no one, cleric or lay, in the present age to write it.[6] Rousseau did not even mention Montesquieu here. He, after all, had also recognized that 'it is necessary to the society that it should have something fixed; and it is religion that has this stability', but all his careful considerations of the relative values of various religions in different societies could scarcely hide his distaste for all of them.[7] That was clearly not what Rousseau had in mind. However, he could not supply the needed book any more than Montesquieu. It must, after all, be very difficult to compose a volume of spiritual advice designed entirely for the use of *other* people.

When Rousseau addressed his fellow authors, especially Voltaire, he did not speak in the tone of injured dignity that he used in his formal replies to the attacks of the Parisian and Genevan authorities. To the *corps littéraire* he spoke as one of the suffering people accusing its decadent oppressors. There were, after all, some good and kind vicars who helped the poor, and religion, even at its worst,

[1] *Lettres Ecrites de la Montagne*, III, 160–5, V, 185.   [2] *Ibid.* I, 123.
[3] *N.H.*, Part III, Letter XVIII; '*Préface*' *à Narcisse*, 971–2.
[4] *Lettre à Voltaire*, 320–1.   [5] *Lettre à Christophe de Beaumont*, 58.
[6] *Rousseau Juge de Jean-Jacques*, III, 972.
[7] *Spirit of the Laws*, II, XXVI, 59; XXIV–XXV, 25–57.

did much to restrain men from devouring each other in the scramble for wealth and distinction. It did soften men in a society in which there were no genuine communal bonds. The men of letters, in contrast, were eager to destroy the last vestiges of a faith that saved men from their lowest ambitions, and did so in order to release the strong and rich from the remnants of shame and pity. All his memories of early poverty and humiliation as an apprentice and as a valet asserted themselves against them. It was this part of his real self that could not endure to see Voltaire sneering at the faith of the poor. The self that always half felt that he ought to have remained in Geneva and completed his apprenticeship to become a craftsman like his father, that drove him away from Paris and that made him again earn his bread as a copyist, rose in sheer hatred against those who had never known the condition of the poor. What could be more revolting than a man living amidst luxury, as Voltaire did, enjoying every sort of good fortune, busily destroying the hope and consolation of the poor by painting a picture of a malevolent providence?[1]

Of himself Rousseau could say with perfect candor, 'I have never adopted the philosophy of the happy men of this century.' He had chosen one 'more appropriate to his heart, more consoling in adversity and more likely to encourage virtue'.[2] Adversity was what he shared with almost all other men. That is why he did not, like the rich, Voltaire among them, think that 'the poor are too stupid to feel'. Philosophers always find it convenient to think the common people insensitive to suffering, just as the politicians scorn them, but 'the people are mankind, those who do not belong to the people are so few in number that they are not worth counting.' And they would not be missed if they were to disappear.[3] Rousseau was one of the many when he accused Voltaire of pure malevolence in destroying the faith that made the life of the poor tolerable. He had felt their need, shared it and believed what he and they had to believe in order to endure the sufferings of the world. Voltaire, on the other hand, amused himself by destroying what he did not personally need.[4] The priesthood for all its wickedness at least preserved

[1] *Confessions*, I, 43–4; IX, 429; *Rousseau Juge de Jean-Jacques*, II, 849; 'Lettre à De Leyre', 5 octobre 1758, *C.G.*, IV, 64.
[2] *Rousseau Juge de Jean-Jacques*, I, 727.　　　[3] *Emile*, 186–7.
[4] *Lettre à Voltaire*, 320–21; *Emile*, 276; *Rousseau Juge de Jean-Jacques*, III, 971.

opinions which had some social value. The fashionable atheist destroyed beliefs without providing a substitute.

Much of Rousseau's self-righteousness came from his belief that he had escaped from the moral evils of the literary life. No one had to be as mean and destructive as most intellectuals were, therefore. He admitted freely that in many periods of his life he had been no better than other men in his situation. His early writings were filled with the bile of his long years of frustration and servitude.[1] As an author in Paris he had been just like the other scribblers. These experiences made it clear to him that his reprehensible conduct was the result of the situations in which he found himself.[2] That was, however, not an excuse, but only an explanation for his conduct. He had not only escaped domestic servitude, but had also learned to overcome his bitterness and had ceased to frequent Parisian society. Those who did not make comparable efforts were, therefore, the objects of his scorn. For while no man in society can completely escape the pressures of opinion on himself, no one need lose himself completely in it, and even more, no one is obliged to mislead others.

Victimhood was the most fundamental condition of all men, but there were different forms of subjugation. The clever and successful were self-made victims, the poor and oppressed were not. The authors of the age were, in their way, enslaved, depending as they did so utterly on public favor. They could, however, throw off these bonds at any time, just as rich men could be happy if they wanted to be, even though they were rarely capable of it. The poor man and the slave do not have that choice. They are doomed to their misery. All of Epictetus' moral strength could not save him from physical torture. 'Neither head nor heart [could] save him from the sufferings of his conditions.'[3] Rousseau was not taken in by elegant chatter about the joys of indigence and the pains of wealth. He knew it to be a pompous bit of sophistry that encouraged the rich to ignore and to exploit the poor.[4] The ability of an Epictetus to

---

[1] *Confessions*, VIII, 368.   [2] *Lettres à Malesherbes*, I, 1132; III, 1135-7, 1140.
[3] *Emile*, 186-7.
[4] 'Tant de pompeux discours sur l'heureuse indigence m'ont bien l'air d'être nés du sein de l'abondance', *Epitre à M. Bordes*, 1131. There was a fairly extensive literature which sang of the joys of poverty in Rousseau's time in order to shame the vices of the nobility. Robert Mauzi, *L'Idée du Bonheur au XVIIIᵉ Siècle* (Paris, 1960), 165-74.

rise spiritually above his circumstances, far from excusing the shame of slavery only proved its utter wrongness, its unjustifiable denial of man's moral potentialities.[1] The tax-burdened and frightened peasant whom Rousseau met in France had not lost his capacity for generous hospitality, but his oppressors had lost their sense of justice. Rousseau, however, learned to hate injustice on that visit.[2] He therefore knew that no one had to remain indifferent to the sufferings of other men.

The spectacle of injustice ought to arouse indignation. Rousseau was not prepared to confuse the moral and psychological weakness from which all men suffer with a self-excusing moral fatalism. He did not think that anything much could or should be done to salvage corrupt societies, but he did not believe that anyone was doomed to be either an active oppressor or an unmoved spectator. The burden of public prejudice could always be lightened by retreating into oneself and listening to the voice of pity and conscience. If there were no perfect moral triumphs, one need not cooperate with the powers of duplicity within or around one either. He was convinced that he had, in his solitude, learned to resist all these corruptions. In this he was, no doubt, deceiving himself, but that hardly affects the truth of his moral observations.

[1] *Emile*, 423; Vaughan, I, 467 (*Première Version*); II, 28 (*Contrat Social*).
[2] *Confessions*, IV, 163–4.

4

IMAGES OF AUTHORITY

DISPELLING ILLUSIONS

The march to self-enslavement is clearly spontaneous, even if ill-intentioned men force their weaker fellows along. Rousseau did not believe that in the normal course of events much could be done about it. Occasionally a small country like Switzerland or Holland, perhaps Corsica, might still retain some degree of freedom and justice. For most of Europe that was quite out of the question. The history that had produced nothing but servants and masters ensured a future that could only be worse than the past had been. Utopia was Rousseau's way of exposing the prevalent degradation. It showed how far men had departed from the possibilities that were open to them. Better opinions were not psychologically impossible. Spartan republics were imaginable. And the restoration of the Golden Age by individuals determined to escape from Paris was thinkable. Even the education of children who would grow up free from *amour-propre* was not inconceivable. The likelihood that any of these enterprises would succeed was minimal, but they were not impossible. Moreover, the contrast between the probable and possible was what these utopias were meant to show. As such they illuminated the misery of mankind's actual situation.

How was one to imagine a sudden break in the history of either a group or of a single person? Men's inner resources were too limited to make self-restoration a plausible notion. Only an outside force could rescue them. That force was the personal authority of a great man.

That man in general needs a master is clear enough when one considers the misery that he drifts into by passively reacting to his situation. What is needed is someone so extraordinary in intelligence and moral strength that he can restructure the environment in which men live and thus indirectly compel them to turn away from their present course. The Spartan republic and the household that a Great Legislator and a God-father respectively might build would be such settings. Possibly a great teacher might, as Emile's tutor does, devote his entire life to saving one child from the impact of society. Someone completely outside the prevailing system of opinions might cure and prevent the wounds that social life usually inflicts on men. Rousseau provided portraits of such men of authority in almost every one of his works. Clearly he found them fascinating and deeply attractive. They were far more than mere mechanical contrivances, invented to give utopia a start. The authority that radiates from great men was obviously a form of psychological power that appealed to Rousseau directly. That was due at least in part to his own sensitivity to relations of authority. He longed for a paternal protector and also feared such men. He was constantly and intensely aware of his own desire for dependence, as well as of the dangers of domination that he might thus invite. From the painful experience that inevitably came with these dispositions, he was, as always, able to draw a public message that his figures of authority embodied.

Paternal authority was not only a personal solution for Rousseau in moments of helpless weakness. While his own experience made him sensitive to both the advantages and limitations of authority, he looked beyond the consumers of authority to those who exercised it. If the Greater Legislator is a figure that owes too much to Plutarch to arouse much psychological interest, Rousseau did draw one portrait of a man of authority that is unforgettable. M. Wolmar is the real hero of the *Nouvelle Héloise*, because he is omnicompetent and perfect. He cures the ill, saves the weak and builds a model estate. He is in fact, as Rousseau makes perfectly clear, God, and he is better and kinder than God. God gave men a freedom which they are too weak to use well and then left them to suffer. It is only in a human image that the goodness ascribed to God can really be made manifest. It is not therefore only the catastrophic state in which most men find themselves that justifies authority. The history of men's vices shows the need for it also. The man of authority, the genuinely good and capable man, who educates, saves and builds, is inherently admirable. He automatically arouses moral aspirations in those around him, because to know him is to become aware of morality. Without these qualities teachers are mere masters, fathers are domestic tyrants and legislators are mere Hobbesian despots. The miracle of the true man of authority is that he subjugates the will of his pupils so that they may develop enough inner strength to throw off the yoke of personal servitude.

The most obvious difficulty would seem the impossibility of finding such men of authority. This, however, troubled Rousseau relatively little. He wanted to believe in his Plutarchian heroes, and such figures as the Legislator, Emile's tutor and M. de Wolmar show how well he could imagine men capable of reordering the lives of others. All he had to show was that such men were possible. What *did* trouble him was the worth of even the most beneficent and necessary authority. On one hand he was completely convinced that a liberating form of authority was possible and the only means of helping men out of their present muddle. Good and wise chiefs know how to 'prevent, cure and palliate' that mass of abuses and ills that overwhelm us.[1] The possibility of 'forcing men to be free', through complex psychological devices (though not through the punitive means implied in the actual context of that famous phrase) was, for him, a real one. Yet Rousseau never forgot that authority meant submission. Even the most self-liquidating forms of authority involve subordination, and that is in itself the essence of evil. Rousseau therefore doubted whether authority could accomplish its true ends. It might cure and palliate, but once men needed a master, they would never be able to do without one. Authority may keep them from evil, but it does not liberate fully or permanently. It only perpetuates dependence. For all his belief in the creative powers of great men, Rousseau never quite overcame his fear of them. Nevertheless, these misgivings did not outweigh his acute sense of the self-destructiveness of untutored men. Here, as always, a negative impulse, a critical rather than a reforming zeal, was his ultimate inspiration.

Personal experience, moreover, only added to Rousseau's perplexities. His view of authority grew directly out of his own inner confusions. His correspondence bristles with declarations of independence. 'First of all I want my friends to be my friends and not my masters.' He wanted to be happy in his way, not according to

[1] Vaughan, I, 207 (*Inégalité*).

their ideas.[1] In the end he concluded that his need for personal
liberty was such that he was simply not made for any civil society.[2]
'He has ideas of independence', wrote the ever-observant Boswell,
'that are completely visionary and which are unsuitable for a man in
his position.' Boswell did not refer merely to Rousseau's social
station here. 'Behold the man he is, and tell me if such a man does
not need a great deal of affection from his fellows—and consequently
if he does not depend on them as we all depend on one another.'[3]
That was, of course, the trouble, and Rousseau knew it only too well.
The Calvinist spinster who had raised him had seen to it that he
became positively 'fond of acts of submission'. She had, as he knew
perfectly well, crippled him morally and sexually.[4] Hume was not
exceptionally perceptive when he noticed that Rousseau was at the
mercy of those whom he loved, even of his little dog.[5] He ought
also to have realized that Rousseau resented and feared those whom
he suspected of exploiting his softness.[6] Eventually that fear led to
exaggeration. And although Rousseau certainly was victimized, not
everyone conspired to tyrannize over him, as he believed they did.
He was, therefore, torn all his life between an urge for perfect
freedom and a longing for submission and for a return to childhood
under the parental care of Mme de Warens or Maréchal Keith. If
patronage was always rebuffed at first and the offer of every royal
pension produced a crisis, Rousseau also longed for a supervising
father. As Saint-Preux, Rousseau's imaginary self-portrait, had
addressed Wolmar, so he later would call Maréchal Keith *mon
bienfaiteur et mon père* and speak of himself as the *fils cadet*.[7]
Patronage could be endured only if it was transformed into pseudo-
paternity. It was Hume's failure to recognize this that led to their
dreadful quarrel in England. Thus Rousseau's first response to the
approaches of his future patron, M. de Luxembourg, was an outburst
of plebeian resentment. 'I hate the great, I hate their estate, their

[1] 'Lettre à Mme d'Epinay', 26 mars 1757, *C.G.*, III, 44; 'Lettre à Diderot', *C.G.*, III,
50; *Lettres à Malesherbes*, II, 1137. [2] *Rêveries*, VI, 1059; *Confessions*, I, 38.
[3] *Boswell on the Grand Tour: Italy, Corsica and France, 1765–1766*, ed. Frank Brady
and F. A. Pottle (New York, 1955), 300. [4] *Ébauche des Confessions*, 1157.
[5] 'Lettre à la Marquise de Barbantane', 16 février 1766, *C.G.*, XV, 62–3.
[6] *Lettres à Malesherbes*, III, 1141.
[7] *Confessions*, I, 56; XII, 596–9; 'Lettre à Milord Marechal', 8 decembre 1764, *C.G.*, XII
122–4; 'Lettre à Mme. la Comtesse de Boufflers', 28 decembre 1763, *C.G.*, X, 278–80.

hardness, their prejudices, their pettiness and all their vices.'[1] This, however, presently changed to 'Ah, M. le Maréchal, I hated the great before I knew you, and I hate them even more now that you have made me feel so well how easy it would be for them to make themselves adored'.[2] He would have wanted to seek him out, Rousseau later wrote to his patron, even if they had been equals. How was he to treat him now, without forgetting himself?[3] For he did not wish to forget the inequality between them, little though it mattered to M. de Luxembourg. Rousseau only wanted to transform grandeur into paternity and to replace class distinctions with emotional subservience. Much as he hated inequality he did not want equality either, and positions of superior and inferior were to be maintained.

Deeply rooted as these psychological tendencies were, they were exacerbated by Rousseau's experiences with the powers that be. To be sure, his distaste for impersonal relationships in any form, and especially for those involving subordination, would have made it difficult for him to accept regular employment of the usual sort. However, Rousseau was also a man of supreme gifts forced to endure every social indignity that society could inflict. If in Rousseau's case apprenticeship, vagrancy and domestic service did not lead to a rejection of all authority, they did fill him with a deep contempt for all the cruel and incompetent masters of this world, in fact for all actual masters. Being themselves corrupt, they can only maim and hurt those doomed to serving them. Had M. de Montaigu been a decent man, Rousseau, his secretary, imagined that he might have made a passable career for himself in the diplomatic service. Had M. de la Roque been a kind man, he would have given his valet, Rousseau, the courage to confess a theft rather than to callously allow an innocent girl to be blamed.[4] The reason why servants cheat and steal is that the masters are usurpers, liars and fools.[5]

It was not difficult for Rousseau to draw the obvious conclusions from these experiences. Actual authority was exercised only to

[1] *Lettres à Malesherbes*, IV, 1145.　　　　[2] *Confessions*, X, 527.
[3] 'Lettre à M. de Luxembourg', 30 avril 1759, *C.G.*, IV, 231.
[4] *Confessions*, VII, 327; II, 87.
[5] *N.H.*, Part IV, Letter X.

maintain a destructive and false order. 'Wherever I look, I see only masters and slaves, not a people and its chief.'[1] The result is that no communication and no genuinely binding relationships are possible at all. 'Neither master nor slave belongs to a family, but only to a class.'[2] His travels up and down the entire social ladder had shown him only too clearly that 'the great know only the great and the small only the small'.[3] Enforced class isolation means mutual hostility and irresponsibility—pride and cruelty at the top, envy, servility and dishonesty at the bottom. What is astonishing is that in spite of these experiences and perceptions Rousseau should still have looked for 'chiefs' and longed for individuals who possessed qualities that justified submission to their authority. Moreover, to a certain degree, he even expected such persons to come from those very upper classes whose vices he had so eloquently exposed. It is not the offended plebeian Saint-Preux, but his patron Lord Bomston, an English aristocrat of immense wealth and power, who delivers the most scathing of all Rousseau's denunciations of the hereditary nobility and who proclaims the cause of equality.[4]

This ambivalence emerges even in Rousseau's view of political authority. On the whole he thought monarchy completely vicious. Even elective kings tend to be tyrants.[5] Nothing amused him more than the Abbé de Saint-Pierre's belief that reform was in the 'true' interest of kings. Far from it, replied Rousseau. Their interest lies precisely in exploiting and oppressing their subjects.[6] Masters never prefer any interest to their own, and most statesmen are positively malevolent.[7] Rousseau was outraged by M. de Mirabeau's notion of a 'legal despotism' as a cure for all political ills. What a contradiction in terms! There are only two alternatives, Rousseau replied. One might have the pure rule of law in which all personal authority is entirely eliminated. That is pure democracy. If this should be impossible (as he thought it was), then one should accept the most perfectly arbitrary, unlimited personal rule. That is the rule of a God. The trouble with this was that it would in fact bring on rulers like Tiberius and Nero, who could only inspire despair. However, there

---

[1] Vaughan, II, 31 (*Contrat Social*).   [2] *Emile*, 369.   [3] *Ébauches des Confessions*, 1150.
[4] *N.H.*, Part I, Letter LXII.   [5] Vaughan, II, 446–7, 461, 464 (*Poland*).
[6] Vaughan, I, 244 (*Économie Politique*); 389–92 (*Jugement sur la Polysynodie*); II, 77 (*Contrat Social*).   [7] Vaughan, I, 358 (*Fragment*).

are only two options, democracy, which is for angels, or the most perfect Hobbism.[1] This stark either/or is very revealing. It is a genuine conflict between ideals, not a choice between the possible and the impossible. Neither one of the ideals is at all likely to be realized, but both are valid. The actuality of bad kings does not invalidate the ideal of beneficial personal rule any more than the actuality of illegality destroys the idea of the pure rule of law. They are merely part of different visions of salvation. The Spartan republic is the utopia of virtue; the rule of a paternal despot is what prevails within each one of the happy families of the Golden Age. Neither can be recreated, and indeed neither has ever existed. Both merely remind us of what we might be.

The choice between these two possibilities must be made, if only to understand what they imply and what men's potentialities are. In making his own choice Rousseau did not exactly prefer personal authority to impersonal law, but he thought that the latter was less effective in moulding men. It does not reach deep enough into the human heart to divert men from their destructive inclinations and the empire of opinion.[2] A Great Legislator is needed not only for that, but to make law possible at all. Even if law is to rule, men must be educated to accept it.

It has occasionally been suggested that Rousseau, in providing Corsica and Poland with constitutional plans, imagined himself to be a real legislator.[3] In fact, he thought nothing of the sort. In a most revealing passage he explained that he could never fulfill the role, precisely because he lacked the necessary personal qualities.[4] He declined, for that very reason, to participate directly in Corsican affairs.[5] No one had a clearer view of the differences between the life of action and the life of observation, and he knew himself to be capable of only the latter. At most he might help to guide some future statesman.[6] At times he claimed that he did not even wish to lead his contemporaries, but only to warn them against false

---

[1] 'Lettre à M. de Mirabeau', 26 juillet 1767, *C.G.*, XVII, 155–9.
[2] Vaughan, II, 64 (*Contrat Social*).
[3] E.g. Jean Starobinski, 'La Pensée Politique de Jean-Jacques Rousseau', in Samuel Baud-Bovy *et al.*, *Jean-Jacques Rousseau*, pp. 83, 99.
[4] *Rêveries*, VI, 1057–9.   [5] *Confessions*, XII, 650.
[6] Vaughan, I, 350–1 (*Fragment*).

prophets.[1] Not that he was modest. He alone among authors had revealed the nature and history of the human heart.[2] Now knowing the human heart was certainly one of the main prerequisites of legislative as of all other authority, but it was not the only one. Rousseau certainly could dream of being a leader, but he knew that it was a mere fantasy. If he had the ring of Gyges he would certainly use it to make mankind happy. It would lift him above all partiality and weakness, but not even in a dream could it make him into a man of action. His force was bound to remain 'negative'. He would remain human, the equal, in spite of himself, of those over whom he should rule.[3] The personality that radiates authority eluded him. It was with Saint-Preux, not with Wolmar, that Rousseau identified himself.[4]

M. Wolmar is, in fact, Rousseau's most perfectly realized figure of authority. Just because Rousseau dreamt that he himself might be the beneficiary of such a man, he was able to bring out very clearly what he expected an omnipotent father to be and to do. Such a man does not tell people what they ought to do. Far from it. He draws them to himself because they long for his approval, and to be at one with him. This alone is the source of every real form of authority, in politics as in personal life. The man who wants to mould a people in fact needs the same qualities as a father who rules his children or a tutor who is capable of raising a child properly. And in a sense all are soul-surgeons, men who prevent or cure the diseases that affect the human heart in every society whether it be the family or the polity.

In his own lifetime Rousseau seems to have known only one such man. That was Claude Anet, Mme de Warens' factotum, and Rousseau's immediate predecessor as her lover. This, Rousseau noted several times, was an extraordinary man, the only one of his kind that he had ever seen. Slow, composed, thoughtful, circumspect and cold, he treated those around him like children, and so made them happy. He managed to do what Rousseau could never do: to keep order in Mme. de Warens' affairs. He did this because she, like Rousseau, and everyone else, esteemed and feared him, and did so

---

[1] Vaughan, I, 342 (*Fragment*). [2] *Rousseau Juge de Jean-Jacques*, I, 728.
[3] *Rêveries*, VI, 1057-9.
[4] *Confessions*, VIII, 355; *Rousseau Juge de Jean-Jacques*, II, 778.

because they could not bear his disapproval. Rousseau knew exactly where Anet's power came from and why he could never emulate him. It was force of personality alone. He had neither the *sang froid* nor the firmness of Anet. Though he was brighter and better educated, he lacked that quality that made people instinctively seek Anet's approval.[1] Even though he did not say so, Rousseau also resented Anet deeply. In his novel the least attractive character, the worthless valet, is called Claude Anet.

It is a measure of what Rousseau thought real authority might be that no one resents M. Wolmar, the perfect man of authority. That is because, among other things, Wolmar is God. Saint-Preux does not want to love the man who has married Julie, but he nevertheless *does* love him.[2] Wolmar cures him of all his ills, and restores his self-esteem because paternal love is irresistible, as Saint-Preux discovers.

Who is Wolmar and what does he do? Born somewhere in Eastern Europe, he is rich and a member of the highest nobility.[3] After an active and adventurous life of travel and soldiering he settles down in his later years to marriage and to running a model estate, Clarens. We are told nothing of his appearance in the novel, but in a letter to his illustrator Rousseau insisted that Wolmar's gaze must be *fin et froid*.[4] Along with his vast experience among every class of men, Wolmar is distinguished by a total absence of any passion. He needs no one, certainly not God. His only active love is for order; his one aversion, to see men suffer. His only interest in life is to read the hearts of men. That his penetrating eye has supernatural powers of looking into the hearts of others is frequently noted by all who know him.[5] This talent is the source of his unfailing judgment.[6] In Wolmar, alone among men, action and observation are not distinct. He acts to learn, and observes in order to act.[7] He not only knows men completely, but he identifies entirely with his

---

[1] *Confessions*, v, 177–8, 201–6, 264–5.   [2] *N.H.*, Part III, Letter XVIII.
[3] *Ibid.* Part III, Letter XVIII.
[4] 'Lettre à M. Coindet', decembre 1760, *C.G.*, v, 295. The coldness of the true sage was often noted; e.g. *Rousseau Juge de Jean-Jacques*, II, 861–2.
[5] *N.H.*, Part IV, Letters XI-XII.
[6] 'What then is required for the proper study of men? A great wish to know men, a great impartiality of judgment, a heart sufficiently sensitive to understand every human passion, and calm enough to be free from passion.' *Emile*, 206. Just so Wolmar.
[7] *N.H.*, Part V, Letter XII.

plans for them, with the creation of order. In this he is indeed like God. The reason Wolmar does not believe in God is that he *is* God to all intents and purposes. Certainly he has all the attributes that Rousseau ascribed to God, self-sufficiency, justice, love of order. If he is not God, he certainly does God's work.[1] Not only does he create peace through justice on his estate, he returns corrupt or ill men to that natural moral condition in which God wants them to remain.[2] His power of attracting others has an immediate impact. To know Wolmar is to desire his approbation.[3] In this also he is like God.

Wolmar is capable not only of running a model estate, he is also the soul-surgeon who heals the moral wounds of those whom society has in some way deformed. He undoes all that fantasy and false opinions have created, and so makes men out of mere victims. To see how great a man Wolmar is, one must appreciate the depth to which those whom he helps have sunk. The evils he erases are the best proof of his goodness.

Saint-Preux is Rousseau's portrait of man destroyed by society. 'We are meant to be men, laws and customs thrust us back into infancy.'[4] Saint-Preux remains a child because he has been victimized by his situation. The prejudices of an inegalitarian society prevent him from becoming either a citizen or the head of the family. His illusions and disordered passions keep him from developing a will. Lord Eduard, his friend and protector pleads with him to emerge from childhood and to be a man before he dies. He has nothing to fear from his passions. Only his illusions distract him.[5] Saint-Preux cannot respond to this advice, because his natural passions have become distorted. It is not enough to tell a man of thirty to grow up. He must be made capable of it and given a motive for asserting his will. If he could help himself he would not be so utterly miserable.

[1] 'La véritable Grandeur consiste dans l'exercice des vertus bienfaisantes, à l'example de celle de Dieu *qui ne se manifeste que par les biens qu'il repand sur nous.' Oraison Funèbre du Duc d'Orleans*, O.C., II, 1277. (My italics.)
[2] 'Dieu veut que nous soyons tels qu'il nous a fait', *Lettre à Christophe de Beaumont*, 88–9. God says to man, 'Je t'ai fait trop foible pour sortir du gouffre, parce que je t'ai fait assez fort pour n'y pas tomber.' *Confessions*, II, 64. In a sense the Wolmars of this world do better than God. They retrieve men from the abyss, rather than leaving them to suffer the consequences of weakness.
[3] As soon as Saint-Preux has met Wolmar he says, 'Je commençait de connoitre alors quel homme j'avois à faire, et je résolus bien de tenir mon cœur en état d'être vu de lui', *N.H.*, Part IV, Letter VI.   [4] *Emile*, 49.   [5] *N.H.*, Part V, Letter I.

Evidently he needs more than good advice, and it is Wolmar who takes complete charge of Saint-Preux to liberate him from his obsessions. To understand why Wolmar has to assert such complete authority over Saint-Preux, indeed has to reconstruct his past for him, one has only to recognize the full extent of the younger man's illness. It is the evil that justifies the cure as much as Wolmar's inherent superiority.

What exactly is wrong with poor Saint-Preux? He is afflicted by a complete disorder of his erotic and intellectual powers. He cannot love without suffering and he has an all-devouring memory that makes him incapable of self-awareness and of action in the present. The origin of both these troubles is that he is not, and cannot be, the master of his own destiny. To Saint-Preux and Lord Eduard this seems to be entirely the fault of the 'barbaric' prejudices of Julie's father.[1] Why, however, should these prejudices make him feel that suffering is the true mark of love? Julie knows that there is more to Saint-Preux's misery than her father's humiliating refusal to permit their marriage. She frequently reproaches Saint-Preux for being led entirely by those around him, of having no will-power of his own.[2] She is certainly in a position to know. Whenever she tells him to go away, he goes. When she recalls him, back he comes, just as obediently.[3] His submissiveness is, in his own eyes, his greatest claim upon her love. At no time does he make a plan for both of them or suggest that she follow him. It is Lord Eduard who, behind Saint-Preux's back, tries to persuade Julie to elope with her lover. When the young man finally leaves her, he puts himself entirely into Lord Eduard's care. 'Do as you please, milord. Rule me.'[4] And for ten years Lord Eduard makes every decision for him.

Why is Saint-Preux so utterly lacking in self-esteem? He knows that true self-esteem is the source of real honor and morality, unlike the false pride of Baron d'Etange which is based on mere opinion.[5] And he is firm and self-assertive whenever he confronts Julie's father directly. Why then does he grovel so before the daughter? Why does he suffer so, even at the moment of supreme felicity?[6]

[1] *Ibid*. Part II, Letter II.　　　　[2] *Ibid*. Part II, Letter XXVII.
[3] *Ibid*. Part I, Letters III, XVI, XLII, LXV; Part II, Letter XII.
[4] *Ibid*. Part II, Letter X; Part III, Letter XXIV.
[5] *Ibid*. Part I, Letter XXIV.　　　　[6] *Ibid*. Part I, Letter XXIII.

Why is his love, as Lord Eduard remarks, such an abuse of his powers?[1] There is more than class humiliation here, though that plays its part. There is also the suffering that men cause themselves when their desires exceed their capacities.[2] This cupidity is not directed at things. Indeed, domination is its primary aim. The baby's second cry is, after all, already an effort to subjugate his mother. The desire for power after power over people is the first and the chief source of our self-abuse. Saint-Preux knows from the beginning that he cannot possess Julie completely. That is because he does not really want to *live* with her, but to *die* with her. No sooner has he kissed her than he longs to die in her arms.[3] As soon as he leaves her he laments that 'the image of death' is now all that he has before him, but that image accompanied him on his one night with her also.[4] When she decides to marry Wolmar, he admits that he wishes she were dead, but that he may not love her enough to stab her.[5] When he returns to see her, years later, they visit an isolated place where he used to dream of her. On the way back he barely restrains himself from throwing both of them into the lake.[6] And finally when he again spends a night at an inn where he stopped after leaving her for the first time, years earlier, he dreams that she is dead.[7] Wolmar knows what that means. In a cold letter he tells Saint-Preux that one only dreams of the death of people whom one wishes to kill.[8] That is what it means to have a penetrating eye that reads the hearts of men! In the end of course Julie does die and that is a necessity since the whole novel moves to that end. Whether she be Christ or Woman, she is the spirit of love that everyone, except Wolmar, wants to sacrifice. And so it is done. When Saint-Preux has been liberated from his miseries and she has fulfilled her maternal functions no one needs her. She is indeed perfectly ready to die.

Saint-Preux's longing for death comes from a sense of futility. That is a social disease. There are no social tasks worthy of his real powers for him. He is neither a father, nor a citizen, nor a man. He is in fact a philosopher.[9] Unlike most he is without any *amour-propre*

---

[1] *N.H.*, Part II, Letter II.
[2] *Emile*, 44.
[3] *N.H.*, Part I, Letter XIV.
[4] *Ibid.* Part I, Letters LXVI, LV.
[5] *Ibid.* Part III, Letter XVI.
[6] *Ibid.* Part IV, Letter XVII.
[7] *Ibid.* Part IV, Letter XVII.
[8] *Ibid.* Part V, Letter IX.
[9] *'Préface' à Narcisse*, 967.

or ambition, but he is not free from the other defects of intellectuality. Both Lord Eduard and Julie note the disparity between his intellectual and emotional powers. It is clear to both that Saint-Preux's absorption in speculative philosophy has atrophied his passions. Why does he write good books, instead of doing good deeds?, asks Lord Eduard.[1] Saint-Preux is kind and gentle, but his inability to really love is part of that emotional dissipation, that lack of real feeling, that Rousseau ascribed to all intellectuals. It is not merely an unjust society that denies Saint-Preux his proper place. He has chosen mutilating preoccupations. Reflection makes men miserable by keeping them from enjoying the present. They are torn between tormenting desires and regrets.[2] That is certainly poor Saint-Preux's trouble. Unlike most philosophers he does not take his malaise out on others. He turns all his anger back upon himself. That is why he is a pure victim and worth saving. That, also, is why Julie loves him so, even when he exasperates her with his incessant jealousy, feebleness and instability.

Lord Eduard, who is English and a political animal, thinks that all of Saint-Preux's troubles would disappear in a free republic where he could marry his Julie and be a citizen. He is not wrong, but neither is he altogether right. There are pains created by association that go even deeper than those of injustice. Reflection can stimulate the imagination, foresight and memory until the sense of reality is totally destroyed. Saint-Preux is not given to thoughts about the future, but his memory is completely out of control. The yearning for the past is for him what ambition is to harder men.

Enduring love between the sexes is never natural, as sexuality is. Love depends on memory, and that is a faculty that is not awakened until men leave the state of nature.[3] Nor does love normally last. Its natural course is to decline. Because Saint-Preux was separated from Julie at the height of his love, he keeps his feeling artificially alive in his imagination.[4] As soon as he leaves her he begins to live in the past. Eternal regret becomes his permanent torment.[5] He is the victim of an all-devouring nostalgia.

[1] *N.H.*, Part II, Letter LXXVII; Part V, Letter II.   [2] '*Préface*' *à Narcisse*, 970.
[3] Vaughan, I, 215–16 (*Inégalité*).
[4] *N.H.*, Part III, Letter VIII; Part IV, Letter LXIV.   [5] *Ibid.* Part III, Letter XX.

While Rousseau disagreed with Locke's opinion that both love and memory were natural, it was from Locke that he and his contemporaries had learned to recognize the immense psychological importance of the memory. The association of ideas which creates all knowledge and understanding is nothing but the work of that faculty. To Locke personal identity, the sense of selfhood, itself depended on memory.[1] He was, moreover, deeply aware of the dangers of a distorted memory. Erroneous and obsessive patterns of association were at the root of all intellectual and religious errors and delusions.[2] Rousseau was inevitably more concerned with the moral suffering caused by aberrant associations. Moreover, he thought that self-awareness was an immediate sensation, a feeling resembling, though not quite like, Descartes', 'I think, therefore I am', rather than a recollection. Moral self-consciousness was, however, wholly a matter of remembering. Man is a moral being and has a conscious moral life *only* when he has a memory. Without memory there is no conscience. Conscience is our ability to regret our misdeeds and to feel pleasure in remembering our good acts. Memory alone creates moral self-awareness.[3] This and our ability to enjoy pleasant memories are the positive aspects of the faculty of memory.[4]

The painful side of memory was, however, a more constant theme for Rousseau. Memory is a form of opinion, Wolmar observes, and so it is easily turned into illusion that can be an escape from selfhood for people who lack self-confidence. It keeps them from accepting themselves, from living in the present.[5] Happiness and health, however, are to be found only in the ability to live in the present, to take each day as if there were neither yesterday nor tomorrow. Memory induces reflection which is crippling, inhibiting and destructive. It keeps us chained to a past that is illusory.[6] And it is not only guilt or a pleasant past that can force us back. Saint-Preux is not troubled by a bad conscience, but only by a dreadful sense of what might have been. Indeed the whole novel is suffused with nostalgia, as Saint-

---

[1] *Essay*, Book II, Ch. 27, ss. 9–25.   [2] *Ibid.* Book II, Ch. 28, ss. 7–16.
[3] 'Lettres Morales', 358–9, 362–3, 365, 368, 371–2.
[4] Georges Poulet, *Études sur le Temps Humain* (Edinburgh, 1949), 158–93. This is a remarkable account of the 'good' that Rousseau ascribed to memory. It is not much concerned with the negative aspects.   [5] *N.H.*, Part IV, Letter XII.
[6] Vaughan, I, 150, 178 (*Inégalité*); *Emile*, 44–5; *Rêveries*, V, 1046.

Preux sees life entirely filtered through regret. Like all artificial
faculties memory is not limited as our natural powers are. That is
why it can lose all proportion. Most of our present ills would amount
to little if the memory of past pleasures did not add regret to them.[1]
Nostalgia that is overpowering can destroy all other emotions.

Rousseau was himself the victim of nostalgia, but he did not discover it as a distinct emotional affliction. It had been discussed for
decades, especially in Swiss medical circles. Young Swiss mercenaries were known to suffer so severely from homesickness that
they often could not perform their duties. The sound of native
melodies, especially the *ranz des vaches* would make them so
nostalgic that they became ill. Indeed, it had been recognized for
some years that this was a moral illness that brought about physical
sickness, either directly or through complex physiological processes.
Rousseau had heard of the learned works on this subject and in one of
his writings on music he noted that the *ranz des vaches* had no strong
emotional qualities as music, but it deeply affected the Swiss abroad,
because it was a *signe mémoratif*.[2] Saint-Preux is a perpetual
victim to such mnemonic signs. Every object associated in any way
with Julie immediately arouses his nostalgia. During the ten years of
separation these objects have, in fact, tied him to her completely.

As soon as Wolmar sees Saint-Preux he realizes what is the matter
with him. There is no romantic dramatizing of nostaliga here. There
is nothing beautiful or significant about it as far as Wolmar is concerned. Saint-Preux is sick and he should recover and put his life to
some use. His self-confidence, and so his freedom, have to be restored.
He must become 'himself' again.[3]

The trouble with Saint-Preux, as Wolmar says, is not that he is in
love with Julie de Wolmar, but that he is obsessed by his love for her
as a young girl—who no longer exists. The hardest slavery, Rousseau
wrote, is that imposed by a passion from which one would like to
deliver oneself, but cannot.[4] Saint-Preux cannot forget. Wolmar's

---

[1] *Pensées*, XLVI, 1309.
[2] I owe all my information to Jean Starobinski, 'La Nostalgie: théories médicales et
expression littéraire', *Studies in Voltaire and the Eighteenth Century*, XXVII (1963),
1505–18.
[3] Much as M. Gaime once restored young Rousseau's self-confidence. *Emile*, 226–7;
Confessions, III, 90–1.   [4] *Pensées*, LXXI, 1313.

method is therefore to 'cover the past with the present', so that Saint-Preux will recognize Julie as she now is, a wife and a mother, and himself as a man who has long had a life apart from hers. To bring about all this Wolmar begins by asserting a complete authority over Saint-Preux. He 'takes possession of him', and Saint-Preux is only too delighed to find himself a child again, with Wolmar as his father rather than his host.[1] And from the first Saint-Preux knows that Wolmar is the image of God. That is, he alone is really a man.

To release Saint-Preux from his memories, Wolmar makes him relive the past, step by step. He must see and touch everything that he saw and touched when he first knew Julie. He is forced to seek out everything that can arouse his memory and make him relive the past. He does so, however, in the present and in the company of a woman who is no longer the same woman as his former mistress. At each moment, profound though the mnemonic shock is, Saint-Preux realizes that he also has changed and he begins to be liberated from the past. The final almost violent trip that he and Julie take to the rocks upon which he once scratched her name finally shakes him free. That, he says, was the 'crisis of his madness'.[2] It passes and Saint-Preux begins to live in the present, to enjoy Clarens and to disentangle his destiny from his past.

It is all Wolmar's work. How does he proceed? He never preaches, never reproaches, never punishes. What he does is to arrange situations which force Saint-Preux to face reality: first the reality of Mme de Wolmar as a woman whom he no longer loves, then himself as a man capable of making decisions for himself. These situations are created with infinite care, the environment being structured in advance.[3] Often it is done against the wishes of Julie and Saint-Preux, as when Wolmar departs, leaving them alone for several days.[4] Sometimes it involves deception, as when Wolmar's collaborator, Lord Eduard, puts Saint-Preux in a contrived situation where he seems obliged to help his patron, and to take charge of the latter's life and future.[5] In both cases Saint-Preux is forced into self-recognition and so into freedom. He is cured of nostalgia and of insecurity.

[1] *N.H.*, Part IV, Letter VI.   [2] *Ibid*. Part IV, Letter XVII; Part V, Letter II.
[3] For the best account of this see Etienne Gilson, 'La Méthode de M. de Wolmar', in *Les Idees et les Lettres* (Paris, 1932), 275–98.
[4] *N.H.*, Part V, Letter XII.   [5] *Ibid*. Part II, Letter XII; Part VI, Letter III.

As Julie says of herself, Wolmar 'returned her to herself', and now Saint-Preux is again sane; Wolmar, she notes, has been his 'liberator'.[1]

It is a slow process. At first Saint-Preux becomes completely dependent on Wolmar and feels unsure as soon as the latter's watchful eye is removed.[2] After passing all the contrived tests arranged for him, he is, however, not only prepared to accept Wolmar's offer to bring up his children, but he no longer fears Wolmar's 'oeil éclairé' when it reads his heart.[3] He does not become a second Wolmar, to be sure; such is not his bent nor his station in life. Even when he is restored to himself he remains in need of Wolmar's guidance. His first response to a difficult situation is to lament Wolmar's absence: 'where are your paternal cares, your lessons, your insight? What shall I do without you?'[4] When he finally does recognize that he is now a free and competent person, he is still aware that this has been Wolmar's work, not his own. It is then that he calls the former his benefactor and his father, and notes that 'in giving myself wholly to you I can offer you, only as to God himself, the gifts that I have received from you'.[5]

In the final test in which Saint-Preux discovers his will Wolmar forces him to protect Lord Eduard, who has for so many years looked after Saint-Preux. The young man is meant to prevent Lord Eduard's marriage to a prostitute. It would have been very much to Saint-Preux's advantage to let this happen, for it would force Lord Eduard to settle in Switzerland and Saint-Preux could then remain near him and Julie. He never thinks of it, but acts with great ingenuity and perseverance to save his patron. When he succeeds he knows that he is a man. He is now ready to assume the post that Wolmar had promised him. For Wolmar has given him a task sufficiently demanding and interesting to give purpose and direction to Saint-Preux's life. He is to bring up the Wolmars' children. That is a life-time's occupation. Saint-Preux will always need Wolmar, if not as a father, as a patron. Wolmar himself accepts responsibility in advance. 'Live in the present', he tells Saint-Preux, 'and I shall

---

[1] *Ibid.* Part III, Letter XVIII; Part IV, Letter VII; Part VI, Letter XII.
[2] *Ibid.* Part IV, Letters VI, XV.   [3] *Ibid.* Part V, Letter VII.
[4] *Ibid.* Part V, Letter XII.   [5] *Ibid.* Part V, Letter VIII.

answer for the future', and that is also Julie's cousin's advice: let Wolmar manage.[1] Saint-Preux cannot expect to be Wolmar's equal, but he has been liberated from himself and from the need for a healing authority. As a member of the community that Wolmar has created at Clarens he remains under his penetrating eye, but not as a patient.

Although Wolmar has done much for his wife, he does not have the authority over her that he exercises over Saint-Preux. He does not even try.[2] Her regeneration is her own work, even if it is only a partial cure that is completed only when she commits sacrificial suicide. Neither Wolmar nor Saint-Preux can influence her, because she has a rare strength of character. She also exercises authority, through her capacity to inspire what is really a very servile sort of love and devotion.[3] This all-attracting, but also subtly hateful portrait was entirely in keeping with Rousseau's general view of women. Women rule men and make of them whatever they please.[4] 'Do you want to know men? Study women.'[5] Clearly Rousseau did not like this monstrous regimen of women. Paris, the very epitome of modern corruption, was entirely ruled by women.[6] Indeed, women were responsible for most of the moral evils of this world, but Rousseau could not help admiring authority, even in this case. The result was a considerable uneasiness. He composed two brief essays to show that women had been important in the great events of history and that in civic virtue and military heroism women were really the equals of men.[7] This did not deter him from claiming that 'the law of nature bids women obey men', because men are active and strong, while women are passive and feeble.[8] To be sure, husbands ought to treat their wives well, but just or unjust, women must submit to the commands of their spouses.[9] However, in the end Rousseau decided that this submission was itself only superficial. Julie also rules at Clarens and when Emile's tutor resigns his authority over his

---

[1] *N.H.*, Part IV, Letters IX, XII.   [2] *Ibid.* Part IV, Letter XIV.
[3] *Ibid.* Part V, Letters III, X; for a religious interpretation of the relationship, see Pierre Burgelin, *La Philosophie de l'Existence de Jean-Jacques Rousseau*, 447–55.
[4] 'Lettre à Lenieps', 8 novembre 1758, *C.G.*, IV, 115–16.
[5] *Letter to d'Alembert*, 82.   [6] *N.H.*, Part I, Letter XXI.
[7] *Essai sur les Evènements Importants Dont les Femmes Ont Été la Cause Secrète*, *O.C.*, II, 1257–9; *Sur les Femmes, ibid.* 1254–5.
[8] *Emile*, 322, 370–1; *Pensées*, VII, 1300; *Letter to d'Alembert*, 87–8.   [9] *Emile*, 333, 359.

pupil, he says, 'My weighty task is now ended and another undertakes this duty. Today I abdicate the authority which you gave me; henceforth Sophie is your guardian.'[1] If anything, her authority is greater even than that of the man who ruled Emile so completely, for she rules over an adult, not a child. It is not a blessing. Throughout his novel Rousseau put the joys of friendship into glaring contrast with the anguish that men and women in love cause each other. Claire and Julie are a support and comfort to each other. Lord Eduard and Saint-Preux are models of what human beings really owe each other. In the end Lord Eduard chooses to remain a bachelor on civic grounds. He does not wish to increase the already excessive number of peers.[2] But then Lord Eduard is English. He has political obligations. Wolmar wants Saint-Preux to marry Julie's cousin, but Claire refuses him out of devotion to Julie's memory.[3] In any case it is clear that everyone will be better off in the single state. Moreover, the duties of a tutor permit no other distractions. Certainly Saint-Preux does not need to be dominated by another woman.

If the authority of women over men is not good, their influence over their children is rarely wise. Though they desire the happiness of their young, most are too stupid to bring them up properly.[4] The ignorance of women is, however, not the only flaw in parental authority, a subject to which Rousseau gave much thought. Of all the actual and inevitable forms of authority it is the most important. In all corrupt, that is in all contemporary societies, parents are the agents who transmit false traditions and habits from one generation to the next. Children are sacrificed to social vanity, cast too early into the conventional mould and, thanks to the ambitions of their fathers, forced into unhappy marriages.[5] Rousseau was, moreover, anxious to minimize the legitimate scope of paternal authority in order to prove, as Locke had, that it could not serve as a model or justification for absolute monarchy.[6]

It is not just the socializing and political functions of the family

[1] *Ibid.* 444.   [2] *N.H.*, Part VI, Letter III.
[3] *Ibid.* Part VI, Letters IV, XIII.
[4] *Emile*, 5, 87. Rousseau regretted that the law gave them too little power over their children mainly because he thought maternal affection less harmful than paternal harshness.
[5] Vaughan, I, 205 (*Inégalité*); *N.H.*, 'Second Préface'; *Emile*, 48, 149, 163.
[6] Vaughan, I, 185 (*Inégalité*); I, 237-40 (*Economie Politique*); II, 80 (*Contrat Social*); *Emile*, 423.

that make it a suspect institution under present circumstances. It is also inherently inefficient as a way of educating the young. If a child is to be brought up for his own sake, to become a good and happy man, he needs constant attention. To be the perfect tutor of a single child is a lifetime's work.[1] It is a sobering thought. Nothing less than a full-time tutor for each child can bring about the regeneration of men through education. And where are tutors to be found? Rousseau doubted whether any man was really fit for it.[2] The tutor, to be sure, need not have the magnetic personality, the immense social experience, nor the wealth and rank of a Wolmar. A reformed Saint-Preux will do. Indeed, a tutor should be no more than a man and should show his pupil that he is only human, a person with weaknesses and needs.[3] Nevertheless, his talents like his responsibilities must be immense. Rousseau himself had been a wretched failure as a tutor. His inability to exercise authority had been his undoing, as he recognized perfectly clearly.[4] His *ideas* on education, however, were fully developed very early, and he adhered to them with unusual consistency. From his first to his last letter on the subject one point was, moreover, always emphasized: the tutor must have complete and absolute authority over his charge.[5] No one, not even the parent, may interfere.

Not only must one 'be a man before [one] can train a man', so that one may 'set a pattern he shall copy', one must also be able to control everyone around the child if one is to be his master.[6] The tutor, as a man, must also play God, for he must create an environment, a new 'natural' situation in the midst of society for the child. Because the threats from within and without are so great, he must be able to exercise an unlimited preventive authority.

It is clear from the discussions between the Wolmars and Saint-Preux that the education he is to give their children is to be the

---

[1] *Emile*, 19.   [2] *Ibid.* 17; *N.H.*, Part IV, Letter XIV.
[3] *Emile*, 208, 299–300. That is why a Saint-Preux would do.
[4] *Confessions*, VII, 267–9; *Emile*, 18.
[5] Rousseau made this point in his first essay on private education written in 1740, 'Mémoire Presenté à M. de Ste. Marie Pour l'Education de son Fils', *C.G.*, I, 367–99, and he repeated it many years later in advising a nobleman on the rules to be followed by the governess of the latter's daughter, 'Lettre au Prince de Wurtemberg', 10 novembre 1763, *C.G.*, X, 205–17; *Emile*, 20. The tutor, not the father, Rousseau insisted, chooses a wife for Emile, *ibid.* 369.   [6] *Emile*, 59.

same as Emile's. Saint-Preux even mentions that he has written something on education.[1] It is agreed that the main task is to prevent the empire of opinion from destroying nature. At Clarens the children will be isolated from society at large and their environment controlled. A benevolent authority will check their slightest inclination toward domination and vanity. They also will learn the true law of nature: to obey necessity and no one and nothing but that. Their tutor is to be guided by nature at every step, moreover. That means two things. First of all the character, the given self of each child, is to determine the exact upbringing most likely to allow him to flourish. That is also Emile's tutor's principle. He is, however, never called upon to discuss Emile's personality, for Emile is not given one. Julie speaks of her boys' characters, but Emile is 'child' in general. As Wolmar explains, each child does have characteristics that belong to man in general, as well as his personal traits. The former are set stages of growth through which all men must pass. Emile's education is specifically concerned with these, with the learning, physical, moral and intellectual appropriate to each age, especially the earliest years where nothing must be forced or imposed upon him. There is to be neither retardation nor forced progress.[2] This is above all a preventive project. The young Wolmars and Emile are to be saved from all the miseries that Saint-Preux had to suffer. That is why he is such an ideal tutor and why he is so delighted when Wolmar offers him the job. It is at last a way of making good use of his talents.[3]

To become entirely unlike Saint-Preux, Emile is taught never to desire anything that he cannot reach single-handed. He will not be allowed to develop any artificial passions and is to know nothing of habit and routine. Memory is not to be stimulated and imagination is not to be aroused. He will grow up simple and direct without *amour-propre* but confident, as he has every reason to be, in his ability to take care of himself. Emile is not ignorant, but reading and speculation are not stressed. He has a useful trade to keep him busy and to protect him against reversals of fortune and the fear of such changes. In the end he marries a young woman who has been

[1] *N.H.*, Part V, Letter VIII.   [2] *Ibid.* Part V, Letter III; *Emile*, 10–11, 157, 216–17.
[3] *N.H.*, Part V, Letter VIII.

especially brought up for him. They settle down in the country to recreate the patriarchal Golden Age together. If his country should call upon him to serve it he would do so, but that is most unlikely. Honest men are no longer in political demand. Emile need not expect to be called from his rustic retreat.[1]

To bring up children in this way demands, Julie explains, that a constant and absolute authority be exercised over them. 'The laws of liberty' cannot otherwise be enforced. Moreover, the force of public opinion and the dangers of denaturation are so great that only an incessant control over a child's daily life can keep them at bay. A child is to be educated *against* society and he must be protected against parents, neighbors and servants who would press their false values upon him. The tutor's direct authority over the child must be complete, because the child is always so defenseless, so exposed to external influences. The question is not, to rule or not to rule over the child, but who is to create his environment for him and to what end? Is convention or virtue to create the man? If the tutor is to replace society, he must have more than equivalent means to arrange the child's life, to structure his experiences and to replace all other human examples and influences. 'Negative education', which is the tutor's method, is far from being effortless or unplanned.

What then is 'negative education'?[2] It differs from conventional education not only in its ends, but also of necessity, in its entire method. Its aim is to make a self-sufficient adult who lives at peace with himself.[3] To achieve this one must at all costs avoid trying to impose a foreign, social character upon the child. His natural self must not be inhibited in any way. On the contrary, everything must be arranged so that the child may learn everything that he has to know, without losing his natural characteristics. 'Fit a man's education to his real self, not to what is no part of him.'[4] 'Negative education' is negative in that it prevents the imposition of an artificial, socially devised and socially oriented self upon the child. It prepares him for knowledge by protecting him against error.[5] If Emile is docile to a

---

[1] *N.H.*, Part V, Letter III; *Emile*, 15–16, 33–5, 44–9, 55–8, 65, 71–6, 124–6, 128, 155–63, 171, 217–18, 435–9.
[2] *Rousseau Juge de Jean-Jacques*, I, 687; *Emile*, 16, 57. [3] *Emile*, 6.
[4] *Ibid.* 157, 216–17; *N.H.*, Part V, Letter III. 'Give nature time to work before you take over her business.' *Emile*, 71. [5] *Lettre à Christophe de Beaumont*, 71.

degree and if his will is at the mercy of his tutor, it is because the latter has made himself loved and has made himself the child's only model. He rules over the child's will by pre-arranging experiences and situations, not by any sort of direct imposition.[1] He never bullies and rarely, if ever, punishes.[2] He demonstrates and manipulates. Like Wolmar he does not hesitate to employ stratagems and deceits. His whole art lies in 'controlling events'.[3] He does not give orders, and, again like Wolmar, is everywhere without being seen.[4] If Emile is in this way buffeted and protected at every point, he is compelled to *do* only one thing: to learn for himself.[5] In this sense he is forced to be free by being negatively educated. That is, he is prevented from becoming weak, and self-destructive, as he most certainly would have come to be without his tutor's care.

The tutor's authority is indeed immense, but so are the evils he must forestall. Far from relaxing with the years, moreover, his control must in fact increase as Emile becomes more exposed to both inner and external threats to his balance. During Emile's childhood the tutor had only to manipulate the environment in order to give nature a chance. Emile only needs challenges to help him grow, not orders or direct instructions. These would only stunt his spirit and encourage deceit. When Emile reaches sexual maturity the relationship alters drastically. Religion and book-learning are introduced and, far more important, he must now be subdued. As a young child he was allowed to be self-assertive and to learn by doing. At twenty he must be made utterly docile. Now he is allowed only a mere 'show of freedom' so that the tutor can be the master of Emile's will.[6] Now is the time when the young man enters society and now more than ever he must be kept 'from being altogether artificial'.[7] Because he has never been forced to obey as a child Emile is, in fact, not rebellious now. He is obedient, meek, mild and, in short, docile to a frightful degree.

While Emile is a child one would not expect him to enjoy full freedom under any circumstances. However, he remains dependent on the tutor's protective guidance even as an adult. At the end of

[1] *Emile*, 84-5.   [2] *Ibid.* 55.   [3] *Ibid.* 209.
[4] *Ibid.* 84-5, 88-9, 107, 177.   [5] *Ibid.* 169.
[6] *Ibid.* 291-2, 295, 297-300.   [7] *Ibid.* 281-2.

Emile, the pupil, now fully grown and about to become a father, still feels in need of the protective presence of his tutor. 'Advise and control us', he begs, 'as long as I live I shall need you. I need you more than ever now that I am taking up the duties of manhood.'[1] As he had said earlier, 'Resume your authority. I place it in your hands of my own free-will.'[2] Even more revealing is the story of what happens to Emile and Sophie once the tutor does leave. The sketch for a sequel to *Emile* that Rousseau left unfinished begins with Emile's lament, 'If you had not left us, I should still be happy!'[3] As soon as the tutor departs Emile and Sophie cease to be able to cope with the difficulties that beset them and commit one mistake after another until their marriage and their happiness are destroyed. Emile's education continues to stand him in good stead. He bears adversity admirably. But he does not know how to avert or end the troubles that afflict him and his wife. He cannot control his situation. What is impossible for the perfectly reared Emile, who possesses every virtue except the quality that controls men and events, is certainly not possible for lesser men.

THE TRUE ART OF RULING

Wolmar's good works are not limited to curing love-sick youths. He is also the creator and master of a model estate, Clarens. As befits a man of his spiritual powers, enormous experience and various skills, he naturally exercises authority over an entire community.[4] The end of Wolmar's managerial cares is not his property so much as the peasants and servants who work for him. They must be kept on the land and away from Paris. To that end rural life must be made more acceptable to them than it usually is. In running his estate Wolmar does not have political powers at his disposal. His people can leave his employment whenever they wish. If they are to stay at Clarens Wolmar must gain authority over their wills. He must manage their lives in such a way that they will not want to go away. That is no great difficulty for Wolmar. He is a master of the art of ruling the wills of other men, as the helpless Saint-Preux discovered.

    Wolmar certainly has all the qualities that would be needed to found

[1] *Emile*, 444.   [2] *Ibid.* 290.   [3] *Emile et Sophie*, 3.
[4] *N.H.*, Part IV, Letter X; Part V, Letters II and VII.

a republic. He has all those supra-human talents that the Great
Legislator possesses, but there is no occasion for him to use them. No
people is available. Instead Wolmar tries to recreate the Golden Age.
That also requires god-like powers. To be the head of a full household and to run it properly, not in order to increase one's possessions,
but to enjoy them and to benefit one's dependants, is to be like God.
In fact, it is to be better than God, who has left mankind to flounder
so helplessly. At Clarens only does one forget one's century and
feel that the Golden Age has been regained.

If Wolmar's personal qualities are not in any degree inferior to
those of the great founders of republics, his task is very different from
theirs. It is even remote from the office of a magistrate. Rousseau
distingushed domestic economy very sharply from political economy
or government. The talents required for the former are essentially
those of a father who is wisest in following his inclinations. That
would only lead to injustice in a republican magistrate. The head of
a household should be partial to his own family and think of nothing
but preserving his patrimony for his own children. They in turn will
defer to him, at first out of weakness, then out of gratitude. No
magistrate should count on such attachments. Law must guide him
and the citizens, not personal feeling. The natural authority of a man
over his wife, though clear, is not that of a sovereign. Pregnancy keeps
her inactive often and he must rule her to make sure that her children
are really his also. It is an authority, however, which looks to unity
and concord in running a family. And it is not complete. There is, as
it were, semi-divided sovereignty in the family. No such condition
may prevail in a republic. Between the head of a household and those
who work for him there is a relationship of exchanged services only.
He has no direct coercive, military powers. In return for their work,
he sees to their maintenance. They can quit his employment, and he
may dismiss them. Because this is an impersonal relationship justice
does enter into it, as it does not among the members of the family
bound solely by ties of affection.[1] If the two forms of authority differ,
it does not follow that domestic government is less difficult than
political rule. Nature speaks too feebly in the actual world to guide
most fathers. And in fact there are no good landlords. Only Wolmar

[1] Vaughan, I, 238–40 (*Economie Politique*).

knows how to be a real father, and it is quite clear at every step that his policy is always the exact opposite of that of all the actual masters whom Rousseau had served.

The primary principle of Wolmar's rule at Clarens is autarchy. Nothing is bought or sold. He does not try to increase his holdings; he merely improves them so that his sons will inherit a model estate. Autarchy is also a moral necessity. How else is Paris to be shut out effectively? The Wolmars are good hosts, but they certainly do not invite visitors. As many people as possible are given work on the land. The going rate is accepted as the basic wage, but it is increased in proportion to a man's efforts and length of service. There is no caprice in all this. It is as certain as law would be. Work is distributed according to talents and strength so well that equals could not have arranged it more equitably. Moreover, there are no quarrels among the workers, because they are each one so deeply attached to their common master. This shared feeling serves to bind them, indirectly, to each other. Servants always imitate their masters, and Wolmar is alone a model worth emulating. Moreover, he tries to make life reasonably pleasant for his people. In a republic citizens are ruled by mores and principles of virtue that have been engraved upon their hearts. Domestic servants and people who work for pay in general can only be ruled by constraint. Wolmar knows that ultimately it is fear of being dismissed or upbraided that moves his workers. He therefore tries to cover their fear with 'a veil of pleasure'.

In these efforts Wolmar's guiding hand is felt, but never seen. It is invisible yet omnipresent. He has to *do* very little, but he must always *be* there. Without his example and his felt presence Clarens would fall apart. All the disrupting temptations would flourish and justice would disappear among the people who live and work there. For Clarens is just as artificial, just as 'unnatural' as any other organized society. The division of labor, inequality, and constraint are just as integral a part of this rural world as of any other society. What makes Wolmar's rule beneficial is its palliative effect and its justice. He prevents the peasants from rushing to their doom in Paris and he saves his domestic servants from the corrupting vices of their situation. They are at least not consumed by envy, promiscuity and dishonesty.

The immense authority that Wolmar exercises over his dependants and neighbors is justified by his method of ruling which can be summed up in one word: justice. A rigorous system of rewards and penalties is administered by a man who is always 'equitable without anger' to his servants. The neighboring peasants are helped to recognize that their situation, for all its hardships, is the best one open to mankind. No one is encouraged to change his social position, but justice renders social inferiority bearable and gives it a degree of moral validity.[1] Each man gets his deserts and respects those of others. However, at no time does Wolmar, or anyone else, claim that inequality and domestic service are natural or agreeable conditions. Wolmar's justice can only render them tolerable. He lessens the force of resentment and his people endure their burdens without complaint. Certainly none of Wolmar's servants want to leave his estate. Life at Clarens, autarchical, isolated from the 'great' world, without any disorder or luxury, and with some sense of common unity and justice, is not perfect, but at least there is less cause for dissatisfaction and hostility than in other societies. More than that even the semi-divine Wolmar cannot do.

Order, regularity, security of expectations and fairness: everything in this stable, harmonious society reflects the soul of the master.[2] And although everyone seems to be doing what pleases himself, it is Wolmar who directs each one, for all are united in their attachment to him. That is because Wolmar not only wants to be well served, but because he is concerned with the moral welfare of his servants and with the order of his estate as a whole. It is his responsibility and he attends to it directly, never acting through, and thus depending on, intermediaries. That is the only way in which genuine authority *can* be exercised.[3] This personal involvement also marks the other efforts that Wolmar and Julie make to soften the anguish of inequality. From time to time they practice 'togetherness' with their servants and neighbors. Festivities and celebrations in which all join are frequently held at Clarens in order that servants and masters might at least share some of the pleasures of life in a spontaneous way, and occasionally recognize their common humanity. However,

---

[1] See also, Vaughan, II, 497 (*Poland*).   [2] *N.H.*, Part III, Letter XX.
[3] *Emile*, 47–8.

this is only palliative, a way of reducing the coldness imposed by inequality. The differences in rank are not forgotten.[1] The brute reality remains, and Rousseau was not disposed to forget it. Even when he was looking for ways of transcending its worst emotional and moral effects, he remained acutely aware of inequality: the heaviest of all chains that society imposes upon us.

Infrangible inequality is the greatest single limit upon Wolmar's powers. It is not the only one. Even he cannot undo what civilization has wrought. The recreation of the Golden Age, like that age itself, is fragile. Julie does not find her happiness there, because she is no longer capable of living in the present, as peasants might. The civilized cannot return to a pre-sophisticated condition. That is the eventual discovery of Emile and Sophie. It is also Julie's. The peasant who needs no education other than that which his situation provides might well evade the impact of civilized life, as long as Wolmar is there to protect him against it.[2] Sooner or later history would no doubt roll over Wolmar's people just as it had destroyed all of Switzerland. 'Neufchatel, unique on earth', was not long for this world, as Rousseau knew only too well. If the villager could only be warned and temporarily saved, the refugee from history was past hope. Escape was a psychological impossibility and the attempt to return to the land could only end in failure.

Wolmar must take men as he finds them and create an environment for them that will prevent their becoming even worse. That is a great achievement. It does not, however, compare in scope or depth to the task of the Great Legislator, the image of political authority. Lycurgus 'turned [the human heart] from its natural course'.[3] He and Numa and Moses each *created* a people. In this they were unique, semi-divine figures. Calvin is mentioned only once, in a footnote and then as a legislator whose work did not endure any too well.[4] It was Plutarch who had fired young Rousseau's imagination and who continued to dominate it.[5] Perhaps historical imagination

---

[1] *N.H.*, Part V, Letter VII. That also is the reason why Rousseau urged festivals so much upon the Poles. And indeed his Polish project presents a strange mixture of domestic and political government. Vaughan, II, 434–5 (*Poland*).

[2] *Emile*, 9.   [3] *Ibid.* 8.

[4] Vaughan, II, 52 (*Contrat Social*); 427–30 (*Poland*).

[5] *Confessions*, I, 9; VIII 356; *Rousseau Juge de Jean-Jacques*, II, 819; *Lettres à Malesherbes*, II, 1134.

was not among Rousseau's strong points. Perhaps the Legislator is altogether too much the sum of all the qualities that modern leaders so conspicuously lacked. Certainly of all his images of authority the Great Legislator is the least genuine, the most wooden, one-dimensional figure. Rousseau admitted that 'the comparison of that which is with that which ought to be had given him *l'ésprit romanesque* which had always drawn him far from actuality'.[1] When he built a dream world out of familiar materials and scenes, a Swiss Clarens inhabited by men and women who emerged, however much altered, from his own experiences, Rousseau was totally convincing. Plutarch served him less well. Those ancient heroes were altogether too remote to come alive, much as Rousseau needed to believe in them. One can feel the force of Wolmar's penetrating eye, but one is merely told about the great deeds of the legislators.

Like Wolmar, the Great Legislator is a god. He also is a model for all other men, and just as inimitably above them. He is a public tutor. If Emile's mentor merely prevents the growth of the diseases of association, the Legislator must provide perpetual antidotes for them. He cannot call on nature's helping hand. On the contrary he must defy her. 'He who believes himself capable of forming a people must feel himself to be capable of changing, so to speak, the nature of men. He must transform each individual, who by himself is a complete solitary whole, into a part of a greater whole, of which that individual must, in some manner, receive his life and his being; he must mutilate, so to speak, the constitution of man.'[2] Without this transformation men cannot be subjugated in order to be made free. Without it they can never be expected to live in virtue under the rule of law.[3]

Indeed the rule of law itself is feeble at best. Without a strong will no people can be expected to possess the self-restraint to live in justice. Law in fact is more the expression than the cause of republican virtue. Above all, to structure the will that creates rules, to give a people its life in the first place, requires a single hand and a single voice. Hymns to the rule of law, of course, abound in

---

[1] 'Lettre au Prince de Wurtemberg', 10 novembre 1763, *C.G.*, x, 217.
[2] Vaughan, I, 324 (*Fragment*); 478 (*Première Version*); II, 51–2 (*Contrat Social*).
[3] *Ibid.* I, 245–8 (*Economie Politique*).

Rousseau's writings. Only law is compatible with freedom.[1] Only law is a 'joug salutaire'.[2] Only under law can the dependence of man on man be ended.[3] Only law can subject men without constraining the will. Law liberates.[4] The great problem of politics is to make governments the guardians, rather than the enemies of law.[5] That is only a small sample of a recurrent theme. However, there were qualifications. The first was that law is psychologically ineffective. It can condition only external behavior. Public opinion and mores alone can touch the heart.[6] And to be truly effective public authority must penetrate to the very heart.[7] To do this requires more than law, it depends on continuing education.[8] Secondly, laws do not grow spontaneously in society. The Great Legislator must not only invent them, but create the moral climate that is needed for their acceptance. Lastly, and this is the greatest weakness, law is not self-perpetuating. Like all the works of men, even the best institutions decline under the inevitable impact of moral weakness. And once corruption has set in, there is no stopping it.[9] If Sparta and Rome fell, what can endure?[10] Law ultimately is what personal authority can give society for a while; it does not replace that force, of necessity a personal one, which can alone touch the human heart. That was the way of those ancient political paragons, Moses, Lycurgus, Numa and Solon.[11] Of such men, alas, modern history knows nothing.[12]

The ancients who knew how to rule, did not argue or appeal to the interests of the people. They controlled the affections of the heart especially by using non-verbal symbols to move people to civic emotions. Objects and music appealed to the eye and ear. Every sense was stirred to evoke thoughts and feelings associated with the fatherland. 'The mind was forced to speak the language of the heart.'[13] Language itself was sonorous and designed to arouse, in the

---

[1] Vaughan, II, 37 (*Contrat Social*).   [2] *Ibid.* I, 126 (*Inégalité*).
[3] *Emile*, 49.   [4] Vaughan, I, 248 (*Economie Politique*).
[5] *Confessions*, IX, 404–5; Vaughan, I, 246 (*Economie Politique*).
[6] Vaughan, I, 322 (*Fragment*).
[7] *Ibid.* I, 248 (*Economie Politique*).   [8] *Ibid.* I, 330–1 (*Fragment*); II, 426–7 (*Poland*).
[9] 'Lettre à Vernet', 29 novembre 1760, *C.G.*, V, 270–2.
[10] Vaughan, II, 88, 91 (*Contrat Social*). 'Le Corps politique, aussi bien que le corps de l'homme commence à mourir dès sa naissance.'
[11] *Ibid.* II, 427–9 (*Poland*); I, 314–20, 330–2 (*Fragment*).
[12] *Ibid.* I, 338 (*Fragment*).   [13] *Emile*, 286–8; Vaughan, II, 429–30 (*Poland*).

open air, a sense of civic unity. The poetry of Homer, the drama, the melodious rhetoric of the public speech all spoke not to dry reason and calculation, but to the primary emotions. That is what is meant, no doubt, when Rousseau spoke of the Legislator's ability to 'persuade without convincing', and of his acting directly upon the will.[1] This is also that 'inner force which penetrates the soul' without which the moral bond is too feeble to hold men together.[2] To say as monarchs do, '*tel est mon plaisir*', does not require an emotive language or a treasure-house of symbols that call upon every one of the senses.[3] The Legislator must need all of these if he is really to fortify the soul of his charges against all the awful evils that civilization holds in store for them. Without so profound a transformation, without calling on all the feelings of men, they cannot receive a new character and a new will. Without those they will inevitably fall victim to all the iniquities of association.

The main source of the Legislator's strength in this extraordinary enterprise is his own personality. He is a man-god who, though he knows our nature thoroughly, does not share it. His tasks and his powers have nothing in common with the more usual forms of political authority.[4] He neither coerces, nor argues. Everything is done by the force of personality. A magnetic personality transforms lesser men. The political future of Corsica could be left to the 'soul and heart' of General Paoli.[5]

Force is self-defeating and reason is wasted on disoriented, simple people, as it is on children, like Emile. Only direct experience and the force of example can really touch men.[6] It is useless to say, 'be good' to them; they must be made so. How are they to be reconstructed?[7] The Great Legislator has only one means at his disposal: illusion and stage management. And indeed it is not everyone who can make himself appear an agent of God and speak for Him.[8] The altering of public opinion, the revolution in attitudes

---

[1] Vaughan, II, 53 (*Contrat Social*).   [2] *Ibid.* I, 483 (*Première Version*).
[3] *Essai sur l'Origine des Langues*, 407–8.
[4] Vaughan, I, 477–83 (*Première Version*); II, 51–4 (*Contrat Social*).
[5] 'Lettre à M. Buttafoco', 26 mai 1765, *C.G.*, XIII, 334–6.
[6] 'Lettre à M. l'Abbé de Raynal', juin 1753, *C.G.*, II, 49. The multitude, Rousseau wrote, are sheep; they need examples, not arguments.
[7] Vaughan, I, 250–1 (*Economie Politique*); 476 (*Première Version*).
[8] *Ibid.* II, 54 (*Contrat Social*).

that impinge upon behavior can only be done by an example so impressive that it inspires the wish to imitate. Like Wolmar, the Great Legislator must change each individual directly, must impress himself upon the inner life of each future citizen.[1]

To change public opinion, popular judgments of right and wrong, he must also engage in the most detailed stage-setting. In all this the guiding hand must remain hidden. To rule over public opinion one must not only be above it, but out of its sight.[2] It is suggestive power that gives people new ambitions, and social instead of private aspirations. That also is why festivals, ceremonies and all other simple and striking ways of structuring the environment to press new feelings upon the populace are so important. All are necessary to protect the public self against the alluring calls of the private self, of *amour-propre* and the false empire of opinion.

Creative legislative authority that 'mutilates the human constitution' and reduces each person to a particle of a greater whole cannot be effectively exercised at all times. It can only be attempted in the youth of peoples. That is why Brutus and Rienzi failed.[3] For legislation is foresight and prevention. Only very few people are in a material or psychological position to be able to bear this salutary yoke. An isolated people, small in number, just out of nature, which has reached a stage that is exactly like Emile's adolescence, might be educated. If to 'the simplicity of nature the needs for society have been added without any of its vices', then there is some hope. Even so, the Legislator has much to destroy before he can give a people good opinions.[4] A young people has no memories; that is its main virtue. What nostalgia is to individuals, traditional prejudices are to a people. On occasion a Lycurgus could 'wash away' the past.[5] This itself was possible for peoples only if they suffered experiences so intensely shocking that they obliterated their past from memory. That is what happened to Sparta at the time of Lycurgus, to Rome after the Tarquins, and to Holland and Switzerland in the course of their liberation. For the large, old, decrepit nations of Europe no

[1] Vaughan, II, 51 (*Contrat Social*).   [2] *Ibid.* I, 246–7 (*Economie Politique*).
[3] *Ibid.* I, 331 (*Fragment*); 489 (*Première Version*); II, 54–6 (*Contrat Social*); *Letter to d'Alembert*, 74.
[4] Vaughan, I, 491 (*Première Version*); II, 60 (*Contrat Social*).
[5] *Ibid.* I, 183 (*Inégalité*).

such prospect existed. Corsica might be saved from civilization; that was all.[1]

Even in Corsica Rousseau feared there might be no great inclination for eternal simplicity.[2] Nor was the absence of suitable subjects for legislation and the disappearance of great men in the modern age all. Rousseau's sense of the hopelessness of man's position reached its height in his conviction that even the best trained Spartans will eventually fall victim to the spiritual diseases that association always engender in men.

The conclusion that creative legislative authority would fail was not fortuitous. It was all but inevitable, given Rousseau's psychological assumptions. For it is not merely the fatal attractions of false social values that threaten the good republic. It is not only civilization that is bound to creep in. Perpetual denaturalization cannot be maintained except by perpetual tutorial vigilance. The difficulties of full socialization were so great because Rousseau was so deeply aware of the individuality of each person. Each one of us has a self which forms the core of our character. This personal self is not inherently hostile to other selves, nor does it thrive in permanent solitude. Indeed 'our sweetest existence is relative and collective and our true self is not entirely our own'.[3] Solitude is not the answer, but neither is society. In fact there simply is no solution.

The best education, whether civic or private, tries to establish a harmony between the self and the environment. Unfortunately, no environment, however well planned, can displace man's pre-existing self, his inborn personality. Happiness lies precisely in avoiding injuries to this self. Independence and self-esteem can only flourish if one's integral character is preserved. To that end one must claim the ability to withdraw into oneself and to be oneself, even in the midst of society. 'Let us begin by again becoming ourselves. . . by conserving our soul.'[4] Only then can we find within ourselves that *moi humain* which is the essence of our selfhood and of our shared humanity. That is not only true for men living in corrupt society.

---

[1] *Ibid.* II, 55–6, 61 (*Contrat Social*). Poland was a mere afterthought. Vaughan, II, 441 (*Poland*).

[2] He feared that his ideas 'differed prodigiously from those of the Corsicans'. 'Lettre à M. Buttafoco', 24 mars 1765, *C.G.*, XIII, 150–3.

[3] *Rousseau Juge de Jean-Jacques*, II, 813.   [4] 'Lettres Morales', 369.

The citizen, however much denatured, however conscious of his civic self, has still an individual self, an inner life of his own, and it is bound to assert itself as soon as the vigilant eye of the Legislator is removed. The Legislator can only work to postpone that dangerous hour, and that is what he does.

A cohesive community cannot be built by those who cherish the *moi humain*.[1] That is why civic education and the education of the individual have nothing in common. However, having invested the natural self with such deep roots and recognized its profound value, Rousseau was in no position to argue that the Legislator could easily supply the citizens with new communal selves. That is why the Legislator's task is in fact superhuman. It is because men would have to be recreated if society were to be just that he is both necessary, and doomed to failure. For the *moi humain* that is the source of all our goodness is also the fountain of all our aberrations.

Civic man needs a new self to replace his feeble natural equipment for social life. He needs a character that can withstand the assaults of *amour-propre*. The wholly military education, the games, the ceremonies and the other appeals to his senses are designed to achieve that. Instead of a weak and divided self the citizen is to have an inner strength that derives wholly from his sense of being a part of a greater whole and of having a 'patria' that is genuinely his. He does not need knowledge for that. He needs only to be saved from error and illusion.[2] Self-esteem is the best protection against these.[3] Pride is what keeps a people attached to those mores and opinions that the Legislator has stimulated in them. It protects them against conspirators who would create inequality and against foreign enemies. There is, above all, no time for reflection, idleness and intellectuality in the good society.[4] The Spartan situation keeps men moving. Perpetual public activity and stimulation by public objects prevent passivity, drift, illusion and their social expression in exploitation, oppression and deception.[5]

All this is created by that supreme illusionist, the Legislator. It is the force of a magnetic personality alone that forces a character upon

---

[1] Vaughan, I, 255–7 (*Economie Politique*).
[2] *Ibid.* 341 (*Fragment*); II, 429–30 (*Poland*).   [3] *Rêveries*, VIII, 1079.
[4] '*Préface*' à *Narcisse*, 970.   [5] Vaughan, II, 344–5 (*Corsica*).

a disoriented multitude. For quite unlike later nationalists Rousseau did not believe that the national self had any basis in nature. On the contrary, its creation does violence to all our spontaneous tendencies. National character was, for him, no 'soul' at all, and in no sense a free emanation arising from the disparate selves of individuals. It was not even an historical accretion. There is no group mind apart from the Legislator. Moses *created* the Jews. He gave them their distinctive, national identity. Before him there was only an inchoate herd. This was the example the Poles were to follow in *giving* themsleves 'a national physiognomy'.[1] This was just what Peter the Great had failed to do. By merely imitating others he had not been able to devise a collective personality suited to the human material in his hands. Not that he had destroyed the Russian soul, there being no national souls. He was merely a Pygmalion who had no talent.[2] Whatever national character a republic is to have, and it must have one, can only be an artificial imposition from above. This character and will, being alien, are always frail structures. Because the Legislator must do more than just integrate existing personalities into a more coherent whole, his work does not endure. Laws and mores cannot withstand the assaults of nature for long. For in the last resort the *moi humain* is indestructible.[3]

The sheer hypnotic power of a great personality can achieve what neither force, reason nor inclination can produce, but it is not an enduring triumph. That was, indeed, exactly what Rousseau meant to say. If the enormity of men's errors justifies such immense authority, it also renders it, ultimately, ineffective.

Freedom is what puts man out of nature and freedom to 'perfect' himself (how ironic that word is meant to sound!), puts man into a psychological position which prevents him from ever finding a real home on earth.[4] Unlimited in his ability to develop every sort of artificial deformity of his powers, there is no way to control his capacity for self-destructive behavior. It is, therefore, because men are free that they need masters. It is when Emile reaches adulthood that he cries out for his tutor. The Polish peasants and burghers who

---

[1] *Ibid.* I, 355–6 (*Fragment*); II, 428, 432–3 (*Poland*).
[2] *Ibid.* II, 56 (*Contrat Social*); 487 (*Poland*).
[3] One can constrain individual character, but one cannot change it, according to Wolmar. *N.H.*, Part V, Letter III.   [4] Vaughan, I, 149–50, 178–9 (*Inégalité*).

are to be freed and raised in rank are chosen carefully for their merits, but it is just when they reach civic maturity that they need guidance most. They are to be watched, protected and helped, not because they are poor subjects, but because they are *free*.[1] It is they who must have an orderly environment and a directing hand. After all, even that part of the public that really desires the common good needs guides.[2] How much more so the more feeble mass!

To Rousseau it did not appear that genuine authority limits freedom. The real tension was between authority and equality. Personal authority is not merely compatible with freedom; it creates the latter. In its healing form, in ordering the disrupted passions, it is psychologically liberating. In ordering the environment it allows men to retain an integrated self and to preserve their independence. Wolmar and Emile's tutor are nothing if not tolerant, especially in matters of faith and opinion.[3] Freedom, in any case, was for Rousseau not a matter of doing as one pleased, but of *not* being compelled, either from within or from without, to do what one does *not* wish to do.[4] Inner compulsion is thus a most severe form of enslavement. That is why an ordered existence is needed to support men in a free condition. That also is why moderate desires, a capacity to live in the present and dependence only on things are the prerequisites of the very possibility of a free life.[5] All of them, however, depend on an educative, preventive, curative and ordering authority. Authentic authority liberates. It gives liberty to those who are incapable of creating it for themselves. Better a will dominated by a tutor, than no will at all.[6]

The strong then liberate the weak, but the distance between them remains. Nothing can alter the fact that Saint-Preux will never be Wolmar's equal, nor Emile his tutor's. However, though its extent is no less than the difference between God and man, this inequality is a natural one, and, as such, relatively unproblematic. It is only the addition of social inequalities to those of nature that creates our

[1] Vaughan, II, 501 (*Poland*).   [2] *Ibid.* II, 51 (*Contrat Social*).
[3] Rousseau was proud of his tolerance. Only intolerance is prohibited by the civil religion, after all. Vaughan, II, 133–4 (*Contrat Social*); *N.H.*, Part V, Letter V; Part VI, Letter VII; *Rousseau Juge de Jean-Jacques*, II, 811.
[4] *Lettres à Malesherbes*, II, 1137; *Rêveries*, VI, 1059; *Lettres Ecrites de la Montagne*, VIII, 227–8.
[5] *Emile*, 48–59, 125–6, 436; *Pensées*, XXXI, 1305.   [6] *Emile*, 196.

great miseries. If Rousseau's images of authority show any one thing it is the intensity and consistency of his hatred for all forms of personal dependence and social inequality, and for their psychological roots, weakness and *amour-propre*. It is these that cause even loving parents to destroy the happiness of innocent young people like Julie and Saint-Preux. It is these that make even the best constructed republic a fleeting palliative. It is these that render even the serene life at Clarens galling to most of its inhabitants. *Amour-propre* and inequality are, moreover, inseparable from social life as such. In society their worst consequences may be cured, palliated and, in the case of a chosen few, prevented from arising. The evil itself remains ineradicable. In his last years Rousseau felt that under prevailing conditions peace was worth more even than freedom. For freedom existed only in the heart of the just man.[1] In short, things being what they are, peace, order and quiet were the best anyone could hope for.

This resignation was not merely a matter of old age and exhaustion. It was implicit in Rousseau's work all along. Indeed, it is less Burke's traditionalist rhetoric than Rousseau's psychological insight that has set the most severe limits on all hopes of easy reform. *Emile* is anything but a manual for those eupeptic schoolmasters who imagine that it is possible to reconstruct society by fiddling with the curriculum and altering the atmosphere of the classroom. A regenerative education *against* society and apart from its strains and prejudices would require one perfect tutor for each newborn child. Apart from Swiss peasants, each child would need the constant attention of a man who was himself above society. Where are such teachers to be found? Yet this is the only way to cure denatured men through educative means. To be sure, it is neither morally nor psychologically impossible, but it is historically very unlikely. Society, being what men have made it, and expressing, as it does, the most deep-seated psychological deformities, is not readily altered. The great men, whose personalities can impinge upon the consciousness of those whom they wish to improve, can effect some real, though never complete, alleviation. Such men, always rare, have now, however, ceased to exist altogether. In their absence nothing can be done to morally reconstruct the European world.

[1] 'Lettre à Moulton fils', 7 mars 1768, *C.G.*, XVIII, 147-50.

That made the need for a utopian vision all the more compelling. It alone could keep the sense of man's moral possibilities alive and it alone could warn those who were not yet wholly corrupt of the dangers that beset them. Only utopia could expose, judge and shame the civilized world as it deserved to be.

5

'ONE NATION, INDIVISIBLE . . .'

THE POLITICS OF PREVENTION

The Great Legislator practices preventive politics in much the same way as the tutor gives Emile a negative education. Both create an external environment that will forestall the moral deformation that has been the lot of 'man in general'. Both also manage to create a deep attachment to themselves in their respective charges. Their influence is thus as profound as it is apparently effortless. There is, however, a rather obvious difference. The tutor is raising one child, while the Legislator is dealing with 'a people', that is, with a considerable number of adults. The startling fact is that Rousseau spoke of 'the people' as if it were Emile. That, indeed, was only one of his personifications. The sovereign, the public happiness ('*le bonheur publique*'), the general will and the body politic are all personifying metaphors, and very conventional ones at that. Together they form the main subject of Rousseau's political thought. That in itself is not particularly odd. All political thought is a matter of metaphors. The complexity of an endless series of relations between people could not be imagined, could not even be felt, without such organizing images.

The mere fact that Rousseau concentrated consistently on a few political personifications is not, in itself, notable. It is what he did with them that is entirely peculiar to him. The personifications allowed him to bring his moral and social psychology to bear on the great question of politics: can civil society be justified? And his quite deliberate use of traditional metaphors permitted him to show just how damaging and erroneous all prevalent answers were. In giving these well-worn commonplaces new meanings he carried his psychology into a political context, and also exposed the falseness of the conventions that these metaphors had embodied. It was a marvellous exercise in rhetorical economy, but it did not succeed perfectly. For, as Rousseau realized with some bitterness, few readers were able to understand the *Social Contract*. Its elusiveness has become notorious.

There is nothing neutral about Rousseau's personifications. They are neither ornaments, nor descriptions. On the contrary, they are part of that 'moral truth' that reveals how people feel in specific situations, and in that exposure there is a judgment. What matters is the moral impact of situations on those who must live within them. Rousseau's moral psychology always involved consumers and creators of social environments. That was unalterable. Society always makes people. The question is not whether society should or should not mould its members. The real issue is how to imagine an environment that benefits those who must bear its pressures. How is one to envisage a social cure for the diseases of association? How might the rift between inclination and duty within each person be healed? The biography of Everyman was a 'genealogy of vice'. Under what conditions might Everyman be restored to a condition free of his traditional miseries? That is the subject of political psychology. It also makes Rousseau's use of personifications far less bizarre than it might seem. They are collective patients.

Rousseau's view of 'the people' is that of an outside observer. The Legislator considers only the physical and social conditions that must be created for it. The reactions of the people, of Everyman, are only what one would expect of most persons in these situations. The interplay between situation and individual is known in its main movements, even if the 'individual' is a composite 'man in general'. He is not any special person, in his entirety, but only the bearer of a number of responses common to all men in society. The sovereign also is treated in terms of the conditions which permit, or rather fail to permit, the exercise of the people's civic rights and duties. The happiness of the people is again not a personal feeling peculiar to any person, but the sum of circumstances which allow simple people to feel secure and contented. The general will, like any will, is that faculty, possessed by all men, that defends them against destructive impulses and influences. It is general because each citizen can guard himself and his fellow citizens against the dangers of *amour-propre*, the empire of opinion and institutionalized inequality. Everyman's overriding self-interest is to prevent inequality and his will is pitted against all those forces within and outside himself that promote it. The body politic, lastly, only shows the conditions under which governments aid or destroy the people. The first function of all these personifications is to illustrate how man might respond to a civil order and to show what a legitimate society would be like. For that Rousseau had to consider only the conditions which were likely to stimulate the least painful responses to the inevitable inconveniences of civil life.

Although there is nothing anthropomorphic in Rousseau's metaphors they have their disadvantages. Even though it is clear that he had no notion of a group mind or of any social purposes apart from those of the individual citizens, his personifications do create an impression of excessive civic uniformity. Rousseau, of course, did think that, in spite of men's natural differences, they were in many aspects quite alike. This was true especially of the vast majority of people who possessed no exceptional talents. It is for them that civic society exists. Their similarity is most notable in their reactions to the process of association. That is what gives Everyman's agonized passage into civilization and Emile's education their plausibility. Rousseau may very possibly have overestimated the pain caused by inner and social conflict. He believed that nothing was more terrible than the tension between nature and society, and that social iniquity was mainly responsible for that suffering. Given these assumptions, he can hardly be accused of ignoring individual needs in favour of public ends dissociated from feelings. 'Everything that destroys social unity is worthless; all institutions that put a man in contradiction with himself are worthless.'[1] This harsh sentence against Christianity could just as readily be applied to civilization as a whole. It expressed completely what Rousseau meant to prevent in his vision of a just civil order. It is not social cohesion as an end in itself. The end is the unity within each man. Social peace is merely the reflection of that inner harmony which had marked natural men in contrast to the civilized. Because this need was a general one, it could be described in a composite figure of a man, or of 'the people', without unduly distorting the experience of actual men.

The great convenience of Rousseau's personifications for joining his moral psychology and his vision of justice does not exhaust their uses. Because they were all rich in conventional associations,

[1] Vaughan, II, 128–9 (*Contrat Social*).

Rousseau could, by redefining them, express, in a word, the full extent of his radicalism, and his utter contempt for prevailing political opinion. Who were 'the people' in common usage? They were everybody who was nobody, the vulgar multitude, the 'feet' of the body politic. That was not Rousseau's meaning. 'The people is mankind; those who do not belong to the people are so few in number that they are not worth counting. Man is the same in every station of life; if that be so, those ranks to which most men belong deserve most honor.' The European peasants, not their masters, are to be the object of all consideration and their welfare the sole end of politics. No one else matters at all. 'If all the kings and all the philosophers were removed they would scarcely be missed and things would go on none the worse.'[1] When Rousseau spoke of the people the word was not just meant to cover, without discrimination, all those who might be living in a given place at a given time. It meant those who are now the poor, and quite specifically, *not* the rich in talent or goods.

The 'sovereignty of the people' is also a metaphor containing a negation. The word sovereignty has scarcely any meaning at all apart from absolute monarchy. It is the chief attribute of the man who can say *tel est mon plaisir*, and make it stick. That he should be able to do this was no less the will of God than it was necessary for social order; such was the meaning of sovereignty in the old régime. By taking this fear- and awe-inspiring power, so wholly associated with monarchical government, and attributing it to the people Rousseau was able to tell simple men in a phrase how immense he thought their rightful claims were. The sovereign people implies the destruction of sovereignty as a relation between rulers and ruled. It is the anti-monarchy, and not a new sovereignty in any intelligible sense.

The general will was certainly Rousseau's most original contribution to the language of politics. The phrase has remained his own and rightly so. However, both Montesquieu and Diderot had used it before him.[2] Montesquieu used it vaguely to signify public

---

[1] *Emile*, 186–7.
[2] Montesquieu, *The Spirit of the Laws*, I, XI, 153; Diderot, *Droit Naturel*, in Vaughan, I, 429–33.

opinion. That was Rousseau's meaning as well, though by no means
a casual one. The initial purpose of his notion of the general will was
to reject Diderot's idea. For Diderot the general will expressed a
vague benevolence felt quite naturally by men for mankind in
general. For Rousseau the general will pursued nothing but hard
personal interest, even if it was an interest that citizens shared.
Nor was its content vague; 'it always tended to equality'. Far
from concerning itself with all mankind, it owed its inspiration
to xenophobia. It can come to men only when they acquire
that *moi commun* which arises out of close and exclusive association
with their fellow-citizens.[1] It is general because the prevention
of inequality is the greatest single interest that men in society
share, whatever other ends they might have. Nothing could
be more remote from the cosmopolitan and aristocratic values
of Voltaire and the Parisian intellectuals. As d'Alembert had
noted, it was a 'ridiculous heresy' to say that the *philosophes*
believed in general equality.[2] It was not a mistake Rousseau was
likely to make about them. He knew perfectly well that they spoke
for the interests of exceptional men, and that his alone was the
'voice of the people'.[3] That also was why his definition of the 'public
happiness' began with a rejection of conquest and commerce as fit
objects of policy. These serve only the interests of the great and
proud. What peasants want is to live in security and abundance. That
is the public happiness, derived from life in a civic order, and
expressed in a quiet satisfaction with things as they are.[4]

The body-politic was the oldest and the most tradition-ridden of
all Rousseau's metaphors. Partly he meant to show, as that personification had always done, that governmental authority could be
justified. He did that by taking the magistrates out of the head or
soul, and reducing them to mere organs of the body, with no will of
their own. That was enough to undo the traditional view of
monarchical authority.[5] For *Leviathan* more was needed. To dispose

[1] Vaughan, I, 460 (*Première Version*); Vaughan, II, 33–5 (*Contrat Social*). For more
detailed accounts of Rousseau's response to Diderot see René Hubert, *Rousseau et
l'Encyclopédie* (Paris, 1928), 31–49, and Jacques Proust, *Diderot et l'Encyclopédie*,
359–99.
[2] Grimsley, *Jean d'Alembert*, 183. [3] Vaughan, I, 243 (*Economie Politique*).
[4] *Ibid.* 325–9 (*Fragment*). [5] *Ibid.* 241 (*Economie Politique*).

of Hobbes' 'atrocious despotism', government had to be pictured, less as a member of the body politic, than as the principal cause of its diseases and ultimate death. As the body dies, so does the artificial man, the state, and it is government that inevitably brings about the destruction, unless it is checked with improbable zeal by 'the people' as a whole.[1]

Negative in this as in everything, Rousseau's metaphors are the vehicles that took human needs into battle against the forces of inequality. Even when Rousseau wrote about a policy or an institution that he recommended, it was always a matter of attacking the existing system. Not equality, but the destruction of inequality matters, all the more so since the psychological predisposition to inequality is a manifest part of the experience of association. That is why the Legislator must instruct a people before it is even capable of knowing what citizenship means. When one remembers who 'the people' are, the necessity for a Legislator becomes all the more evident.

The people, as Rousseau never forgot, are not very intelligent. It may know its own interests, but it needs help if it is to defend them effectively.[2] Without a Legislator to guide men, they will never acquire a character or become aware of themselves as a people, who 'collectively' are citizens subject only to laws they have made for themselves.[3] Like Emile at adolescence the people needs instruction and examples. Interest brings men together, but to become all that they might be as a people requires more. To be ready for its Lycurgus the people must not yet have rooted prejudices, must be 'pliable', isolated from foreigners and, in sum, have the 'simplicity of nature joined to the needs of society'.[4] Only such a people can be saved for liberty and from the master's yoke. To avoid that is indeed its main aim.[5] To that end it needs civic pride, while Emile needs Stoic self-control. Both, however, know how to find their fulfillment in isolation.

The best way to avoid both war and inner confusion is simply to keep the people apart from all others. Philosophers, to be sure,

---

[1] Vaughan, II, 91 (*Contrat Social*).
[2] *Ibid.* 50–1 (*Contrat Social.*)
[3] *Ibid.* 34 (*Contrat Social*).
[4] *Ibid.* 60 (*Contrat Social*).
[5] *Ibid.* 40 (*Contrat Social*).

pretend to love Tartars and other distant nations, but that is only to save themselves the trouble of having to love their fellow-citizens. For ordinary people it is more important to avoid foreigners, indeed to dislike them. To prevent that dreadful 'mixed-state', half social and half natural, the people needs a 'smaller social group, firmly united in itself and dwelling apart from others, [that] tends to withdraw itself from the larger society. Every patriot hates foreigners; they are only men, and nothing to him.' It is not a perfect situation, but it does avoid the perpetual war and despotism of monarchies and the cold indifference of philosophers.[1] These are the conditions the Legislator must, at all costs, prevent from arising.

Commerce and conquest, the policies of monarchical states, are far from the people's interest. The Legislator induces the people to be neither so rich as to tempt other nations, nor so poor as to be itself tempted to engage in these forms of international relations. A modest self-sufficiency is the first condition to be met.[2] There are also powerful psychological reasons for isolation. Emulation is always bound to lead to trouble. Nations only copy each other's vices.[3] Had not the French corrupted the Swiss?[4] Emile might be allowed to travel: he is not a citizen, but even he must be warned against the dangers of foreign influence to his inner integrity.[5] Self-possession, like civic loyalty, is frail. Lord Eduard is pleased that the English are nothing but Englishmen, since they have no need to be men. An Englishman's prejudices spring from pride, not from *amour-propre* as do those of Frenchmen.[6] This idea came to Rousseau from Montesquieu, who in one of his panegyrics on England, had noted that 'free nations are haughty, others may properly be called vain'.[7] Like many of his contemporaries Rousseau enjoyed comparing

---

[1] *Emile*, 7; Vaughan, I, 251 (*Economie Politique*); 326 (*Fragment*).

[2] Vaughan, II, 58–9 (*Contrat Social*).   [3] '*Préface*' à *Narcisse*, 964.

[4] Vaughan, II, 323 (*Corsica*).   [5] *Emile*, 418.

[6] *N.H.*, Part II, Letter IX; *Emile*, 416. Rousseau was evidently familiar with much of the 'national character' literature of his time. Lord Eduard was, however, a specifically political figure and Montesquieu alone had concentrated wholly on that aspect of the English scene. To miss that is to miss both what Lord Eduard is meant to convey and the immense influence of Montesquieu upon Rousseau. That is why the purely literary approach in general does such scant justice to the *Nouvelle Héloise*, e.g. George R. Havens, 'Sources of Rousseau's Eduard Bomston', *Modern Philology*, XVII, 1919, 125–39; see also Albert Schinz, *La Pensée de Jean-Jacques Rousseau*, 339–41.

[7] *Spirit of the Laws*, I, XIX, 315.

the 'character' of various peoples. He very much regretted the uniformity to which life in the capitals of Europe had reduced their inhabitants. Only isolated peoples can retain ways that are integrally their own and express their particular experiences.[1] The masked people of capitals are not just faceless; they are without character or self-esteem. The Legislator must see to it that the people acquires a character suited to it and capable of withstanding foreign influences which simply disintegrate that independence that comes from having a clearly felt sense of self-hood.[2] In prehistoric times, for which Rousseau had a real understanding, the bare needs for subsistence and all that bears upon it, climate and soil, mould men entirely. That is, however, not men's condition now.[3] For Rousseau climate was not, as it was for Montesquieu, a perpetual influence upon men's lives. Once they emerge from animality, moral forces dominate their lives and characters. The history of the Jews had taught Rousseau that.[4] In history, it is psychological, not physical resources that cause a people to survive or to perish.

The people's character, for Rousseau, was in no way separable, either as an end of policy, or as a subject of study, from the ways of its individual members. To show how shared conditions affect the behavior and opinions of individual persons was all he had to show. That is why he talked not of Spartan maternal behavior, but of just one truly awful Spartan mother. That, also, is one of Lord Eduard's roles in the *Nouvelle Héloise*. Rousseau did more than just put Montesquieu's phrases about England into his mouth. He made Lord Eduard a perfect embodiment of those traits that Montesquieu believed the English owed to their liberty.

Without illusions about himself or his country, Eduard is wealthy, but never acquisitive. As Montesquieu had noted, opulence and personal merit are all that matter in England. Lord Eduard is as generous as he is rich, takes no pride in his ancestors, serves the laws rather than the king, loathes the court and is totally indifferent to public opinion. He immediately recognizes Saint-Preux's worth and the two become the closest of friends. To be sure, he is no Wolmar, far from it. He has violent passions, and his deep Stoicism cannot

---

[1] *Emile*, 415–18.   [2] Vaughan, II, 428–30, 432 (*Poland*).
[3] E.g. *Essai sur l'Origine des Langues*, 383–95.   [4] Vaughan, I, 351–7 (*Fragment*).

save him from them. His manners are direct and the same toward all. No false politeness and no delicacy for him. He is not at all stupid, but completely unintellectual. Because he is proud, and not arrogant, he has none of the class prejudice that dominates Julie's father. And it is he who denounces the latter mercilessly for having sold his military services to the king of France and for adhering to tyrannical notions. No one buys Lord Eduard—nor does he buy others. He himself is a model of personal independence because the people still count for something in England; even the simple sailors whom Saint-Preux meets have a feeling for real merit and a sturdy character. Freedom creates character, even in modern England.

Nevertheless, it is Lord Eduard, quite in keeping with Montesquieu's own pessimism, who notes that the laws do not rule in England; it is merely the last country in which they still exist.[1] Above all, it is he who in dissuading Saint-Preux from suicide, brings out with great force how enormous a distance separates modern man from the heroes of antiquity.[2] The republic and its virtue are so remote from modern man that its heroes cannot be copied. Self-control and a melancholy awareness of present ills are all that the ancients can now teach us. It is the English hero who must recognize this most perfectly, because he was the only conceivable rival to the moral supremacy of ancient virtue. Montesquieu had wavered. Rousseau was certain: Rome was incomparably greater than England.

The historical reasons for the character of the English or any other people were beyond Rousseau's range of thought. It was not his ambition to be an inferior Montesquieu. Psychology was what he understood and it enabled him to create a living character who also personified English freedom. Lord Eduard, quite apart from his intrinsic interest as one of the best drawn figures in the *Nouvelle Héloise*, is important for an understanding of Rousseau's notion of a people's character. In spite of the enormous differences in their

---

[1] *N.H.*, Part I, Letters XLV, LX, LXII; Part II, Letter II; Part III, Letters XXII, XXIII; Part V, Letter I; Appendice I, 'Les Amours de Milord Eduard Bomston.' *Spirit of the Laws*, I, XI, 156-7. Thus Montesquieu did not choose to 'examine whether the English actually enjoy this liberty or not ... it is established by their laws; and I inquire no further'. I, XI, 162; XIX, 307-15.

[2] *N.H.*, Part II, Letters XXII, XXIII; *Lettres Ecrites de la Montagne*, IX, 255.

style of thought, Rousseau's debt to Montesquieu was enormous. It was Montesquieu who had shown that a people's character is not the cause of its collective conduct, but part of a social whole which it reflects and sustains. It is both an expression of a people's physical and political experience, and also its chief source of strength in maintaining those institutions which best suit it. It is that active force that must inform the law if it is to be appropriate to the physical and moral needs of the people. It is, moreover, a sensitive disposition, which like the personality of a human being can be crushed, as despotism can crush people who once were free. In that complex of related and mutually dependent actions and responses that are summed up in the word 'society', the character of a people plays the most vital part in maintaining the integrity of the whole. That is why Rousseau felt so strongly, knowing the true lesson of Montesquieu, that a people must be given a character by the Legislator. It must be moulded for strength and survival. *Secretly*, therefore, when he seems to concern himself with regulations, that master psychologist stimulates the mores and opinions of the people which alone can give it an enduring character and institutions capable of enduring.[1]

Character is pride and the structuring of the people's opinions has no more important end than to replace *amour-propre* with self-esteem.[2] That is a sense of inner self-appreciation that makes people indifferent to the opinions of outsiders, as it guards individuals against that servile and self-destructive Parisian concern for 'what is done'. To feel secure men must have a sense of the importance of their own part in the social whole. How else can pride be extended to public objects? Only in a small society is that ever possible. People cannot even have an awareness of society as a single whole unless they know each other.[3] In large states, where people are strangers to each other, public sentiment just evaporates.[4] To be sure, citizens should not be crowded together as they are in Paris and other large cities, 'where man's breath is fatal to man'.[5] They should meet regularly, but live apart. The agrarian republic is perfect for

---

[1] Vaughan, I, 322 (*Fragment*); II, 64 (*Contrat Social*). (My italics.)
[2] *Ibid.* II, 344–5 (*Corsica*).   [3] *Ibid.* I, 251–2 (*Economie Politique*).
[4] *Ibid.* 294 (*L'état de guerre*).   [5] *Emile*, 26.

that. Men do not live in cities there; they only meet to conduct public affairs in them. Then they return to their own land, which their simple minds identify directly with the fatherland. That is why patriots grow in the soil.[1]

Size is not only important in creating attachments to the land and fellow-citizens. It makes the assertion of rights and the identification of interests much less difficult. Interest is what brings men into society and keeps them there.[2] The consciousness of common interests is citizenship. Justice itself is not divorced from *amour-propre*. It is, like pride, only well-understood, expanded and properly directed self-interest.[3] In a small state this is not difficult because the identity of interests is genuine and evident.[4] Given very meagre intellectual capacities of the people, the scope of society should not exceed their faculties.[5] If they cannot understand what is going on people will dissociate themselves from their fellows. Moreover, a man's vote does not matter much to him, or to anyone else, if it is only one among many.[6] He then feels powerless and loses interest in the state. Size and complexity thus always work against the interests of the people and in favour of those who have special abilities and wealth.[7] Rousseau had learned that in Paris. That, indeed, is why the cohesive community is very much the anti-capital. Its virtues arise mainly from the absence of those conditions which created Paris and its counterparts all over Europe.[8]

In the absence of social bonds, moreover, the *esprit d'état* of the magistrates will assert itself and they will become overbearing with no active public to restrain them and no patriotism to shame them.[9] In addition to that, the difficulties of governing a large territory and a huge population cannot but increase the need for concentrated governmental power. The inevitable result, as Montesquieu had shown, was that large states are ruled by monarchs who presently

---

[1] Vaughan, II, 110–13 (*Contrat Social*); 347, 351 (*Corsica*); *Emile*, 326.
[2] Vaughan, I, 455, 470, 493–4 (*Première Version*); II, 32 (*Contrat Social*).
[3] *Emile*, 215.
[4] Vaughan, I, 484–5 (*Première Version*); II, 56–8 (*Contrat Social*).
[5] *Ibid.* I, 126 (*Inégalité*); II, 57 (*Contrat Social*).
[6] *Ibid.* II, 66 (*Contrat Social*); *Emile*, 427–8.
[7] Vaughan, II, 66–8 (*Contrat Social*).
[8] *Emile*, 286–7, 418.
[9] Vaughan, II, 431–8, 472 (*Poland*).

become despots.[1] In short, everything that has gone into the making of the old régime was to be avoided. The small, isolated city, the peasant republic, its opinions and mores carefully instilled by a Legislator and maintained by patriotic feeling, is the sole defense against civilized tyranny.

The conditions that impinge so deeply upon the people's feelings and ways are part of a psychological strategy. These defenses against inner and outer threats are, however, useless unless those interests which lead men to join in a social contract continue to be served. That is why the Polish project is such a superficial fantasy; as Rousseau well knew.[2] Polish patriotism does not support the military policies of the ancients and it does nothing for the vast majority of the people, who are excluded from its political life. Without sovereignty, in fact, the people has exactly nothing. The Legislator's art is described in loving detail in the Polish project, but it says nothing about the real ends of republicanism. For that one must read the *Economie Politique*, the true Spartan utopia. It has its Legislator, but it also has a general will and a *vox populi, vox dei*, which alone make it possible for the people to achieve its permanent interests. Without freedom and justice no republic can be said to exist. And without equality there is no liberty.[3] All the hypnotic powers of the Legislator were in vain if inequality, the root of all vice, was not checked. Rousseau never doubted the truth of Montesquieu's remark that 'a free nation may have a deliverer: a nation enslaved can only have another oppressor'.[4] No single savior can replace the conditions necessary for freedom.

To illuminate the conditions required for justice, Rousseau turned from the Legislator and the character of the people to another personification, the sovereign. Rousseau admitted explicitly that for him the words 'the sovereign' was a personification. It was his name for 'the will of all [which] is the order, the supreme rule' in society.[5] The writers of the monarchical tradition, and above all Hobbes, had certainly paid their respects to that will as it was expressed in the social contract which establishes civil societies. Rousseau

[1] *Spirit of the Laws*, I, VIII, 120; Vaughan, II, 77–81 (*Contrat Social*).
[2] Vaughan, II, 443 (*Poland*).   [3] *Ibid.* 61 (*Contrat Social*).
[4] *Spirit of the Laws*, II, VIII, 309.   [5] *Lettres Ecrites de la Montagne*, VI, 203.

entirely agreed with that, but for purposes of his own. What he wanted to show was that these contracts, so long misinterpreted by absolutist theory, were invalid because they were never enforced and could not be enforced unless the people was sovereign. That is why, in spite of the title of his most celebrated book, the social contract itself plays an insignificant part in his political thought. It is the ordinary people, 'the all' whose will rules, that matters most. Their sovereignty is meant to express their supremacy within civil society, a supremacy which it is always in their interest to retain and which must always be protected against usurpation. Sovereignty thus personifies the most important interest of all. And it is never anything apart from the interests of the men who come together to live in society, and who recognize the rules under which their interests are to be secured.[1] The justifiable civil society is one in which the people's interests, and none other, determine the rules: not kings and not representative parliaments, but the people are sovereign. That is the chief value of the personification. It brings home, as no other word could, whom the people, the nobodies, are to replace. The great question of politics is how to protect the people against its own incompetence, and against fraud and usurpation.

All societies are based on some agreement, some commonly accepted conventions. That is merely a definition of society. Moreover, men generally come together for the same sorts of reasons: to ensure their preservation and to supply their needs.[2] The contract, the decision to create a civil society, expresses nothing else. It does not come from any new moral awareness or civic sense. It creates these eventually, and the differences between societies depend on that development. The terms of the contract are, in fact, exactly the same for every civil society, whatever its moral and political quality may be.[3] In every case it is an agreement that replaces possession with property.[4] Instead of having to defend his person and his things as best he can, each man now agrees to respect the possessions of every other man and to

---

[1] Vaughan, I, 457 (*Première Version*); II, 35 (*Contrat Social*).
[2] *Ibid.* I, 455 (*Première Version*); II, 32 (*Contrat Social*).
[3] *Ibid.* I, 181 (*Inégalité*); II, 31–2 (*Contrat Social*); *Emile*, 424; *Lettres Ecrites de la Montagne*, VI, 205.
[4] Vaughan, I, 245 (*Economie Politique*); II, 37–9 (*Contrat Social*).

join with everyone in protecting these. From now on his safety and his goods are his, not because he has the strength to ward off attacks upon them, but because his potential aggressors have agreed that they are his to have and hold in undisturbed peace. He, in turn, not only recognizes their right to this, but all join together in order to protect each one whenever the need for it arises. *If* this arrangement really comes to mean in actuality what it says, it is a very advantageous exchange in which all gain.[1] 'All' means, of course, those who are not exceptionally strong and shrewd: the people. For them only, after all, is it true that 'no one' loses anything to any other person, since all give up identical powers and all gain an identical security.[2] They, indeed, give up only a precarious hold on their safety in return for collectively assured protection. The easy possibility of aggression was of no use to them, in any case. To be sure, if a man now fails to abide by his agreement he may be punished. That is implicit in the accepted obligation to protect each person through collective action against any aggressor.[3]

This is the origin of every civil society. It is also the birth of law and justice. Without property, without mutuality of rights and duties, there can be no sense of justice. Any individual will, like little Emile, feel a sense of injustice when someone simply deprives him of the work of his own hands. Justice, as a general social feeling, as the sense of what is due to others, no less than to oneself, can arise only out of rules that establish property, that define 'mine' and 'thine' and the rights and duties implicit in those words. However, unless we also learn to care for our brothers as we do for ourselves it is ineffective.[4] The emergence of a sense of justice is transforming for those who enter civil society, *any* civil society. It is not, however, a feeling that can prosper under all circumstances.

It is only when men *really* recognize and accept mutual obligations, and when the rules *really* apply to everyone of them in exactly the same way, that justice can be said to be more than a frustrated hope.[5] If the strong continue to dominate the weak, and the rules do not replace, but only legalize the power of masters, then nothing at all

[1] Vaughan, I, 456–7 (*Première Version*).　　　　[2] *Ibid.* II, 32–3 (*Contrat Social*).
[3] *Ibid.* I, 457 (*Première Version*); II, 36, 46–8, 63 (*Contrat Social*).
[4] *Ibid.* I, 259 (*Economie Politique*); 494–5 (*Première Version*); II, 48–9 (*Contrat Social*).
[5] *Ibid.* I, 471–4 (*Première Version*); 44–6 (*Contrat Social*).

has been gained by anyone but the rich. A man obeys himself only if he follows a rule that he knows to be necessary and advantageous. If he follows rules that limit him, but impose no restraints on other men, then the rules are not in his interest and he cannot be presumed to have agreed to them simply because he is silent. Consent may not be the most uncomplicated word in the political vocabulary, but it does not mean slavish endurance of domination. To have said so was the atrocious error of that 'untruthful child', Grotius.[1]

Not the mere existence of a social contract, but mutuality of obligations under rules that are impersonal demands, and not the wishes of any one person, makes justice. That is also what is meant by replacing the inequality of physical powers by civil equality.[2] It is not mere consent that imposes obligation. Only an agreement that binds all equally, and therefore excludes the possibility of personal domination, is obliging.[3] Only this condition makes the social contract a plausible justification for the 'chains' of civil society.

The real problem of justifying civil society is, then, to find ways of making the social contract effective. As usual, Rousseau's mind took a negative turn. What he really wanted to make clear, after all, was how unjust all actual societies were. He therefore concentrated on the conditions that reduce the contract to futility at best, and to an instrument of enslavement at worst. Without the work of the Legislator no contract can ever come to much. The people cannot be expected to have the wits needed to protect its newly awakened sense of justice against its own *amour-propre* or against the wiles of the conspiratorial few.[4] In fact, most social contracts are fraudulent, mere deceptions, as Rousseau showed in the *Discourse on Inequality*. All societies at present live under rules designed by the rich in order to oppress the poor.[5] The poor were lured into submitting to a contract by the rich. The pretense of the contract to bind all equally deceives them. In fact when there are rich and poor the effect of the contract is to prevent the poor from attacking the rich

[1] *Emile*, 421–2; Vaughan I, 130 (*Fragment*); II, 25–31, 41–2 (*Contrat Social*).
[2] Vaughan, I, 459–60 (*Première Version*); II, 39 (*Contrat Social*).
[3] *Ibid.* I, 274 (*Economie Politique*); 467, 475 (*Première Version*); II, 45 (*Contrat Social*).
[4] *Ibid.* I, 183–9 (*Inégalité*).
[5] *Ibid.* 190 (*Inégalité*); Vaughan II, 39 (*Contrat Social*).

without inhibiting the powers of the rich in any way whatever. When there are rich and poor there are always two kinds of rule, the legal one set by the contract, and the real one exercised by the rich who dominate everyone and everything without restraint.[1] Such a contract merely accelerates the abuses of inequality, of which despotism is the ultimate one.[2]

Fraud is not the only means of rendering the contract ineffective. Since it is not a simple agreement, but the creation of a new civic consciousness, it is imperative that the sense of justice should be sustained and continually asserted. The people cannot develop an artificial social conscience, which is justice, spontaneously. Mere natural compassion is not enough now. Justice is an attitude that has to be nurtured. It is a question of the psychological growth of 'the sovereign'. Civic obligations must not just be accepted once and for all, but must be explicitly and regularly reassessed and reaffirmed. Not only must every citizen participate in the original contract, but he must at any time be free to reconsider his allegiance. If he rejects it, he should be free to reconsider his allegiance and should be free to leave the polity, without hindrance, difficulty or fear for himself or his family. Without that, tacit consent is a fraud, not merely a silence. For consent to be explicit, genuine and personal, the possibility of opting out must exist. Once a man has accepted the contract he obviously cannot leave to escape from his duties, whether they be personal debts or military service in time of war.[3] That would be a private act of war against the polity, not a free act of dissociation. With that in mind, however, no one is bound by the contract who has not agreed to it.[4] All contracts say that. Few mean it.

The contract also lapses if the people cannot assemble at stated times to consider the rules that bind all of them, and to reaffirm their intention to abide by them. There is no other way in which the sense of justice can be kept alive. It is also the only way of keeping governments within their legitimate bounds. That, indeed, is the main political function of these assemblies.[5] The purpose of the

---

[1] Vaughan, I, 181–3 (*Inégalité*); 268 (*Economie Politique*); II, 346 (*Corsica*).
[2] *Ibid.* I, 190–1 (*Inégalité*).
[3] *Ibid.* II, 102, 105, 44–6 (*Contrat Social*).   [4] *Emile*, 424.
[5] *Lettres Ecrites de la Montagne*, VII, 230.

assemblies of the people has nothing to do with modern notions of legislation. They are not called to make or remake laws, but to reassert the people's willingness to abide by the contract and to live in justice. That is why the fewness and antiquity of laws is the very best proof of their validity and worth.[1] There is nothing wrong with tacit consent so long as the opportunity to make it vocal is always present.[2] The open and frequent affirmation of faith in the rules is an expression of the sense of justice that the rules have kindled and a means to their preservation. The sovereign *does* very little. Sovereignty is the people's determination to live without masters and under rules accepted by it, even if fashioned for it by the Legislator. This is what separates an 'association' from a mere 'aggregation'.[3] The acts of periodic recollection are not a blind adherence to tradition as such; on the contrary, by returning to its foundations the people reinvigorates a present and immediate commitment to justice, to a single virtue.

Justice is also not a matter of self-government in any very extensive sense. It does not imply any sort of action or adaptation to change. It is, rather, an effort to prevent all change. The sovereign people abides by an ethos that has been created for it by the Legislator. It is he who is the sole 'architect' of the edifice that the people maintains.[4] That is why Rousseau quoted Montesquieu with such approval: 'At the birth of societies the chiefs of the republics make institutions, and later the institutions make the chiefs.'[5] The psychology of justice demands participation in public acts of civic loyalty and defense against usurpation. It does not call upon the people, for all its sovereignty, to make new laws or to exercise governmental functions. It does mean that the *moi commun* is sustained, that each citizen, even the least important, is treated with the consideration due a 'sovereign', and that the citizens, because they are equal and just, care for each other.[6] These dispositions are found only among the people, not among privilege-seeking groups. That is why the people is fit for sovereignty, and why the great in their cruelty and the intellectuals

---

[1] *Confessions*, IX, 404–5; Vaughan, II, 91–3 (*Contrat Social*); *Lettres Ecrites de la Montagne*, VII, 231.
[2] Vaughan, II, 40, 91 (*Contrat Social*).   [3] *Ibid*. 31 (*Contrat Social*).
[4] *Ibid*. 54 (*Contrat Social*).   [5] *Ibid*. 51 (*Contrat Social*).
[6] *Ibid*. I, 126 (*Inégalité*); 241, 250–1, 253–4, 256 (*Economie Politique*).

in their indifference are not.[1] Justice is, in short, a state of mind created by civic experience. Its ultimate victory comes when the little *moi humain* is totally absorbed by love of the public good. This is what sovereignty does for the people.

If Rousseau had been able to abandon the traditional vocabulary of politics occasionally, he might have saved his readers at least one confusion. Because the term sovereign has as its corollary the term subject, Rousseau thought it necessary to put it to at least some use. The just society is evidently a society without subjection. Rousseau wanted to say just that. The citizen is the very antithesis of the usual subject. What he did say was that the people consists of citizens who are the sovereign, and of subjects who submit to the law of the state.[2] This disastrous explication seems almost to make the people as neurotic as the Vicar at his self-divided worst. In fact, exactly the very opposite is implied. Not two selves, but an undivided self is the mark of the citizen, who, being tormented by neither *amour-propre* nor oppression, finds that his duty is also his inclination. He is internally whole because he lives in a social environment in which his interests are perfectly served, and subject and sovereign are 'identical correlations united in the term, citizen'.[3]

If he expressed himself awkwardly, Rousseau, however, did not misrepresent a very essential aspect of his view of citizenship by speaking of sovereign subjects. It brings out perfectly the extent to which the people is a beneficiary of justice in society, rather than its creator. In the perfect Spartan republic the people is taught to understand and even to love its laws by carefully constructed pre-ambles.[4] That is how men absorb the meaning of their laws, as Plato had so well explained.[5] Such an education is nothing if not wise in a patriotic republic, as the Legislator well knows. It also says something about the people's sovereignty. It is a condition free from personal oppression, but it is not self-determination in a politically active sense.

The people is, quite in keeping with Rousseau's psychology, re-active and passive in its moral life. Its activity, important though it

[1] Vaughan, I, 242–3 (*Economie Politique*). [2] *Ibid*. II, 34 (*Contrat Social*).
[3] *Ibid*. 93–4 (*Contrat Social*); I, 493 (*Première Version*).
[4] *Ibid*. I, 246 (*Economie Politique*); II, 453, 459 (*Poland*). [5] *The Laws*, 723.

be, is at most defensive. It must assert itself constantly, but only to prevent usurpation. It does little else. Personification has, thus, the effect of seeing the people as subjects of a social situation that has been created for them. To be sure, they experience it as beneficiaries, not as victims. The individualizing tendencies of Rousseau's psychology are also evident here. Each citizen is like every other in being just. Justice is, however, described as an external condition and as an inner state of mind. At no time is there a sense of relations *between* people. The 'others' are the situation for the individual citizen, and he remains an isolated entity who reacts to them. Their justice creates that absence of oppression which is the essential feature of a legitimate society. For the individual it is a framework, not a set of relationships. He helps to maintain the structure, but he does so primarily by keeping his own inner civic self intact. The only visible actors in society are the Legislator and the enemies of the people who compete for its opinions. Social change after the initial institution of a people is always a decline, therefore. That is inherent in Rousseau's utopia.

The conspiratorial few are not the only agents of degeneration. Gradually, as the memory of the Legislator fades so do the character and opinions that he gave the people. He is, after all, only a brief interruption in the normal course of history which is a tale of otherwise unmitigated popular self-destruction. Indeed, neither he nor his utopia have any purpose other than to illuminate what might be, in a glaring contrast to what is, was and will be. The picture of a legitimate civil society is that of laws as they might be, men being what they are. It is the interplay between these two, between the unrealized possibility and history, that makes the personification of politics into a dramatic morality play.

Of all Rousseau's celebrated 'bipolarities' none is more dramatic than the confrontation of the possible with the probable.[1] Just because fate is character, a failure of the human will, it is insurmountable, as any doom must be. The dramatic intensity of Rousseau's style of thought is not in its admitting alternative and in-

[1] Jean Wahl, 'La Bipolarité de Rousseau', *Annales Jean-Jacques Rousseau*, XXXIII, 1953–5, 49, 55. I completely disagree with this effort to impose Hegel on Rousseau, and I have only borrowed the excellent term, bipolarity, from it.

compatible moralities. It is not the either/or of Sparta or the Golden Age, but *either* one of these, when it is pitted against men's actual moral poverty, that illuminates, without solving, the deepest and most universal tensions. The juxtaposition of what is and what might be is not a call for action, but a revelation, a psychological event, not an historical one. The sinister accidents that drive men out of the Golden Age and out of Sparta are all of their own making. That is their most significant aspect, because it ensures their recurrence. To understand and to condemn are the only fit responses to this spectacle and Rousseau knew no others. He was not interested in showing how men gradually mould each other. That is the subject of historical narrative. The drama of irresoluble confrontations alone could express warnings, imprecations and denunciations, and, above all, Rousseau's infinite revulsion.

THE WILL AGAINST INEQUALITY

Since the people does not do very much with its sovereignty, why does it need a will? Could Rousseau not have saved his readers from confusion by replacing the term, general will, with the more simple word, consent? He could not, because the latter does not in the least express his meaning. The general will is Rousseau's most successful metaphor. It conveys everything he most wanted to say. It ties his moral psychology and political theory together as no other words could. And the unity of morality and politics was a matter of no small importance to Rousseau.[1] The general will is a transposition of the most essential individual moral faculty to the realm of public experience. Like the personal will it is not directed at the external world or even immediately toward manifest action. It is a regulative power, the defensive force that protects the self against the empire of opinion that threatens it from within and without. On the level of public life that means that the republican people is on its guard against all other states, and that its will protects it against them.[2] It is, as a will, the very antithesis of Diderot's general will, which encompassed the rights of all mankind. It is also an internal faculty, because it defends the people against those disruptive groups that yearn for inequality. As such there is nothing mysterious about the

[1] *Emile*, 197–8, 422.   [2] Vaughan, I, 243 (*Economie Politique*).

general will. It is the will against inequality. That is also why it is general. It pursues the interests of man in general against those 'particular' wills which lead men to seek privileges, especially by forming groups that aim at inequality. The general will is, thus, a specific form of the human faculty of willing, and one that each citizen ought to possess.

The nature and functions of the will as a psychological power, rather than its 'generality', really explain why Rousseau had to attribute a will to the people in its position of sovereignty. The people, the nobodies of this world, is '*par état*' in favor of justice and equality. It knows perfectly well that if exceptions to the rules are made it is not in its favor or to its advantage.[1] That realization is not too difficult, even for men of the most limited intelligence. One does not have to be particularly shrewd to feel cheated and to wish to avoid it. There is nothing complicated about peace, unity and equality. Anyone can appreciate them.[2] Only the *arcana imperii* require subtle minds. The real interests of the people are more easily grasped. There is no great need to alter men's opinions on this score. Let each man have his own opinion and 'what is most pleasing in itself will always secure most votes'.[3] And equality is certainly what is most pleasing to the people, since that is its main interest. There is nothing excessively confident in this. The problem is not that the people does not see its interests, but that it is no match for those who want to deceive and mislead it.[4] That is why the force of circumstances, the external pressures upon the people, always tends toward inequality.[5] That is why the people needs a Legislator so desperately to enlighten it. What happens without him is only too well known.

There is, moreover, a psychological dynamism at work, even in the best of republics, that disorients every citizen. *Amour-propre* arises out of association as such. It is stimulated in the just no less than in the unjust society. Only the family does not arouse it. The people, each individual citizen, that is, cannot be protected against the emergence of competitive feelings. In the *Social Contract*, Rousseau conceded that a self-oriented, advantage- and privilege-

[1] *Lettres Ecrites de la Montagne*, IX, 263.   [2] Vaughan, II, 102 (*Contrat Social*).
[3] *Emile*, 306.   [4] *Ibid.* 239, 243, 248; Vaughan, II, 50-1 (*Contrat Social*).
[5] Vaughan, II, 61 (*Contrat Social*).

seeking particular will remains alive within each citizen. As long as this tendency is not allowed to play any significant part in civic life, it is not a serious obstacle to the prevalence of the spirit of justice, but it must be limited and diverted.[1] To keep particular wills in check within the citizens is the greatest achievement of the Legislator's educative art. That is why he also is said to submit to the general will.[2] The strengthening of opinions that prevent institutionalized inequality is, indeed, his main task.

The fostering of an unwavering will is by no means easy, for nothing was clearer to Rousseau than the feebleness of this faculty. The timid instinct of conscience and the artificially created sense of justice are alike in their weakness. Both emerge best when the individual withdraws into himself for quiet introspection. If conscience is to be awakened, the pains of remorse must be recalled. If justice is to move a citizen, he must remember the dangers of inequality. To achieve these recollections men must withdraw from their fellows and return to themselves. That is why the citizen before voting should consult with no one, but only bethink himself.[3] In both cases the individual, whether he be a man or a citizen, pursues only a strategy of self-fulfillment. It is, however, only if his duty and his personal inclinations are really at one that men can feel both free and virtuous.[4] If the citizen is to prefer the general to the particular will, he must really see that his own interest is served by such a choice. That requires two inseparable conditions: that he live in a society where there are no rich and poor and that he be educated to see his enduring interest in preventing inequality. In an unequal society to be just is far from one's real interest. That is why the mixed state is so painful. Justice is known but not practicable. The just Emile feels a duty toward his native land, unjust though it be, because the very fact that he *does* live in *a* society has given him a sense of obligation and justice. *Any* society, after all, arouses the capacity for justice, even those that deny it. Where justice does not prevail, however, the just man feels his duty as something he owes to himself, to his own self-respect, to his idea of what a man should be. It is

---

[1] Vaughan, II, 103–4 (*Contrat Social*); I, 278 (*Economie Politique*).
[2] *Ibid.* I, 247 (*Economie Politique*); 481 (*Première Version*).
[3] *Ibid.* II, 42 (*Contrat Social*). See *supra*, Ch. 2.
[4] *Ibid.* I, 248–9, 278 (*Economie Politique*).

evidently no part of his non-existent civic life. That is why a just
man must suffer, for his sense of justice is perpetually insulted and
outraged. He wisely withdraws to the Golden Age.[1] Only in a republic is it in the social, as well as emotional interest, of the citizen to
be just and civic-minded.

The mores engraved upon the hearts of the citizens, the opinions
instilled in them by the Legislator, fortify them against *amour-propre*
and against the empire of opinion. Without that the social contract is
meaningless. Without the new rules that instill new opinions men
will have no common feeling for justice and no means of 'forgetting
their primitive conditions'. The pull of nature will overwhelm
that of duty, which, within society, can lead only to competition
and institutionalized inequality.[2] However, the will to maintain
the republic can become a lively personal motive in a properly
educated people, for it is not difficult to share the ends of those whom
we like. The youth's education in perfect equality, the elimination of
the family and the selfish partiality it creates, the incessant games and
assemblies, the military exercises and constant stimulation of a
common pride in a shared past, all have as their end the redirection
of *amour-propre* toward civic self-esteem, and the replacing of opinions that tend to inequality with those that prevent it.[3] The tendency
of men's spontaneous reaction to society is toward personal preference; education must counteract it. For their enduring interest is to
maintain equality, without which liberty is meaningless.[4] Once there
are rich and poor, all is lost.[5] As long as a man feels part of the sovereign, as long as he is actively engaged in some sort of public activity
with his fellow citizens, he is likely to remember his and their common
interest in defending the republic against the forces of inequality.[6]
When he leaves the rites and assemblies, however, he will again think
of himself as a particular person, not as a citizen, and his mind will
turn to personal advantages, rather than to civic interest.[7] The whole

[1] *Emile*, 436–8.
[2] Vaughan, I, 474, 476–7 (*Première Version*); II, 50–1 (*Contrat Social*).
[3] *Ibid.* 248, 250, 255–7, 275 (*Economie Politique*); II, 122 (*Contrat Social*); 344–6 (*Corsica*).
[4] *Ibid.* I, 460 (*Première Version*); 61 (*Contrat Social*).
[5] *Ibid.* II, 330 (*Corsica*).
[6] *Ibid.* I, 457 (*Première Version*).
[7] *Ibid.* 460 (*Première Version*); II, 40 (*Contrat Social*); *Emile*, 426.

policy of patriotism is to make these moments of civic dissociation rare, and to prevent their becoming accepted modes of conduct.[1]

The instilling of proper mores and opinions would be an impossibility, if they did not correspond to the genuine social interests of men. The present 'mixed condition' is morally tormenting because our duty never corresponds to our interests. Men cannot be moved by anything but their interests; their self-preserving instincts and their will cannot respond to anything that ignores and defies these.[2] The general will must, therefore, express the fundamental common interests that all men can accept as both their advantage and duty: the prevention of inequality. The general will is a 'tendency to equality'.[3] Personal non-civic interests survive, but as long as they are not organized into privilege seeking groups, they cancel each other out.[4] The general will, in any case, is not determined by the number of voices that can, at any moment, be heard, but by the one interest that unites the citizens—which may momentarily be forgotten.[5] What that interest is, however, is very well known. It is the replacement of the inequalities of nature by civil equality.[6]

Social disunity is therefore a sign that some members are not as aware of the necessity for justice as they ought to be. That also is why unanimity is a sign of civic vigor in the people. If all agree to a rule it can only mean that all are served by it. Competition divides, shared interests unite. That is evident enough. Unanimity is a sign of concord—except in monarchies where it is a sign of despotism. Absence of conflict is all the more a proof of civic well-being since the general will is not directed at political action which may involve prudential calculations. It is not concerned with government and policy. The general will is, like the personal will, a state of mind, not a specific motive for action. The will creates, sets and strengthens character and standards of conduct. Specific courses of action are left to the determination of magistrates, even when peace and war are at stake.[7]

The difference between moral purpose and government is

[1] Vaughan, II, 95–6 (*Contrat Social*). [2] *Ibid.* 456, 477 (*Poland*).
[3] *Ibid.* 39–40 (*Contrat Social*). [4] *Ibid.* 42 (*Contrat Social*).
[5] *Ibid.* 45 (*Contrat Social*). [6] *Ibid.* 39 (*Contrat Social*).
[7] *Ibid.* 40–1, 76–7 (*Contrat Social*).

particularly clear in the military aspects of civil life. Rousseau was more than enamored of the military spirit. 'Every citizen must be a soldier as a duty and none may be so by profession.'[1] It is a sign of young peoples that they have a militia, not a professional army, which is typical of despotic regimes.[2] At one time Geneva had its citizen army; now the magistrates repress it, as inequality has come to destroy the city.[3] Equality and the armed citizenry were as inseparable as were inequality and professional armies. Had not, as Lord Eduard notes, Saint-Preux's father fought for his country, while Julie's had sold his services to the king of France? Who stood, then, for real valor?[4] The social contract of the far from cosmopolitan people, therefore, makes it a right and duty of each citizen to defend the polity against aggression.

Since there can be no law between polities, but only among individuals within a polity, justice has nothing to say about war and peace. The relations between states are not subject to law and justice. There are neither just nor unjust wars. War is a matter of preservation or destruction.[5] In a just society it is never anything but defensive, since conquests are a danger to the people. However, the duty to fight for one's polity is, under a social contract, always absolute. For wars may be a political mistake, but they are never lawful or unlawful. Citizens must fight for their country just as much as they must pay debts and protect each other's lives and goods. In addition, patriotism is a military virtue, and the Legislator who wants the contract to flourish can base it on no firmer ground than the spirit of martial valor. Military service is therefore a part of civic education and a fundamental duty and right. War and peace, however, are merely questions of prudence and may, therefore, be left to the magistrates. It need hardly be added that military obligation, like any other, is real only within a society that is ruled by a living social contract. In fraudulent civil orders there are no civic obligations or rights, only prudential calculations among which fear plays the most significant part.

Acts of sovereignty are declarations of principle. They sustain the

---

[1] Vaughan, II, 486–7 (*Poland*).   [2] *Ibid.* I, 308–9 (*Fragment*).
[3] *Ibid.* II, 488–9 (*Poland*).   [4] *N.H.*, Part I, Letter LXII.
[5] Vaughan, I, 294–305 (*L'état de guerre*); 448–54 (*Première Version*); II, 37–9, 46 (*Contrat Social*).

spirit of the laws upon which civic society rests. The sovereign people assembled has only one function, 'to maintain the social pact' in its military and proprietal aspects. In considering government the sovereign has to answer only two questions, whether the form of government is acceptable, and whether the men who conduct its affairs are faithful to the social contract binding all citizens.[1] Moral self-defense, not action, is the concern of the general will. That is why agreement among the citizens is so valuable. It proves that they are not competing for private gains, but are really concentrating on common interests. However, unanimity is required only for the original contract.[2] The principle of majority rule may be accepted for all future decisions.[3] Majorities may, to be sure, be diverted from the pursuit of equality. They may be overcome especially by organized privilege-oriented particular wills.[4] When that becomes the habitual state of affairs the republic is dead, because evidently the citizens no longer care for justice.[5] The social bond is then broken and no real grounds for obligation are left, only considerations of prudence and fear.[6] These, to be sure, must determine the moral strategies that each person pursues. They do not liberate men from the instinct of conscience, but that is not the voice of public obligation.

When an individual citizen or even several of them find themselves at odds with the majority, no one need feel aggrieved, nor is the republic in danger. They have accepted majority rule and if their notions are at odds with the general will they have erred, which is only human. To be in a minority does not deliver these men into political servitude, it only forces them to accept, as they knew they would have to, the will of the majority.[7] In a free society, if there is no war and they have no debts, they can always leave if they wish. In such a society the problem of minority rights is not a real one. The supreme interest of the people and the whole aim of the general will is to prevent inequality, and that demands a single state of mind. To reject that spirit is to reject civil society. One may do that perfectly freely, but one may not conduct war

---

[1] Vaughan, II, 102 (*Contrat Social*).
[2] *Ibid.* 105 (*Contrat Social*).
[3] *Ibid.* 32 (*Contrat Social*).
[4] *Ibid.* 42–3 (*Contrat Social*).
[5] *Ibid.* 105–6 (*Contrat Social*).
[6] *Ibid.* 26–7 (*Contrat Social*).
[7] *Ibid.* 105–6 (*Contrat Social*).

against the people by forming privilege-oriented groups which usurp its sovereignty.[1]

In a society that accepts inequality as desirable or inevitable the enforcement of minority rights is indeed the essence of liberty. That was, however, not Rousseau's idea of a just society. The individual is protected in his rights, but the pursuit of inequality is not among these. The people is sovereign only as long as it can and does prevent institutionalized inequality. To that end the majority of the citizens must share a common will. The protection of groups that are opposed to civil equality, its most fundamental interest, can hardly be one of the sovereign's aims. The general will is, in its tendency to equality, opposed to the particular will which strives for inequality. The general will maintains the spirit of the republic, its opinions and mores. The particular wills in the polity oppose them. The former stands for inner unity, the latter for public disintegration. Where only a minority cares for the republic and has a will against inequality its rule is not conceivable. A reign of virtue cannot be imposed. Either the sovereign people protects its interests or it fails to do so, in which case all legitimacy lapses. A lawbreaking individual can be coerced to abide by the conditions of freedom, but not a majority of citizens, since freedom is defined as its will to be free.

It is clear why the people has to have a will. What makes that will general? Partly it is general because it is the will of 'man in general' and not of exceptional men. Mostly, however, generality is a set of limitations upon the scope of the will. It is not any will, but a will to impersonality and to fairness toward all. Sovereignty being a condition, rather than a way of exercising power, is not only inactive, it is also limited by its purposes. The general will can only express itself in rules which apply to every member of civil society, and in an identical manner.[2] For all its sacred inviolability the sovereign may not burden one subject more than another, nor deprive anyone of any liberties and goods except those freely ceded to the civil order in the social contract. No person and no group may be singled out for special burdens or privileges.[3] That

---

[1] Vaughan, II, 42–3 (*Contrat Social*).
[2] *Ibid.* 46 (*Contrat Social*).
[3] *Ibid.* 44–6, 49, 98–9 (*Contrat Social*); *Emile*, 425–6.

not only prevents the emergence of 'estates'. It also precludes arbitrariness. General rules even in unjust societies and even when they aim at socially harmful ends have at least one virtue: they treat those who are affected 'without preferences', without whims. That is why Rousseau thought that even the worst law was better than the best master.[1] In that he may well have been mistaken, but it certainly illustrates how profoundly he distrusted personal subservience of any sort. Clearly he felt that all personal acts of domination were humiliating in a way that even general oppression was not. Rousseau, to be sure, spoke for the people and for himself as an apprentice and footman. Certainly he knew what he was talking about when he spoke about masters. The Legislator is unique just because he inspires laws, as his very name implies.

The absence of preferences and the impersonality of general rules are not the only limitation on a will that is to be general. It cannot, by definition, impose duties that are not genuinely useful to the citizens.[2] Rousseau admitted somewhat ruefully that the decision about what was in fact useful was ultimately up to the sovereign. Who, after all, could decide what the people needed, except the people itself? Is utility not also a convention and an opinion? Rousseau was troubled by this because he was so deeply aware of the people's stupidity. He comforted himself with the thought that if the people were ever to suffer from its own errors, it would hasten to correct them.[3] That is a mechanical evasion, since no one knew better than Rousseau that moral self-injury cannot simply be undone. Moral and social errors are irreversible. The sovereign people need only follow its own interests to live in justice, but there is no guarantee that it will do so. The best hope is to save it from the wiles of its seducers by providing it with good opinions at the time of its civil formation. Without the Legislator the will cannot be sustained or attain generality, which demands more intelligence than the people can command. To know what is really useful is beyond the wits of the people. That is why the rich can dupe it so easily into accepting a false contract. That is also why it needs the Legislator so desperately.

---

[1] *Lettres Ecrites de la Montagne*, VIII, 228.
[2] Vaughan, II, 44, 131 (*Contrat Social*); *Lettres Ecrites de la Montagne*, VI, 202–3.
[3] *Lettres Ecrites de la Montagne*, IX, 263.

The generality of the sovereign's will is its impersonality, its expression in the form of rules which apply to all. That is what its justice and civic equality mean. The great lesson Montesquieu had taught Rousseau was that justice without law is unimaginable. It was Montesquieu who had insisted that it was 'only by the protection of the laws that the equality of nature can be recovered in society'.[1] That was also why Spartan society was no extension of the family. The virtue of republicans owes nothing to the natural partiality of parents. Citizens are bound by impersonal bonds of mutual obligation, and if they learn to love each other it is because they have no other erotic ties. The 'sublime virtue' of republican magistrates arises on the annihilation of parental affection.[2] To think that a republic can be built on the model of the family can have only one result: a society ruled by a prince in whom the love of domination takes the place of an affection he certainly does not feel for his subject-children.[3] Civil society thrives on the redirection of erotic energy, not on its spontaneous movement. Nothing in Rousseau's vision of Spartan community life suggests the extended family group. There is nothing cozy about Rome or Sparta. For those who long for the warmth of family life a retreat to the Golden Age offers the only hope—and an unattainable one. Who, however, is happy in a place such as Sparta? Are Caius and Lucius in their inner integrity as citizens no longer men at all? Do they not yearn for some sort of felicity?

Since happiness is the sole object of men's striving, the legitimate society, like any other human enterprise must be judged in terms of its ability to satisfy the most universal aspiration. Rousseau did not forget it. The sovereign people must feel a 'public happiness'. Like the general will it is a metaphor of personification. For happiness is the most individual and personal of feelings, as Rousseau realized very well.[4] This evidently made it difficult to speak of it as something 'public', and after worrying the notion of '*le bonheur publique*' in several fragments, he used it rather sparingly in his finished political writings. His difficulties with the notion are, however, very interesting, because they reveal how and why he used his metaphors as he

[1] *The Spirit of the Laws*, I, VIII, III.   [2] Vaughan, I, 240 (*Economie Politique*).
[3] *Ibid.* II, 24 (*Contrat Social*).   [4] *Ibid.* I, 326 (*Fragment*).

did. It also shows how aware he was of the complexities that his
subtle moral psychology created for political judgments.

The first and the greatest obstacle to a notion of the public
happiness was that Rousseau did not believe that happiness was ever
attainable. It is not for men. At best a man's happiness is 'a negative
state, measured by the fewness of his ills'.[1] 'Man is born to suffer,
that is what it means to be a man.'[2] The closest Rousseau could
come to recalling a moment of joy was the memory of watching some
peasants celebrating a holiday.[3] Certainly happiness could not be
taught. Emile's tutor does not attempt anything of the sort. Emile
learns how to cope with adversity and to evade misery. His emotional
equilibrium is due to a balance between his needs and his powers.
He does not yearn for anything outside his reach. 'Then alone a man
is not unhappy.'[4] Even natural man is a stranger to happiness.
Absence of pain, health and freedom are all he enjoys.[5] At least he,
unlike social man, does not busily create his own misery. The best
strategy is to follow him in that, and to avoid the worst form of
misery, that for which we are alone to blame.[6] Our happiness
consists in self-content which depends on our ability to avoid
abusing our powers.

What can the public order contribute to such an inward state?
Does the happiness of each person not depend on his particular
'powers', his personality? Rousseau admitted that readily. Happiness
is like religious belief in that it depends entirely on those aspects of a
man's character and disposition which are uniquely his and which
differ greatly from man to man. Governments cannot force men to
be happy.[7] Public control is, in the complete absence of identity of
feeling and need among individuals, an intolerable imposition.
Certainly there is no abstract or collective notion of happiness that
could be dissociated from the feelings of the individuals who compose the public. What they all want in common is 'peace and abundance' which are conditions necessary for happiness.[8] However, that
is not happiness itself, private or public.

[1] *Emile*, 44.　　　　　　　　　　　　　　　　[2] *Ibid.* 183.
[3] *Rêveries*, IX, 1085; *Letter to d'Alembert*, 126.　　[4] *Emile*, 44–5.
[5] *Ibid.* 140.　　　　　　　　　　　　　　　　[6] *Ibid.* 362.
[7] Vaughan, I, 328–9 (*Fragment*); *Lettres Ecrites de la Montagne*, III, 146; Vaughan, II, 133
(*Contrat Social*).　　　　　　　　　　　　[8] *Ibid.* I, 348–9 (*Fragment*).

As with all his personifications, the 'public happiness' was thus a situation created for people in which they might achieve something they desired. In this case it was reduction of misery, a relief from the tensions created within men between nature and society, inclination and duty, interest and virtue.[1] The public happiness then would be much like that absence of pain in which man lives in nature. However, Rousseau did not choose to leave it at that. He also wanted to show that there must be some sort of peculiarly 'public' state of felicity, which was different from private joy, at least in its source, just as the general will differs from the personal will. As one might expect, he began his investigation of that possibility on a negative note. What are the false notions of public happiness now being pursued? Some states, monarchies for example, have no interest at all in the felicity of the people.[2] Others claimed that wealth or conquest contributed to the public happiness. Wealth is a relative notion whose meaning depends on the existence of poverty. The state that seeks wealth through commerce must not only impoverish other states, but also comes to depend on them. Commerce, moreover, makes the use of money necessary, which allows for accumulation of wealth among individual citizens. Domestic inequality is thus the inevitable result of trade between nations. As such it is scarcely a contribution to public happiness.[3] As for conquest, it creates misery among conquerors and conquered alike. Excessive power inevitably accrues in the hands of military and civil officials who plan and carry out conquests. If they are not despots when they begin, they will certainly be that before long. Nothing compares to the misery of conquering peoples, ruined by mercenary soldiers and enslaved by ambitious proconsuls.[4] These are the abuses of civil power that pretend to promote the public happiness. So much for *raison d'état*.

To avoid these now prevalent paths to assured misery was a contribution in itself to the public happiness. The public happiness, like all Rousseau's metaphors, carried a criticism within it. The whole idea of commercial wealth and territorial expansion so

---

[1] Vaughan, I, 326 (*Fragment*).   [2] *Ibid*. II, 77 (*Contrat Social*).
[3] *Ibid*. I, 329, 344–9 (*Fragment*).
[4] *Ibid*. 263–5 (*Economie Politique*); II, 485–92 (*Poland*).

avidly promoted by 'benevolent' despots and their publicists had to be exposed. Voltaire might admire Catherine the Great and Frederick of Prussia, but not Rousseau. He could see perfectly that the happiness of the people was not even part of what they promoted. What was the alternative? Clearly Rousseau did need one if he was to appropriate the phase so glibly misused by 'enlightened' despots for their own ends. A people finds its happiness in perfect obscurity and in independence from all other states. It avoids war and commerce.[1] To that extent the public happiness is the mere avoidance of present policy. Autonomy for the people is what it is for Emile, the proper use of one's powers and the limitation of one's needs.

However, the truly Spartan order must offer more than that. It must have a public happiness that is more than the sum of personal felicities. That would merely be an aggregation of feeling, not a union. The happiness of citizens must emerge from their new relations to each other and the civil law engraved in their heart. It is a pool, as it were, from which each draws his happiness rather than creating his own as best he can.[2] People find their fulfillment in public, not private places. Rousseau did not develop this notion. He abandoned it, in fact. To be sure, public activity is a source of pleasure to citizens, as justice is the necessary condition for well-being. The public assembly was not, however, where he finally looked for signs of happiness. To find out if people are happy one ought not to listen to what they say in any case. People complain when they are free, not when they are miserable.[3] To know whether they are really well off one must look somewhere else. The only one objective proof of good government, the only true sign that a people feels at ease, is a general willingness to have a lot of children.[4] When people feel as well off as is humanly possible, they procreate, willingly and frequently.

In the end then, happiness, even if it is stimulated by a favorable civil situation, expresses itself in the most personal way. Happiness remains individual. In the just society the sort of happiness that man

[1] Vaughan, I, 328–9, 348–9 (*Fragment*); II, 308–9 (*Corsica*).
[2] *Ibid.* I, 450 (*Première Version*); 326–7 (*Fragment*).
[3] *Ibid.* 327–8 (*Fragment*).   [4] *Ibid.* II, 87 (*Contrat Social*).

as man, and not as a particular person with particular sensibilities, can feel in response to his social environment, is a form of security. And men express that feeling in a simple and direct way. Everyone does the same thing in the absence of socially created anxieties; they multiply—whether for their own or the republic's sake is not clear. In any case, there is one common way of showing happiness, rather than perhaps consciously feeling it. In this way one can tell when the harmony of man within nature has really been recreated for the citizen within the republic.

It is clear that the achievements of the civil state, for all the virtue and justice that it engenders, are not really so much greater than that of the Age of Gold. If public virtue is justified by so modest a form of felicity, then denaturation hardly seems worth the trouble. And indeed, it is only thinkable as an alternative to our present miseries. It is, moreover, no more enduring than the Age of Gold. The polity is a body because it also dies. It can function well only as long as the will against inequality is strong enough within each citizen to quell *amour-propre* and to protect him against the empire of opinion. When the will built up within each citizen by the Legislator slackens, when mores weaken and particular wills assert themselves against equality, the republic is dead. The citizens live as persons, the people remains, but its sovereignty, its laws and its inner unity are gone. The sense of justice survives. Its reign is over.

TWO BODIES POLITIC

The body politic was of all metaphors of personification the one Rousseau used most frequently. Sometimes he mentioned it quite casually simply to refer to civil society. Occasionally, however, he went into full anatomical detail and then he had very specific purposes in mind. Moreover, he gave the metaphor much thought, and at least in one fragment, subjected it to a devastating critical analysis. That did not prevent him from doing with it what he had done with other traditional metaphors. He turned it upside down.

Rousseau used the body politic, as it had been so often used before, to demonstrate the necessity of government in a healthy society. However, when he drew his body he assigned to government a bodily function infinitely less important than the head or soul that had so often stood for monarchs, whether absolute or not. That, however, was not Rousseau's only contribution to political physiology. He also provided a second picture of the body politic, one in decay. Far from enjoying *Leviathan's* 'artificial eternity' which only unruly subjects and conquest could end, Rousseau's second body politic was born to die.[1] It dies not because the people disappears, but because the general will is subverted by the magistrates, and justice and equality are destroyed. This body politic was made to convey Rousseau's most radical thoughts. All the earlier bodies politic had defended rulers; his alone attacked all governments. If one of his bodies politic tried to overcome the conflict between authority and equality, the second exposed it. In this there is no real conflict. Rousseau knew that government was necessary, no less than he understood that rulers were the enemies of the people.

In the history of political theory the body politic had enjoyed an immense popularity. Writers as different as John of Salisbury, Thomas Aquinas and Thomas Hobbes all adopted it. In medieval thought the body politic was the social microcosm, which, as such, shared the essential traits of all God's creations. It was a model of hierarchical harmony, created out of human diversity by a beneficent authority, which assigned a proper place to each person and group so that all could perform their functions in maintaining the whole. Everyone has his preordained place in an organism which reflects the divine order.[2] It is a creation, but in no sense is it a forced union. For it corresponds to a common need and end. 'There can be no faithful or firm cohesion', wrote John of Salisbury, 'where there is not an enduring union of wills and, as it were, a cementing together of souls.'[3] The head, however, wears a crown and the soul a mitre in a body of which the peasants are merely the feet.[4] The king has, moreover, responsibilities that no one can share. It is he who has 'the function and duty to bring different acts into harmony by allotting them to different individuals to whom they are appropriate'.[5]

[1] *Leviathan*, ed. by Michael Oakeshott (Oxford, 1947), 127, 209–18.
[2] Anton-Hermann Chroust, 'The Corporate Idea and the Body Politic in the Middle Ages', *The Review of Politics*, 1947, IX, 423–52.
[3] John of Salisbury, *The Statesman's Book*, ed. and trans. by John Dickinson (New York, 1963), 71.   [4] *Ibid.* 64–5.   [5] *Ibid.* 73–5.

Authority from above is what keeps this body together. Such also was Thomas Aquinas' body politic. The efficiency of a monarchical soul was clear to him, both within an established social body, and when a new polity is to be created, as Romulus had once created Rome.[1]

Above all there was *Leviathan* so boldly engraved and described on the opening pages of the book that Rousseau carried like a cross on his back. That artificial monster in the picture has a body made up of men, but the head is not composed thus. It is just a head and it wears a crown. The sovereign, not visible, is said to be the soul. In the full anatomical account the head is not mentioned at all, but it is implicit throughout, that monarchy fits *Leviathan* as no other cranium could. The body politic made monarchical government appear an integral necessity, even if not at all a logical one, when one considers that it was by 'pacts and covenants' that this body was 'first made, set together and united'. It allowed Hobbes from the first to pretend that monarch and sovereign were indistinguishable.[2]

On one occasion Rousseau used the old metaphor in a medieval way, but not to justify political authority. Marriage was, in his view, necessarily a union between unequal partners. The authority of husband over wife was perhaps no more natural than marriage itself, but it was necessary for their harmony. The husband is thus the head while the wife is the eyes of this social body.[3] Rousseau resorted readily to the traditional form of the metaphor when he wanted to express an old-fashioned prejudice. In his political writings he found no occasion to do so.

The fullest account of the body politic, in minute anatomical detail, occurs in the *Economie Politique*, Rousseau's most complete and perfect Spartan utopia.[4] It is also a violent attack upon the intellectual establishment and, indeed, a continuation of the *First Discourse*. The patriot is pitted against the unfeeling, cosmopolitan philosopher, and Cato is again raised above Socrates.[5] The perfect

---

[1] Saint Thomas Aquinas, *On the Governance of Rulers*, trans. by Gerald B. Phelan (London and New York, 1938), 36, 40–2, 91–4.
[2] *Leviathan*, 5, 112, 113–20, 121–9.   [3] *Emile*, 340.
[4] Vaughan, I, 241 (*Economie Politique*).
[5] *Ibid.* 250–1 (*Economie Politique*); *Discours sur les Science et les Arts*, 8.

unity of this Spartan polity is due, in no small degree, to the identity
of interests between the people and its 'chiefs'.[1] Rousseau liked to
speak of rulers whom he admired as 'chiefs'. That seemed to take the
sting out of political authority. Clearly neither the functional
hierarchy of the medieval monarchy, nor the absolutism of Hobbes
could have much application to a society composed of citizens who
have no interest other than equality and liberty. There might be no
feasible solution to the problem of government under law. The rule
of law might be as difficult to devise as the squaring of the circle.[2]
The most perfect personal rule might be the only tolerable alternative
to 'austere democracy' as Rousseau admitted in a despairing letter.[3]
But Sparta was neither. It might be unrealizable, but it was *the* only
satisfactory polity that could be imagined at all. *Leviathan* might
appeal to all the intellectual valets of the 'enlightened' despots, but
he was not Rousseau's idol. Sparta was his answer to those who chose
to flatter Frederick and Catherine the Great.

His own body politic was a distorting mirror of all its predecessors,
but most especially of *Leviathan*. Rousseau's body had no soul.
That locus of the Catholic Church in John of Salisbury's body is
simply eliminated. The sovereign is in the head. It does not, like
Leviathan's sovereign, take the place of the Church in the soul.
There is also no place left, the head being already occupied by the
sovereign people, for a monarch. The rest of the body politic is not
unlike *Leviathan*. The magistrates are the mere organs of the
faculties which are lodged in the head and so cannot move unless
the sovereign wills it. However, they are only joints in *Leviathan*
also. To be sure, in Rousseau's body they are even less than that.
Only the citizens make the body move and work. The main physical
difference between Rousseau's *Leviathan* and Hobbes' is that there
is no place for a crown on the former. The head contains all those
powers of feeling and understanding which react to bodily and
sensory stimulation and it is, therefore, not only the seat of life
itself, it is sovereign because the people, the total body, affects it
constantly. Clearly democracy was the only form of government for
such a body politic. And, indeed, Rousseau readily recognized that

[1] Vaughan, I, 244 (*Economie Politique*). [2] *Ibid.* II, 427 (*Poland*).
[3] 'Lettre à M. le Marquis de Mirabeau', 26 juillet 1767, *C.G.*, XVII, 155–9.

democracy was the form of political organization that best corresponded to the will of his robot. The example of Athens' turbulence
did not discourage him. Athens was no democracy, but an aristocratic tyranny governed by intellectuals and orators.[1] Only in
democracy, after all, does the sovereign feel pain when any
member of the polity is hurt, as does the head of this body
politic.

There was, however, more than a subtle caricature of *Leviathan*
here. Rousseau was also covering a difficulty with a metaphor. The
subordinate physical position of the magistrates only illustrates that
they cannot move without the will of the people. It says nothing of
their activities. And those are extremely extensive in a Spartan
order. The chiefs are to make the people happy by a wise political
economy, a term that covers all the relations of government to
persons and things.[2] Commerce, industry and agriculture are the
mouth and stomach of the body politic and public finance is
the blood which a wise economy, performing the functions of the
heart, pumps throughout the body politic. The later part of the
Economie Politique is devoted to this economy, which it emerges, is
conducted by the magistrates. Clearly the magistracy is an organ,
but, though this is not made at all clear by the metaphor itself, that
organ is the heart of the body politic.

Government enforces the law against any deviant member, and
it is responsible for every aspect of public policy.[3] It is government
that instils patriotism. Old magistrates and soldiers educate the
young. Government protects the poor against the rich, and prevents
the excessive accumulation of riches. It protects the safety and
prosperity of the citizens, and it administers a system of taxation,
agrarian laws and public finances in general.[4] In fact, once the
Legislator has done his work, it does everything. The chiefs are said
to be well-intentioned, to be sure.[5] Everything, in fact, depends on
that. This miracle is the result of law, the bond that keeps the body
united.[6] That, however, only describes a republic: a people united by
mores and moved by a will that prevents inequality and assures an

---

[1] Vaughan, I, 243 (*Economie Politique*).   [2] *Ibid.* 240, 258 (*Economie Politique*).
[3] *Ibid.* 244 (*Economie Politique*).
[4] *Ibid.* 246, 248, 250, 254–5, 257, 259–60, 265, 272–3 (*Economie Politique*).
[5] *Ibid.* 247, 258 (*Economie Politique*).   [6] *Ibid.* 239, 240, 242–3 (*Economie Politique*).

identity of interests. It does not explain it. And indeed in that respect the picture of Rousseau's *Leviathan* is not so unlike Hobbes'; both are attempts to evade conclusions implicit in their respective social contracts.

Sparta and Rome were hardly ungoverned republics; both were aristocracies. Rousseau accepted that as their essential character and as a necessary part of their social triumph: the transformation of men into citizens. The body politic metaphor allowed Rousseau to strengthen the impression that the republic thus artificially recreated the state of nature. The body politic, like healthy man in nature, does not neglect its self-preservation. An integrated whole, it does no injury to itself, but on the contrary avoids any source of pain.[1] When the health of this body is gone, then its instincts, the people's self-love, no longer operates effectively. That is why despotism is not a body politic at all. It is only a master and slaves united neither by law nor love. It is a mere aggregation of people, not a people and its chiefs. It is that combination alone which may properly be called a body politic.[2]

What of equality, however, in this body? Is it not, after all, just like all those medieval bodies politic, a justification of governmental authority, even if not of monarchy? In fact, it is just that. The chiefs may have no interests apart from the general will, but there is a vast difference between those who rule and those who are ruled. The body politic merely seems to show that government is necessary for republican survival. Identity of interests, benevolence and unity, however, are not equality, natural or social.

In his most violent attack on the intellectuals Rousseau had claimed that the well-governed society was so free from *amour-propre* that the conditions of natural equality were totally restored. Not even moral differences are given public recognition; just as in nature psychological inequalities find no occasion to flourish. 'In a well constituted state', he wrote, 'men are so busy that they have no time for speculation. They are so equal that no one can be preferred as the more learned or shrewd. At most he is the best, and even that is often dangerous, because it makes cheats and hypocrites.' No

[1] *Lettres Ecrites de la Montagne*, VI, 202.
[2] Vaughan, II, 31 (*Contrat Social*).

desire for distinction is, therefore, lighted in the hearts of the citizens at all.[1] Now *that* really *is* equality.

To deny the public relevance of moral inequality, to refuse any public recognition to the difference between good and bad is indeed the ultimate step in egalitarianism. In a mood of furious anger and self-deception Rousseau was driven to accept anarchy. That was not his normal attitude. However, the notion that equality meant identity was not merely a passing thought. It was something he had often said and always believed. The state of nature was not one of mutuality, but of isolated men identical because subject to a situation that rendered them uniformly alike. Underdeveloped man has no talents; that is why there is no inequality. The great differences in men's abilities remain dormant. They are alike in their utter dullness. In a society in which the general will is dominant that identity is partially recreated by making men equal, and so, alike in their rights or duties. If that means that not even moral powers are allowed to differentiate men in their public life, then one really has a staggering degree of equality. In such a society election to office must be by lot and government a 'true democracy'. Rousseau recognized that clearly. He also knew that no such polity could exist.[2] He might have added that the Spartan body politic does not even try to be egalitarian in that sense.

The patriotic, the virtue-creating state that reconciles men to society, makes equality impossible. The heroic republic with its Brutus and Cato does not disregard moral differences. It is in fact an extremely competitive society that uses rewards to stimulate moral athleticism among its citizens.[3] Moreover, Sparta is a single-value society. Virtue, whether it be an end in itself, or the means toward ending men's inner conflicts, allows for only one standard of judgment. Patriotic devotion, essentially martial in character, is the only attribute which has any worth. Additional values might, of course, destroy the inner harmony of the citizens. However, by demanding that all citizens strive to achieve one character and to acquire one sort of excellence only, inequality is made inevitable.

[1] *'Preface' à Narcisse*, 965.   [2] Vaughan, II, 107–8 (*Contrat Social*).
[3] *Ibid.* I, 246, 248–50 (*Économie Politique*); 334 (*Fragment*); II, 345–6 (*Corsica*); 433–41, 477–80 (*Poland*).

For certainly all men had never been, nor did Rousseau pretend that they could have been, equal in their capacity for patriotic devotion, military heroism and statesmanship or even in physical agility and toughness, which were so important to the Spartan model citizen. Governments, moreover, not only administer the system of rewards that encourages competition in virtue, its offices are rewards for virtue. Cato is the perfect magistrate, after all, not an ordinary citizen. Was not Brutus a 'chief'? The pursuit of virtue integrates citizens, prevents the rise of destructive opinion and mores, and it restrains rulers. It does not, and was not expected to, create equality.

All this was perfectly clear to Rousseau. Equality of political rights and duties was all that distributive justice demanded in the public sphere. That meant no exceptions to the rules, no special privileges. The inequality to be fought, moreover, was not inequality of authority, but of wealth. Not distinctions as such, but distinctions based on wealth were obnoxious. The government pictured in the *Economie Politique* is legitimate, and expressive of the general will, because all its public policies have one end: the elimination of the power of the rich. As long as the rich cannot buy the poor and the laws are not mere instruments for promoting the interests of the wealthy, the will against inequality is in effect.[1] Only power based on wealth, not power based on authority, is illegitimate. Only wealth reduces the contract to a fraud.[2] The will against inequality is a will against wealth and privilege, not against political rulership.

Governments may prevent economic inequalities that are sufficiently great to make the poor the bought servants of the rich. However, equality does not characterize governments. And as Rousseau knew only too well, the psychology of *ésprit de corps* is always a danger to the people in general. It is not money that corrupts individual magistrates. Each one of them may be a man of the utmost integrity. Collectively, however, they have a will of their own, an interest particular to themselves. In defense of that there is no injustice they will not commit. In the *Economie Politique* Rousseau chose to forget it, to pretend that, as long as no pecuniary ambition

---

[1] Vaughan, I, 267–8 (*Economie Politique*); II, 436, 438–9, 474 (*Poland*).
[2] *Ibid.* II, 346 (*Corsica*).

existed, the magistrates shared and promoted the interests of the people.[1] In short, they are 'chiefs', not masters. Why, however, should they be satisfied with that? They do not love their subjects as fathers love their children; they need a sterner virtue.[2] Why should they submit to it, and to laws that only inhibit their interests? Rousseau did feel compelled to offer an argument here. They are likely to obey the law, since it is by law that they hold authority.[3] It is not a good answer. If they have the enormous powers that the law gives them, they are perfectly free to use it as they please, to protect or to destroy the law and the people whom it serves. He knew that and admitted, even as he contemplated Spartan perfection, that personal interest is always contrary to duty and that lesser associations find their interests served by defying the popular will.[4]

The unity of will that binds a people and its chiefs is based on the strength of virtue, mores and the *moi commun* which all citizens must possess. However, since the interests of governments are not those of the people, magistrates soon cease to be 'chiefs'. The picture of the body politic, which makes magistrates passive organs of the will, gives them an apparent insignificance, and justifies their existence by their lack of independence and power. It is not a true picture of Sparta with its ephors and kings or of Rome with its consuls and tribunes. That hardly mattered to Rousseau. Was Cato not a greater man than Socrates? Was not the great censor incomparably superior to the opinion-makers of modern Europe? Does Rome not show what manner of men the 'chiefs' were able to create? Were they not in every way better and happier than the enervated and enslaved Parisian poor? That was enough. The Spartans and Romans had not been perfect. They were men. That is precisely why they shame modern civilization so, and that was all they were meant to do.

The full body politic that justifies political 'chiefs' was not the only one for which Rousseau had some use. His rhetorical ingenuity went well beyond that. Eventually he invented a body politic that

[1] See *supra*, Ch. III; Vaughan I, 247, 261–3 (*Economie Politique*).
[2] Vaughan, I, 239 (*Economie Politique*).   [3] *Ibid.* 244–5 (*Economie Politique*).
[4] *Ibid.* 242–3 (*Economie Politique*).

showed government to be the seat, not of public life, but of death. He developed this new metaphor rather gradually. It was at first forced upon him by those critics of the *Discourse on Inequality*, who insisted that man was a political animal. To this Rousseau replied that civil society had come late in the history of mankind and that this was not a natural development comparable to the aging of a man. Our relatively recent history is not a necessary bodily growth, but the consequence of external circumstances, many of which even depend on the will of men. He did not, however, as one might have expected, abandon the body politic metaphor entirely at this point. Instead he replaced the old organic body with his own artificial one. Government is what a crutch is to an old man. If mankind is senile then it needs an artificial limb. In short, mankind can be said to be in decay, but it is an artificially induced state and one that depends on man-made devices. That has its advantages. What men have done cannot be undone, but they can at least be warned against continuing on their disastrous course. They can also avail themselves of artificial devices for survival, such as civil society.[1]

Another common appearance of the natural body politic was in conventional law of nations thinking. Rousseau was torn by conflicting urges in this case. On one hand he detested the cosmopolitanism of the intellectuals and admired the martial spirit of Sparta; on the other he hated war and conquest which were, as he knew well, the instruments of despotism. The isolated polity, economically and militarily self-reliant, bound by no ties to any other state was the only answer to these various demands. It provided martial virtue without war and bloodshed. War itself was only the manifestation of incomplete socialization. It was not natural. Men in nature do not fight, they are too aloof from each other. This alert autarchy is what the artificial body politic must imitate. Where law is impossible, the situation of nature, which is *not* a state of war, but one of isolation, is the only safe alternative. The body politic should artificially model itself upon the natural condition of man.

This 'natural' policy among peoples is not open to any states

[1] Vaughan, I, 223–4 (*Lettre à M. Philopolis*).

except just republics. To think that the actual states of Europe could be anything but at war was pure folly. Nothing could exceed the stupidity of the Abbé de Saint Pierre's notion of a law binding sovereign states, and absolute monarchies at that. The deceptions invented by Grotius were worse. His laws of war and rights of conquest were lies that enslaved. Invented to flatter kings and fleece the people, this law of nations was neither law nor did it bind states. Rousseau disliked Grotius particularly because the real social basis of law, the social contract between free persons, could never be understood unless conventional jurisprudence was shown up for what it was; a fantasy at best, a crude deception at worst.[1]

The law of nations which purports to rule the conduct of states in peace and war is, first of all, no law at all. Sovereign states have never been known to live in anything but a state of war. Peace occurs only when the stronger state can see some advantage in not attacking the weaker.[2] In this, however, they do not behave as individuals who have a fight. War is a social phenomenon in which men, organized and policed, are forced to fight men who are in the same condition as their own. The state, whether in active or dormant war is, thus, in no sense like a natural body. It is subject to none of the limitations, physical or psychological, that restrain individuals, even highly aggressive ones. The horror of our present 'mixed condition' arises out of this situation. As individuals men are forced to live under laws. As subjects of lawless absolute monarchs they are forced by these very laws, which correspond to none of their needs, to fight and kill men with whom they have absolutely no quarrel whatever. The conflicts are between the ambitions of only a very few men, the absolute sovereigns of Europe. However, as sovereigns they control 'artificial' bodies politic with which they can engage in military enterprises which are completely unlike private violence. It is again precisely because the body politic is artificial, and not organic, that it is not subject to law. Instead, its members are exposed to force and to the despotism that comes with war. Governments in their relations to each other and to the citizens, in short, are always potential sources of death to the body politic. For despotism,

---

[1] Vaughan, I, 447-54 (*Première Version*); II, 37, 41-2 (*Contrat Social*).
[2] 'Lettre à M. de Malesherbes', 3 novembre 1760, *C.G.*, 247-8.

conquest and revolution kill bodies politic, even artificial ones. The people continues to survive, but not the polity.[1]

The artificiality of the body politic explains why in the present 'mixed', semi-social condition, government is a perpetual threat to the survival of the people. Indeed royal government had ruined men so utterly that no monarchy could be reformed.[2] The artificial character of republican bodies politic, however, had its advantages. Their decline could be slowed by cautious citizens in a way that natural death could not be.[3] That was why Rousseau felt it was worth warning the Genevan people against its magistrates. The *Social Contract*, Rousseau explained in the *Confessions*, had two ends in mind.[4] It was to show how government under law might be achieved, and how necessary this was, since men are whatever governments make them. This is what the first part does. It shows, 'laws as they might be'. Standards are set according to which civil society could be justified, 'men being what they are'.[5] The second purpose of the book was to warn Geneva against the dangers of government unchecked by law. In fact, Rousseau managed to denounce *all* governments in warning the Genevans against theirs.[6]

The *Social Contract* is not a Spartan utopia like the *Economie Politique*. It is the continuation of the *Discourse on Inequality*, as the former completed the *Discourse on the Arts and Sciences*. As such it is not directed at the intellectual servants of despotism; it attacks the masters directly. It deals not with the corruption spread by art and science, but with the burdens of injustice and oppression borne by the people. It does not, therefore, offer a picture of republican perfection, though the standards of political judgment presented in it are drawn from the Spartan model. The *Social Contract* is, especially in its many chapters on government, an account of how republics degenerate and die. It is the political part of the 'genealogy of vice'. That is why Rome is here not described as the perfect city of the *Economie Politique*, but as a polity tense with conflict. All its virtue rests in the assemblies of the rural people. The city is full of

[1] Vaughan, I, 293–305 (*L'état de guerre*); I, 389–91 (*Jugement sur la Paix Perpétuelle*) II, 29–31 (*Contrat Social*). [2] *Ibid.* 416–17 (*Jugement sur la Polysynodie*).
[3] *Ibid.* II, 91 (*Contrat Social*). [4] *Confessions*, IX, 404–5.
[5] Vaughan, II, 23 (*Contrat Social*).
[6] *Lettres Ecrites de la Montagne*, VI, 203–5; VII, 208–9.

rabble. The patricians hate the people. Though the rich are fined for ostentation, there are both rich and poor people in Rome. Eventually the tribunes betray the people and the people begins to sell its votes. That was the predictable end. Nevertheless, with all its faults Rome was completely inimitable in the modern age. The Genevans were not to imagine that the Romans were models for them. They could not even hope to be Athenians.[1] If Rome fell, what hope was there for republics so infinitely less virtuous? The political fatalism is profound. For while he attacked governments as deadly, Rousseau continued to insist that they were necessary. With this the body politic returns to the stage.

The 'body politic' of the *Social Contract* bears no resemblance to *Leviathan* at all. It is not presented in all its parts. The body politic has to be integrated and it needs a 'force' in order to move and act. That force is government.[2] The second characteristic of the body politic is its inevitable end. 'The body politic like that of man begins to decay at birth.'[3] For all his skill in destroying the persuasiveness of the 'natural' body politic of his opponents, Rousseau did not want to discard the organic associations of the metaphor entirely. Its death was no more natural than its life, but life and death are natural experiences. They are also the most dramatic. And Rousseau wanted to bring that to bear upon the spectacle of justice created and destroyed.

The active agent of destruction is government. When it has finally succeeded in overstepping its legally assigned powers, the body politic is paralyzed, but it is not dead. Only when a society has completely dissolved does that occur. Anarchy is not the usual condition of the people, however. Paralysis is more common.[4] It is, in fact, the condition of all unjust, that is all actual, states. The sense of justice is alive in the people, but its will cannot be asserted. The people is powerless and it cannot make the body politic move because the government is completely indifferent to the general will. The mind and soul of a paralyzed person are active. He has a will,

---

[1] Vaughan, II, 104, 113–15, 117–19 (*Contrat Social*); *Lettres Ecrites de la Montagne*, IX, 254–5.

[2] Vaughan, II, 64 (*Contrat Social*); *Lettres Ecrites de la Montagne*, VI, 202.

[3] Vaughan, II, 91 (*Contrat Social*).

[4] *Ibid.* I, 301 (*L'état de guerre*); 318 (*Fragment*); II, 91, 29–30 (*Contrat Social*).

but it is of no practical use to him, because he cannot move his limbs. He is impotent, as is the people in an unjust polity. The general will must unite government and people as the soul and body must be one in a living body.[1] When that link breaks, the man may live, but not well.

When Rousseau introduced government into the true civil society he was explicit about its character. It was to be aristocratic, a body with a real life with a *moi particulier* apart from that of the people and a sensibility, a force and a will common only to its members, and designed to preserve it and to keep its members united. Government means assemblies, councils, rights, titles and exclusive privileges, and no turbulent interference from the people.[2] No wonder that governmental usurpation is the vice that inevitably 'from the birth of the body politic tends relentlessly to destroy it'. It is the one form of organized particular will that is unavoidable, but which, like all such wills, incessantly assaults the general will.[3] Government was, however, necessary, not because it was legitimate, but because 'austere democracy' was not possible and, perhaps, not even desirable, for 'men as they are'. Nevertheless, for all its inevitability, government could not be justified positively. All the arguments that Rousseau raised against those representative bodies which, like Parliament, had feudal roots were perfectly applicable to any form of government. It is not the dangerous notion of shared sovereignty, nor the false belief that people are bound by a fundamental contract to their rulers that made Parliament so dangerous to law and justice. It was, rather, that like any association set apart from the people as a whole, its members possessed interests contrary to the general will. Even as mere agents of the sovereign, magistrates have a particular self and will.[4] The reason why Rousseau came to assert that there is no best government, that everything depends on time and place, seems to have been grounded in the belief that all were bad, if not always equally so.[5] When he was really interested

---

[1] Vaughan, II, 65 (*Contrat Social*).
[2] *Ibid.* 68 (*Contrat Social*); *Lettres Ecrites de la Montagne*, VIII, 224; 'Lettre à M. Marcet de Mézieres', 24 juillet, 1762, *C.G.*, VIII, 35–8.
[3] Vaughan, II, 88 (*Contrat Social*); *Lettres Ecrites de la Montagne*, VI, 204–5.
[4] Vaughan, II, 68, 95–7, 99 (*Contrat Social*).
[5] *Ibid.* 82–7 (*Contrat Social*); *Lettres Ecrites de la Montagne*, VI, 205–6; *Emile*, 422.

only in standards of justice, he said nothing about government at all.[1]

Because the *Social Contract* was less a utopia than a book of warnings, Rousseau took great care to admit all the germs of future destruction to this body politic. There is, at the beginning, legitimacy based on equality which alone can create liberty. However, it is at once made clear that this equality has its limits. No inequalities, apart from those recognized by law or held in virtue of rank, are to mark the distribution of power. No inequalities of wealth that permit the rich to buy the poor and force the poor to sell themselves are to exist. That does not, however, exclude governmental powers at all and it is not inconsistent with those conflicts between rich and poor that led to the decline and fall of the Roman Republic. Such degrees of inequality *can*, unlike those of contemporary society, be regulated and controlled to slow down the steady march to destruction.[2] It justified Rousseau's enterprise. There was room for anger and denunciation, but not for hope or action. 'Austere democracy' might alone be justifiable, but it had to be dismissed so that the body politic might live and die.

It was, however, by no means easy for Rousseau to shake himself free from his rustic dreams. He had made it far too clear that the bonds that tie citizens to each other and to their polity depend on equality and mutuality and not on governmental power.[3] All the virtue, mores and opinions of republican men are ephemeral without these. A people remains a people, with or without its chiefs.[4] And only in a democracy does the execution of laws follow immediately upon the expression of the public will.[5] In short, here alone is there no particular will to misguide, or disrupt the general will or to keep it from its ends. There is no gap between the interests of the people and the conduct of the body politic. No one is imposing anything upon anyone. This is the 'government without govern-

---

[1] The *Première Version* breaks off just at the point where 'public force' enters. This was to begin the discussion of government in the final version of the *Contrat Social*. In *Corsica* only a vague reference to 'guardians of the law' disturbs the rustic peace. Vaughan, I, 461–2 (*Première Version*); II, 64 (*Contrat Social*); 351 (*Corsica*).

[2] Vaughan, II, 61 (*Contrat Social*).　　　　[3] E.g. Vaughan, II, 317, 321–2 (*Corsica*).

[4] Vaughan, I, 468 (*Première Version*).

[5] *Ibid.* II, 75, 100 (*Contrat Social*).

ment', fit only for angels. Men good enough to govern themselves would need no government. That is only another way of saying that democratic government and gerontocracy, which is another form of election by lot, are not possible for 'men as they are'.[1] That may well mean that no civil order can ever be legitimate, if all need governments. For the rustic simpletons, who 'live without masters, indeed almost without laws', are those heads of large families, those happy men of the Golden Age, the peasants of Neufchatel, 'perhaps unique on earth'.[2] If only democracy can be legitimate then civil society is not justifiable, because it depends on rulers. Rustic bliss, however, has nothing to say to socialized men. Pre-social life was moral because it was psychologically satisfying, but men in their stupidity abandoned that condition. Now they need medicine. And civil society is only the cure for social disease. It also is no permanent abode for men.

Of Emile it is said, when he reached adolescence, that he was 'now in the world of morals, the door to vice is open'.[3] It is so with mankind as a whole. Once they come together morality is before men and so is evil, and neither can be wholly evaded. Before joining civil society men might have been 'good and just without knowing what goodness and virtue are'.[4] In this, the true rustic democracy, there is an equality that is more than a struggle against inequality. It is also a world in which men live without ever feeling anything, without really being men at all, in fact. In it 'we would have died without having lived; all our happiness would have consisted in not knowing our misery; there would have been no goodness in our hearts, nor morality in our actions and we would never have tasted the most delicious sentiment of the soul which is the love of virtue'.[5] Rustic man is evidently a 'stupid and limited' creature and not a man or a citizen.[6] We are in this respect worse off than he was, however. For we will not 'become men until we are citizens'.[7] We are like rustic man in being less than human, and worse in every other respect. For having destroyed our capacity for

[1] Vaughan, II, 72–4, 108 (*Contrat Social*).
[2] *Ibid.* 320–1 (*Corsica*); *Letter to d'Alembert*, 60.
[3] *Emile*, 65.
[4] Vaughan, II, 321 (*Corsica*).   [5] *Ibid.* I, 449 (*Première Version*).
[6] *Ibid.* II, 36 (*Contrat Social*).   [7] *Ibid.* I, 453 (*Première Version*).

unconscious goodness, we have not created the conditions for conscious virtue.

All of Rousseau's radicalism and all his resentment are in that phrase: 'we will not become men until we are citizens'. That is the voice of the watchmaker's son. The Spartan model was a marvellous blunt instrument to hurl against the powerful, the rich, and especially at their polished literary footmen. All of them professed to admire antiquity, but, with the sole exception of Montesquieu, they had chosen to forget the social conditions of republican virtue. To admire Cato meant to love the republic, to despise the intellectuals and to hate Paris. The voice of Cato did not go unheard, however. It found a ready response among those whose interests he was supposed to defend. If Catonism has often been the ideology of a declining gentry, it has also had a genuine appeal for the peasantry.[1] Rousseau certainly had them in mind. He was not in the least interested in protecting Baron d'Etange. The peasants had to be rescued from civilization. Wolmar tries to do that, but he is not merely a model landlord, he is God, and even he fails, because he cannot defend his family against the consequences of their world. Sparta fails and the Golden Age is frail, neither can be restored and both illuminate the situation of men who are torn helplessly between nature and society. The intimate society, the wholly un-Spartan friendship group that Rousseau longed for, and that every man really needs, is a mere day-dream. There could be no society 'according to my heart' or indeed to any heart.[2] Self-knowledge had taught Rousseau that Clarens, or some version of the Golden Age, was the most fundamental human need. Public understanding and hatred of oppression moved him to remind men of Sparta. Neither one is actually attainable. History is the story of mankind's inability to achieve either peace or justice.

Rousseau knew that a revolution was on its way, but it promised nothing. He did not need to speak of popular corruption; the stupidity of the people suffices to condemn it to servitude once

[1] Barrington Moore, Jr., *The Social Origins of Dictatorship and Democracy* (Boston, 1966), 491–505.
[2] *N.H.*, Part IV, Letter X; *Confessions*, IX, 414; *Rousseau Juge de Jean-Jacques*, II, 827; *Lettres à Malesherbes*, I, 1132.

rustic simplicity has been lost. The freedom for which the intellectual classes hoped was not in its interest. Rousseau was no defender of
intolerance or intellectual repression, but the interests of the
intellectuals are not those of the people. The people has an interest
in maintaining an order in which there are no intellectuals at all, in
which there are, in fact, Catos to see that none appear. Once the
learned classes exist, the conditions for popular felicity are already
gone. The interests of the clever and talented support civilization.
The people have every reason to prefer rural simplicity. Rousseau
was far from being deaf to art and learning; he just did not choose to
pretend that these embellishments contributed to the moral well-
being of mankind. In a corrupt world they are necessary, but there
is nothing to be said in favor of that world as a whole. The world as
it is demands resignation and prudence, and a careful attention to a
conscience that keeps us from causing harm to those around us. It
offers no occasion for happiness or civic virtue. Nevertheless,
Rousseau did feel bound to do more: to speak the truth, both about
'the history of the human heart' and the world men had made. When
he called upon his readers to choose between man and the citizen he
was forcing them to face the moral realities of social life. They were
asked, in fact, not to choose, but to recognize that the choice was
impossible, and that they were not and would never become
either men or citizens.

6

POSTSCRIPT: CONSIDERING ROUSSEAU

How does one go about interpreting a writer like Rousseau? That question really means: 'what is the history of political thought all about'? And it quite naturally would lead to another: 'why should it be studied' or 'is it relevant'? To be sure, not everyone will be inclined to doubt the relevance of Rousseau's thought, but many of the most brilliant of one's academic friends might. To them one must say that relevance is the most relative of terms. The daily news, the events of one's own life-time, the records of the immediate past and future, however minutely and accurately studied, do not satisfy the intellectual interests of all. For some it would be an act of self-inflicted exile to renounce the past. To integrate oneself into the cultural past, to become a part of that cycle of intellectual and artistic events can be experienced no less intensely or personally than those occurrences which impinge upon our consciousness as we read our mail, our newspaper, our forecasts and our books on contemporary history. To say that only the latter are relevant is to invite a question: relevant to whom?

If one has a sense for abiding as well as temporary human concerns, and if one is not convinced that, intellectually, the latest is also always the best, and lastly, if one regards reflection and observation as self-justifying activities, then one will see the relevance of the history of political theory without difficulty. If, however, one cannot feel touched by anything that is remote in time, one will inevitably have a sense of relevance which will exclude it. Moreover, if one experiences activity solely as a response to the conduct of one's contemporaries, the study of history in general and of the intellectual past especially, will seem vain and pointless. Between these two ways of assessing relevance there can really be no compromise and therefore no argument. They should both be understood clearly and accepted without rancor.

There are, however, ways of trying to reconcile these two views of relevance that are ill-considered. Often one hears an ancient author praised for being up-to-date and modern. That merely means that he has said something that sounds familiar because it is frequently being said now. It would not be very difficult to show that there is much in Freud, in Piaget, in Sartre and even in the sayings of Chairman Mao that comes straight out of Rousseau. So what? Does that enhance his reputation or diminish their achievements? What does it tell us about anyone? What standards of evaluation and what new information can precedence and subsequence yield here? What does it say about the art of illuminating man's discords and discomforts? That it has a history, that is all, and that was scarcely in doubt.

That raises the question of interpreting Rousseau again. It is really a matter of making decisions, and an awful number of them, ranging from the most abstract to such practicalities as how one footnotes. All are worth considering explicitly, however, because all have a bearing on the main subject, the study of political theory. For when one makes decisions about specific ways of interpreting the thought of Rousseau, or any great political theorist, one immediately also chooses one's approaches to the history of political theory in general.

The very delimiting of one's subject matter involves choices of this order. When one decides to concentrate on the work of a specific writer, one must often exclude the most interesting considerations, so as not to stray too far from one's main character. Nothing has been said here, for that reason, about Rousseau's influence upon his readers and their immediate successors. The effect that his eloquence may have had upon various protagonists in the French Revolution had to be left to the historians of that period, most notably to André Soboul. Rousseau is not 'rousseau-isme'. The way in which philosophy may or may not become operative ideology is interesting enough, but it is a part of social history, not of political theory directly. When one is dealing with relatively minor political writers it may often be best to treat them as part of a more general historical survey. We are more interested in what they can tell us about the world around them than in their little ideas directly. We look at their roles as disseminators of opinions, as middlemen, rather than as builders. Here trend-watching

he had the utmost contempt could be cited as profound, moulding influences. One could offer other examples, but it is not necessary. The only past that is worth discussing is that which is specifically mentioned in Rousseau's work and then only as one explanation among others, and never merely for the sake of displaying possible links for their own sake.

If we interpret a man's thought in order to be directly instructed by him, what ought we to know about him? Are there any stable rules of interpretation? Probably there are only recurrent considerations, not canons. How important, for example, is biography, or to be exact, what sort of biography? In Rousseau's case the answer is clear. The private biography is of utmost significance. That is so not only because he wrote so personal an autobiography, but because he thought of his *Confessions* as a public act and an integral part of his moral position. He regarded his public philosophy as an expression of his feelings and thoughts and he also regarded his interior life as a public document of the most general social significance. Not all autobiographies are like that. Some are more purely private, others more public. John Stuart Mill's *Autobiography* does not really enrich our understanding. We would know all there is to be known about his philosophical outlook without it, and we do not learn much about his inner being. It is not at all certain that we would really gain anything by deeper revelations. It is interesting, but not an essential part of an intellectual and artistic edifice. Of the inner life of other philosophers we may know even less, and we do not really care. Only the most idle curiosity could make one wonder about the emotional life of Aristotle or Hobbes.

When one comes to public biography one is again faced with a variety of possibilities that have to be sorted out. What sort of public life is one to consider? There is first of all a realm where public and private life melt into each other. The most typical experiences of a writer are in a sense public. They are what he shares with his contemporaries and they make him, in the common phrase, a part of his age. Some of these experiences may, however, be very insignificant intellectually. Hobbes and Aristotle were, as were many other intelligent men, tutors. It is typical, but insignificant. The social condition of a philosopher's family may influence him deeply, but it is not always so. It is the groups he chooses to speak with and for that count, rather than the views commonly held by men born into his sort of family.

In Rousseau's case family origins matter enormously, not because he was a typical son of a Genevan artisan, but because he was not. His immense social mobility, which took him all over society and of which Rousseau was so aware, was just as completely unique as he said it was. No other member of the intellectual world of his time had lived like that. Moreover, Rousseau continued to live among people (Thérèse's family!) who were completely unlike those whom he wrote for and who read him. That all this contributed to giving the watchmaker's son a special tone, and an outlook entirely peculiar to him, cannot be doubted. It is, however, not certain that what is so important to an understanding of Rousseau, would matter to our understanding of Hobbes or Montesquieu or Kant.

Changes in political experience and association may be a guide to understanding an author. This may be the main task of public biography. In Locke's case, for instance, changes in such circumstances led to changes in his outlook. All his various experiences after he left Oxford are reflected in his writings, the radical Continental friends no less than Whig patrons at home. But his 'origins' seem to matter less than a public life that was *really* 'public' as Rousseau's experiences were not, because he, unlike Locke or Montesquieu, was never near the official world. His political activity, such as it was, his protest on his own behalf in Geneva, came after his work was completed and it did not alter this old and half-mad refugee. Locke's public life affected him deeply and his theory must be read with a view to development, growth and changes of belief. Rousseau began to write only after he reached middle age. He worked incessantly for ten years to complete his novel and his philosophical works. Then came a second period of mainly autobiographical writings. Rousseau's social experiences, felt injustice and contempt for established power went into that late, brief, and concentrated period of political writing. Nothing new was added to them and the works are therefore a compact, single whole. If not in subject matter, the spirit of the autobiographical writings is, moreover, the same as that of the earlier period. In feeling and intention

Rousseau was, thus, eminently constant, even if there were many minor inconsistencies of which he was aware and which he thought quite insignificant. Nothing is gained by hunting down Rousseau's self-contradictions. They reveal nothing of interest. His profound unity is far more imposing than his occasional logical lapses. Only a petty mind could gain any intellectual satisfaction in catching Rousseau in a self-contradiction. It is, indeed, hard to see why anyone would want to make the search for inner contradictions a rule or even an important part of the interpretation of the great political theorists of the past.

What then of Rousseau's general relations to his age? To speak of an 'age' is to refer to an abstraction created by the retrospective imagination. It cannot be said to have any concrete existence except in the historian's mind. To impute to the notion of 'an age' a general moulding power makes very little sense. One must be more selective, especially in the case of a writer like Rousseau, whose mind restlessly moved from the universal to the contemporary difficulties of being human. Moreover, like most intellectuals, Rousseau was more intimately related to others of his own kind than to anyone else. Socially and spiritually they were his ancestors, his family, his friends, and above all, his enemies. The Parisian philosophers were his milieu far more genuinely and completely than any Genevan provincials, of whom he pretended to be one, as long as it suited his purposes. His age was the 'Enlightenment' also.

The first question one might well ask in considering a political theorist's public biography is, therefore, against whom did he write? Political theory is inherently contentious and persuasive. Most great political theorists have a special *bête noire*, as Locke has his Filmer and Bentham his Blackstone. Rousseau had Voltaire. If Voltaire had not existed, Rousseau would have had to invent him. He was the embodiment of everything Rousseau hated. He was, together with Rameau, the greatest creator of civilized art and he was also the enemy of the people. Rousseau had every intention of shoving this old idol off his pedestal and of replacing him. All in all, Voltaire was the most important single person in Rousseau's life. It was, however, a highly impersonal relationship. Voltaire was for Rousseau not only a man, but the sum of all that he distrusted in society, and of the intellectuals' dealings with it, especially their subservience to the powerful and rich. In this way that small part of 'the age' that took part in the salons and in the exciting world of Parisian letters influenced Rousseau most. It did not do so only negatively.

Rousseau did after all learn a great deal from the *philosophes*, especially about psychology. For Locke was the dominating influence on all. The *Essay* was for them a common bond as much as anything else. A discussion of Rousseau's relations to Locke 'places' him so effectively, not only because his ideas were closer to Locke's than to Condillac's whom he knew quite well personally, but also because he argued with and referred to Locke constantly. Above all, he followed Locke in bringing the new psychology to bear upon moral and political theory. Condillac was far too cautious and detached for that. Locke was a general intellectual model for Voltaire no less than for Rousseau. And in that sense Locke's philosophical style, if not any one of his doctrines, constituted 'the age' in which Rousseau lived and which can intelligibly be said to have moulded his thought both in its typical and highly atypical aspects.

The *philosophes* were, moreover, one of Rousseau's primary audiences. The relation of a writer, especially of a political theorist, to his readers is an important part of his public biography, surely. The first thing to remember is that until the nineteenth century the audience for writings such as Rousseau's political essays was very small. Rousseau was one of the most celebrated writers of his age. He owed his fame, however, to a very few people, to the judges and readers of essays that won academic prizes, to the salons and to the very small literary worlds in the cities. The people on whose behalf Rousseau wrote were illiterate and Rousseau did not, as he frequently said, speak to them, but about them. When he complained that he was misunderstood he was, however, wrong. Those who read him understood him very well and had every reason to dislike his abuses. He was certainly not loved, but he was understood by his highly intelligent and knowledgeable audience. Their opinion of him is, therefore, a very reliable guide to his thought. The decent and level-headed d'Alembert can tell us more about Rousseau than most commentators. He is really hard evidence.

The *Nouvelle Héloise* was written for a very different and far larger audience. It was meant for the young and for women, as were most novels at that time. To write novels was a far from acceptable literary activity. History, philosophy, epic poetry, drama, moral fables were still the only aristocratically 'right' genres. Even Diderot, who loved Richardson's novels, never risked his literary reputation by writing one himself. The philosophic fable was as far as he would venture. Rousseau was deliberately and defiantly *déclassé* in writing the *Nouvelle Héloise*, as he took pains to explain in his preface. The *philosophes* found the book hysterical and obscene. The ladies adored it. It was a stupendous success, an all-time bestseller. Did they understand it? The scores of letters that aristocratic, no less than bourgeois ladies, from the provinces and from Paris, wrote Rousseau show a tender response to the love story, to the beauties of nature and an enthusiasm for domestic virtue. These were themes that Rousseau shared with them and with many other writers. He was of course more eloquent and moving, but it was his most typical pages that moved his readers most. The philosophic aspects of the novel were lost on them. Nevertheless, Rousseau felt a deep sympathy for this public and took part in its feelings. His novel was the one occasion on which he could put his private daydreams on paper and find readers to appreciate them. Even if it was only a mawkish taste for sex spiced with piety that Rousseau shared with his young and feminine readers, it does show him, for once, as a figure who reflected, made articulate and moulded the sensibility of his 'age'. It remains a moving book, perhaps because there was so much more to it than sentimentality. It is in the mixture of the typical and very unique, the simple soap opera and the profound psychological novel of character and ideas put together that make it so revealing.

The reception of *Emile* was even more ambiguous. Rousseau clearly did not intend it for parents, but, as he often said, for the wise. The latter understood it perfectly. The *philosophes* were generally critical, and the clergy had it burned and its author persecuted. These were, however, not its only readers. Coming as it did at a time when the whole notion of childhood and the place of children in the family was undergoing the most profound changes, it was inevitably read as a manual for enlightened parents. Even German princes asked Rousseau's advice about hiring governesses for their daughters. These readers had, of course, no intention of educating their children *against* society. They only wanted them to be happier within the civilized order, which was the last thing Rousseau had in mind or even thought possible. The success of *Emile* tells us much about the 'age', but little about Rousseau. Except for the *Nouvelle Héloise*, Rousseau wrote for his intellectual peers, the intellectuals by avocation, even if he only meant to abuse them. They were, after all, his real kin, his reviewers, his critics and his real audience. They were, moreover, if anything even more obsessed by Rousseau than he by them.

What did his contemporaries recognize as great in him, even those who reviled him as a charlatan and a *poseur*? He lived among the most intelligent and competent literary judges. Why did they think that he was so remarkable? His eloquence was universally recognized. Admirers and bitter enemies alike agreed that Rousseau was the most eloquent man of his age. His style is overwhelming. Rousseau, Diderot eventually said, was what one says of the poor draftsman among painters: a great colorist. Rousseau's literary powers were indeed phenomenal and to understand him fully one must give more than a passing thought to how he wrote. There is, however, another quality that his contemporaries did not recognize, partly because they shared it. That is the scope of Rousseau's intellectual competence. Even among his versatile contemporaries he was extraordinary: composer, musicologist, playwright, drama critic, novelist, botanist, pedagogue, political philospher, psychologist. That is not unimpressive. There is nevertheless even more in Rousseau's intellectual scope that seems notable now, though it did not strike his fellow intellectuals. They tended only to marvel at his suspect novelties and 'paradoxes'. We can marvel at the catholicity of Rousseau's social philosophy.

The range of his social thought, much more than his specific admiration for them and for antiquity in general, makes Rousseau an heir of Plato and Aristotle, and a part of the intellectual world they created. That is what one means when one speaks of Rousseau's writings as an aspect of European high culture. It is also what makes him a major, rather than a minor, figure in the history of political theory. The battle between the ancients and the moderns was not really decided in favor of the latter until after the French Revolution. Until then pagan antiquity was admired and known in all its details even by those who adopted a decidedly modern philosophic and scientific outlook. In Rousseau's time the attraction of an un- and pre-Christian world was particularly great. Everyone who was educated at all, and by whatever means, was familiar with classical literature. It defined intellectuality, set it limits and its style. The standard of relevance raised by ancient philosophy still prevailed, even when its content no longer did. Eager to out-do the ancients, Rousseau and his fellows nevertheless emulated them all the more intensely, because all the topics that Plato and Aristotle had touched upon had to be reconsidered. Rousseau was no slavish imitator of either one, but he accepted their example, their vision of what was involved in social theory, without a question. The importance which psychological, pedagogic, artistic, ethical and religious ideas play in his philosophical ensemble and their inseparability from politics, all demonstrate an adherence to a literary and philosophic culture which had its roots in antiquity and of which Rousseau was one of the last representatives. The scope of his theory, therefore, demands that all its aspects be studied without allowing later categories of thought to cut out what was essential for him. There is, moreover, a judgment here also. For surely Rousseau is so penetrating and convincing because his was so comprehensive a structure of ideas about man and society.

Scope is not the only mark of either Rousseau's greatness or of his participation in and contribution to high culture. Literary style is just as important. What is said cannot be separated from how it is expressed. Political theory was a distinct literary form also, and inherently so. All political theorists must, among other things, be competent rhetoricians. The word is not used here in any pejorative sense at all. Quite on the contrary. Political theory is meant to be persuasive. Its style falls somewhere between that pure rhetoric which urges men to open and specific actions and scientific discourse. It aims rather at changing attitudes, at making the reader see his world differently, and so to discover new meanings. That is why not only hortatory, but also expository utterances can be rhetorical.

Postscript

Political theory as a form of persuasion does, however, seem closer to what Aristotle called rhetoric, than the sort of discourse which is clearly scientific or purely formal. The political theorist at his best must, therefore, possess to a preeminent degree those virtues that Aristotle ascribed to a good rhetorician: 'to be able to reason logically, to understand human character and goodness in their various forms and to understand the emotions'. Surely it was the command of these powers that enabled Rousseau to awaken, to shake, to alter the vision and inner dispositions of so many generations of readers.

A grasp of metaphors and of their successful use is what every rhetorician, practical or analytical, must absolutely have. No one who has given any thought to the matter since Aristotle has disagreed with him about that. When one deals with an eloquent writer and an accomplished literary artist, like Rousseau, one can learn a lot from looking at his metaphors. They can show us why he persuades, why he can bring so many associations to bear on each argument. It gives us an insight into how every formulation fits into a far wider context and how a whole range of ideas moves the reader's mind each time Rousseau invites him to reject again the conventional wisdom and the civilized order. The extraordinary skill with which Rousseau deployed his political metaphors is just one example of his ability to move readers, of his celebrated eloquence and of his style. It is what allows us to speak of him as 'great' as much as anything, not only because of the 'effect' on his reader, but also because of the inner structure, the construction of evocations that tie his daydreams, his experiences, his knowledge, his moral convictions and his observations into a single whole, like a mosaic.

The uses of literary criticism for interpreting political theory are generally very extensive. A study of rhetoric, of modes of expression, may have more to offer than linguistics and the analysis of ordinary language. When one looks at political metaphors, for instance, one wants to know how they work, what makes them effective within the context of a writer's general purposes. One does not want to judge their legitimacy or validity or their grammatical correctness. Again, the analysis of ordinary language is too indifferent to the broad objectives of speech and especially to complex purposes such as those of political theory to be able to tell us how and why it is persuasive and convincing. It is most effectively applied to discourse that occurs within a far more specific and defined context, such as that of legal language, for example. It is at its best in dealing with single sentences which are self-contained contexts and when the wider intentions of the speaker need not be considered. The literary criticism of I. A. Richards, for example, seems more promising and might well be applied to the interpretation of other political theorists. Machiavelli and Hobbes particularly come to one's mind here, both being notably eloquent and extremely careful literary craftsmen.

There should, however, be nothing restrictive in one's use of literary criticism. It is only one form of interpretation among others. There can be no possible advantage in thinking of political theory as an 'autonomous' literary form, impervious to historical and psychological considerations. Rousseau reading Plutarch is decidedly not Keats reading Chapman's Homer. The criteria of relevance must remain distinct since political literature is a specific form of persuasive prose. It is a form of literature, but its ends, its character, its content and meaning must never be forgotten in consideration of literary technique. Nevertheless, if there is much political thought in novels and poems, there are also characteristic literary qualities in political theory, the description and analysis of which is most revealing. It has its limits, to be sure. It can tell us much about a writer's intentions, but one ought to be careful not to infer too much from language. A change of metaphors may reflect an alteration in society; more likely it expresses only a new attitude peculiar to the writer, and even that has to be carefully investigated. Indeed, the greatest benefit of rhetorical analysis might well be that it will inhibit the tendency to speculate without evidence.

The analysis of metaphors turned out to be a laborious business. Not only did Rousseau use the term 'body politic', for example, over and over again, but he mostly used it very casually as a synonym for civil society. However, there is no way of knowing when the use of a metaphor is meaningful and when it is not, unless one has looked at each occasion of its appearance. That was bad enough. The history of this one is also especially long and intricate, but only a very small part of it seemed at all relevant to Rousseau. One might write a history of its use as an independent project, and one must know its past to see its implication at any given point. However, much of that work did seem a trifle useless in the end since so little mattered. The future of the 'organic' theory of the state did not require much attention. It is plain that the pseudo-medieval defence of hierarchy and tradition which the organic conceptions of the post-Revolutionary era brought forth is utterly remote from Rousseau. It seemed redundant even to mention it, especially as it would have involved unwanted reviews of, and arguments with, other interpretations of Rousseau.

In discussing Rousseau's style one need not limit oneself to rhetorical analysis. The consideration of his special literary strengths will make clear why some of his works, not always the best known, are especially illuminating. Rousseau was clearly a dramatic writer. He could, when he chose, entertain an eighteenth-century theatre audience enormously. However, that was not what he wished to do. He wanted to attack and shake, not to amuse. The conventions of the stage of his day did not permit that, and Rousseau's contempt for the theatre of his age was amply justified. As a remarkable critic he continued to show how stage-struck he was, and how well he understood the art of the dramatist. He had, however, to discover another vehicle for expression and he found one that was, perhaps, inherently more suitable, given his discursiveness: letter-writing. Rousseau's letters, private, public and semi-public, are among his best works because they enabled him to have his say in a manner that really fitted his temper.

The variety of his letter forms is extraordinary. At their best all have two characteristics, they are tense and dramatic because they are addressed to a specific reader, real or imagined or a bit of both, who inspires a public statement about Rousseau's inner state. They are public confrontations of personal feelings. That is why they are so revealing and so important to an appreciation of Rousseau. Thus, the *Nouvelle Héloise* is written in letters which permit both self-revelation and dramatic clashes between the characters. There is little action here, which is just as well. Rousseau had no talent for epic drama at all, as his feeble efforts at such writing show. He could, however, create a drama of feeling well enough, and letters suited that peculiarly well.

Postscript

The sequel to *Emile* is also written in letters, but it is really a monologue, Emile's autobiography. Rousseau had also written such an autobiography in his four letters to Malesherbes, the censor, and, as such, an obvious father figure. These letters have the same aim as the *Confessions*, to show how pure Rousseau had remained in spite of his situation and how he had reacted emotionally and intellectually to his environment. Because he had a specific person to persuade and because he stuck to essentials in this compressed version of his memoirs, the letters to Malesherbes are not only perfect, but indispensable for his readers. They are dramatic since there is another personage to be confronted and who determines their form. And they tell us almost everything that must be known about Rousseau as a verbal self-portraitist. The equally semi-private letters to Voltaire share these characteristics even if they deal less with feelings than with ideas. The scarcely veiled hostility, the enormity of the challenge, make these letters a duel more than a mere exchange, and because they are so sharp, so angry and so deeply felt, they again tell us all there is to know about the watch-maker's son's view of 'celebrated Arouet'.

Rousseau's supreme effort as a letter writer is the *Lettres Morales* addressed to Mme d'Houdetot. They are both personal and impersonal. He is not openly addressing her as the woman whom he had so passionately loved or as the mistress of another man, although these circumstances color everthing. Here Rousseau did, however, display his naked heart. Many of the phrases from the Savoyard Vicar appear here also, but the message is a very different one. Rousseau spoke openly of his total skepticism, of his conviction that men lived amid illusions of their own devising and of the impossibility and worthlessness of any knowledge other than that gained by introspection. In this complex way Mme d'Houdetot was to be convinced to look into her heart from time to time, to withdraw from the external world and to retreat into herself. Since Rousseau was no longer part of her world, it was clear why he wanted her to abandon it. For he obviously hoped that within herself she would find some memory of him and would be united with him not as a lover, but as a guide in the interior realm. The mixture of personal and philosophic persuasion is enormously effective. It is, moreover, the clearest and most reliable account of Rousseau's real beliefs, because here he was anxious to be himself and to be remembered as such. That is why they are so important.

The openly public letters, those that Rousseau wrote in reply to the Archbishop of Paris and the Genevan authorities, are quite different. They are essentially forensic in rhetoric, not drama. They are exceptionally well argued, informative and clear. One reads them like any item by item defense for the points they score, and one is quite certain at the end that Rousseau left his opponents in pretty poor shape. Here again style and purpose merge and one learns readily what to expect in the various literary modes in which Rousseau chose to present his views. Without recognizing their form they would often remain unnecessarily obscure and partial. How it is said tells us what is meant no less than the aim of speech determines its style.

In sum, then, one must consider biography, both public and private, circumstances and audiences, and also, the range and structure of arguments and their style. There are beside these enduring concerns of the art of interpretation many minor decisions that have to be made as one goes along. What is one to do about the secondary literature? Rousseau has never failed to arouse commentary. The stream of interpretative works has been steady, as is the case with almost no other political theorist. Most of it did not worry me, even though it had to be read. In footnoting, only open and clear arguments, specific debts for ideas and, above all, sources of information seemed to me worth recording. Courtesy has to be observed, but there was no point in noting down everything I had read, unless there was some obvious reason for it. The history of the Rousseau literature is now a subject in its own right anyhow. Moreover, the books to which I am most deeply indebted could not be readily footnoted because their impact tended to be general. The present book, evidently, shows the influence of Bertrand de Jouvenel's essays on Rousseau and of the writings of Jean Starobinski at every turn. The former has demonstrated the depth of Rousseau's political pessimism, but psychological nuances do not arrest his attention. Starobinski is not as conversant with the history of political theory, but his general knowledge of psychology and of

Rousseau's in particular are a wonder. To put these two together seemed in itself to justify a new book on Rousseau. Of other books, Schinz' older work seemed to me to retain a real value and Fetscher's study of Rousseau's politics was very instructive, even when I disagreed with it.

I limited the footnotes referring to other commentators to the necessary honest, polite and helpful minimum. However, I footnoted as minutely as possible every sentence referring to the work of Rousseau. It was, first of all, a necessary form of self-discipline. It forbids one to say anything about Rousseau that cannot be shown to refer to his own words. If it leads to pedantry, that is a price I was willing to pay in order to eliminate any self-indulgent speculating and the inaccuracy that mars so much writing on political theory. It should, I hope, also help the reader, who can return to Rousseau for his own critical review more easily that way. This consideration also governed the editions I used. Whatever was most easily and usually available to me and to those whom I knew to be likely readers seemed best. Vaughan, the better English translations and a combination of the Pléiade and Hachette editions of Rousseau's work were used on that principle. It is hoped that this will prove convenient for as many people as possible. The Dufour edition of Rousseau's correspondence is, of course, a trial to all who have ever had to use it. It was a relief to have Mr R. A. Leigh explain why it is so confused. He is about to put us all in his debt with a far superior collection, but it was not yet sufficiently far along to be used here.

This has been, then, a general account of some of the decisions that anyone who would write this sort of book would be likely to face. There is nothing self-evident about making these choices. They are difficult and uncertain and many are certain to be other than sound. The fact that so many and such diverse considerations arise does not help. There are all sorts of pitfalls. One can easily over-identify with Rousseau and see everything his way. Or, since he was so often irritating, one can get very angry at him. Neither will do. Nevertheless, there is no cause for complaint. To have read Rousseau with some care is to have thought about all that is most relevant to political philosophy and to the intellectual imagination in general.

APPENDIX

A brief Summary of the *Nouvelle Héloise* and *Emile et Sophie ou les Solitaires*

Since there are no complete readable translations of either the *Nouvelle Héloise* or of *Emile et Sophie ou les Solitaires*, I will try to offer brief accounts of the contents of these novels for those who cannot read them, so that they might more easily follow my argument.

The *Nouvelle Héloise* is written in letters, which was a form Rousseau had surely adopted from Richardson. It suited him well, since it permits a maximum of self-revelation and confrontation of characters. The novel begins with Saint-Preux (that is his nickname), declaring his love to Julie d'Etange. As he is merely the tutor of this daughter of a nobleman, he assumes from the first that he will be rejected. This does not happen, and they presently become lovers. Julie's letters are at first mostly addressed to her cousin, the more level-headed Claire, who is eventually in everyone's confidence and who acts as a sort of one-woman chorus throughout, observing, predicting and lamenting. Julie's father, though not her mother, is inflexibly opposed to the marriage of the young lovers. Julie hopes to force her father to consent by becoming pregnant, but she has a miscarriage.

At this point Lord Eduard Bomston, an immensely rich English peer and a friend of Julie's father, appears. He takes a great liking to Saint-Preux, but the latter suspects him of having designs on Julie. In a jealous rage he challenges Lord Eduard to a duel. This disaster is finally averted and Lord Eduard's generosity is proven by his efforts to persuade Baron d'Etange to permit the marriage. This fails and he and Saint-Preux go off to Paris, from where the latter writes Julie a series of devastating accounts of life in the capital.

While they are gone Julie's mother discovers the correspondence and is very upset, and soon after she falls ill and dies. Even though the two events are unrelated Julie feels guilty and thinks that she is to blame for her mother's death. In this state of mind she consents to renounce her lover and to marry M. de Wolmar, an older man whom her father has chosen for her. During the wedding she undergoes a profound inner change, a conversion to virtue. She now feels ready to accept her duties as a wife and mother. In her pursuit of virtue she is at every step helped by her extraordinary husband, a man as wise as he is good. Although she cannot bring herself to tell him of her relationship with Saint-Preux, he knows and forgives everything.

Saint-Preux is thrown into utter despair by Julie's marriage and contemplates suicide. He is dissuaded by Lord Eduard, who finds a position as engineer on a vessel going on a trip around the world for him. After ten years Saint-Preux returns and is made welcome by Wolmar and his wife. Julie now has two children and her life is wholly devoted to them and to running a model estate at Clarens with Wolmar. The rest of the book describes these efforts, Julie's virtue, Wolmar's wisdom, the beauty of their English garden and the prosperity of their estate. Julie's only sorrow appears to be that Wolmar is an atheist. He never speaks of it, always attends church for the sake of appearances, but he is a convinced unbeliever. This disturbs Julie, although Wolmar never tries to alter her faith. The more beneficent Wolmar is, the more he does to cure Saint-Preux of his old infatuation, the more religious and miserable his wife becomes. In the end, as it seems certain that Saint-Preux will marry Claire and settle down at Clarens to become the tutor of the Wolmar children, she tells him of her profound malaise and boredom. There is a short break in the story just before this that deals with Lord Eduard's amorous adventures in Italy. An appendix is also devoted to this delightful subject.

The final section is brief. Julie jumps into a lake to rescue one of her children, catches cold and dies. She is very happy to die, because she is now perfectly aware that all her virtue has not helped her to forget Saint-Preux. She loves him as much as ever. As she dies she gives an account of her tolerant and loving religious beliefs, but her greatest hope is to be reunited in heaven with Saint-Preux. Wolmar looks thoughtful, but never admits to conversion.

This is a very inadequate account of the *Nouvelle Héloise*. It is meant only for those who cannot read this remarkable work. For all its mawkish mix of sex and piety it is not only a genuine novel of ideas and character, it is often very moving, and it is not at all difficult to see why several generations of readers shed gallons of tears over it.

Only two chapters of *Emile et Sophie ou les Solitaires* were completed. In the *Confessions* Rousseau said that this sequel to *Emile* would illustrate the principles of negative morality, that is of avoiding situations of dependence in which one might benefit from harming others. It is not, however, clear from the parts that he wrote how he would have developed the theme. We only know that he *may* have contemplated an exotic ending to the tale, but that is mere hearsay. The finished sections are, however, pure Rousseau in style and content. What we have are two letters from Emile to his old tutor. Emile does not, however, expect the tutor to receive them. They are, in fact, an autobiography, which is to deal explicitly, not with the events of Emile's life, but with his ideas and feelings. The letters are addressed to the tutor in order to allow Emile to explain how his life collapsed as soon as his mentor left him, and how in spite of disaster his good education saved him. Having lost everything, he was still self-possessed and uncrushed by despair.

The tale is simple. As soon as the tutor leaves Emile and Sophie and their two children everything begins to go wrong: Sophie's parents die and then her little daughter. She is in despair and to cheer her up, Emile takes her to Paris. In spite of the tutor's warnings, Emile is gradually moved to emulate the ways of the Parisians and a frivolous life soon kills all real passions in his heart. He soon ceases to love anyone. Sophie, in turn, also enters society and falls into bad company. She finally admits to Emile that she is pregnant by another man. Emile becomes completely enraged, and when that passes, leaves his family and Paris. Blessing his solid education, he takes a hard look at his situation and accepts necessity as he has been taught to do without a murmur. As a man willing to live for himself, unmoved by common opinions, he decides to give up his son and wife, since he could not learn to live with her once she became the mother of a child that was not his.

As soon as he has made this decision he feels calm again, delivered from both anxiety and hope. He decides to begin life all over and gets a job in a carpenter's shop, but then decides that he ought to leave

France entirely if he is really to abandon his family completely. After all, the sage lives only from day to day and must learn to forget. He wanders on, working at his trade for subsistence, totally unattached, a carefree vagabond. At Marseilles he embarks for Naples. His ship is attacked by pirates and Emile is sold into slavery by his captors. His first quiet reflection upon his changed condition is not one of regret. What has he lost? Nothing, only the freedom to behave foolishly. He feels more free than ever; for he is again accepting necessity. He is *not* being forced to do anything he does *not* want to do. He is, in fact, not doing anything at all in his heavy chains, and so he feels perfectly free.

As a slave he changes masters several times and eventually he is put to work on a public building and brutally starved and beaten. Recognizing that this treatment is certain to kill him off in about two weeks, he decides to organize a strike which, should it fail, would only bring about his death a little sooner. The strike is sufficiently successful to come to the notice of the master, to whom Emile explains that it would be in his economic self-interest if his slaves were properly fed and cared for, since they would then work harder. The owner sees the point, has the brutal foreman put in chains, and puts Emile in his place. He does his job so well that the dey of Algeria calls for him and makes him his personal slave. As the letter breaks off it is clear that Emile has become the advisor of a ruler of a soldierly and law-abiding people.

Not a single theme of real importance to Rousseau is left out in these thirty-odd pages. That is why I regarded it as a document of such great importance. The happy end of *Emile* is false, especially to the tone of its opening pages, so full of dark foreboding. It is man, not the situation, that is being remade, and Emile's character cannot reveal itself until he *really* becomes a man, that is, a suffering victim.

INDEX

Aesthetic feeling, 83-4

Ambition, 29, 59, 107, 139; emergence of, 50, 76, 158; evils of, 55, 56, 57, 72; social, 77, 86, 96; in men of letters, 111, 113, 114

amour propre: and inequality, 10, 82, 97, 163, 197, 202; redirection of, 16, 19, 21, 28, 160, 182, 187; Golden Age family free of, 23, 25; and knowledge, 24; emergence of, 28, 35, 76, 185; and opinion and prejudice, 76, 86, 88, 89, 90, 91, 158, 171, 174; and the will, 92, 166; and self-delusion, 107; and men of letters, 111, 112; and Saint-Preux, 138; and Emile, 147; and justice, 175, 179

Anarchy, 203, 209

Anet, Claude, 134, 135

Anger, 112

Aquinas, Thomas, 198, 199

Aristocracy, *see* Nobility

Aristotle, 218, 219, 224, 225, 226

Armies, army, 189; *see also* Military

Arts, the, 24, 101, 109, 110-11

Assemblies, 19-20, 180-1

Association, human: artificiality of, 10, 35, 76; legitimate bond of, 18, 20; evils of, 56, 140, 155, 157, 159, 166, 185; process of, 157

Associations, public and private, 10, 91-5, 181

Atheism, 108, 112-14, 118

Athenians, Athens, 19, 201, 209

Autarchy, 152, 153

Authority: paternal, 21, 25, 127, 128, 130, 145; of a master, 127-8; as personified in Wolmar, 128, 129, 134, 135-6, 137, 142-4, 149, 150-4; Rousseau's ambivalent attitude to, 129-33; Rousseau unfit to exercise, 134-5, 146; of women, 144-5; of the tutor, 146-50; in the Great Legislator, 154-8, 160-1; creative legislative, 158-9; and freedom, 161-3; personal, 162; of husbands, 199

Bacon, 64

Beauty, 84-5

Benevolence, 38, 61, 64, 65

Bentham, 221

Bétique, (*Télémaque*) 5

Blackstone, 221

Body politic, 165, 166-7, 169-70, 197-214

Bomston, Lord, *see* Eduard, Lord

Boswell, 130

Brutus, 6, 21, 66, 203, 204

Burke, 163

Calvin, Calvinism, 115, 154

Catherine the Great, 102, 110, 196

Catholicism, 115

Cato: heroic virtues of, 6, 66, 67, 203, 204; typifies anti-intellectualism, 103, 213, 214; 'above Socrates', 199, 205

Change, 11, 28-9, 30

Character: individual, 55-6, 147, 159 (*see also* Individual); national, 160-1, 171-5

Chiefs, 132, 200, 201, 202, 205

Child, children: education of, 17, 22, 24, 34, 45, 49, 143, 145-9; relationship between parents and, 25, 145, 151; potentialities of, 36; procreation of, 196

Choice: necessity of, between natural and social state, 5-6, 15, 30-2, 57, 212-14; ability to make, 38; between general and particular will, 186-7

Choiseul, Duc de, 96, 110

Christianity, 18, 31, 117, 118-20, 167

Church, 77, 80, 97; Catholic, 200

Citizen(s)
  of Sparta: 5, 15-22, 56, 57, 160, 169
  of the just society: 182, 183; interests of, 175, 186-8, 211; military duties of, 189, 203-4; happiness of, 196-7
  rustic man, neither man nor, 212-13

Civilization: 1, 5, 33; man's drift into, 33-4, 44-57; withdrawal from, 22 (*see also* Golden Age, privately created); a system of dependence, 35; cannot mitigate individual suffering, 39-40; a record of suffering, 44; ways of countering worst effects of, 57-74; *see also* Society

Claire (*N.H.*), 106, 145

Clarens (*N.H.*), 23, 61, 63, 142, 144, 145; as the model community 150-4,

237

Index

Index

Enslavement, 33, 35, 43-4, 51
Entertainments, 24, 100
Envy, 112
Epictetus, 125
Equality, 18, 19, 169, 185-97; does not characterize governments, 202-5; *see also* Inequality
Everyman, *see* Man, in general
Evil, 59, 63, 70, 71
External: restriction of will, 72; compulsion, 73

Family, the: destruction of, in Spartan model, 21-2, 187, 193; essence of the Golden Age model, 21, 22-7, 85; and the education of children, 145-6
Fanaticism, 112, 113, 118, 122
Fantasy, 54
Fashion, 71
Fatherhood, 24-5, 58, 69
Fear, 24, 55, 75, 76, 84
Felicity: desire for, 4, 39, 54, 71, 73, 193, 195; impossible in civilization, 33, 56, 60, 62; *see also* Happiness
Fénelon, 4-6
Festivals and ceremonies, 111, 153, 158, 160
Fetscher, 231
Feudalism, 94, 95
Filmer, 221
Flux, 10
Fontenelle, 79
Frederick of Prussia, 196
Freedom, 18, 55, 84, 176; possibilities of, 10, 34, 60; natural, 46, 76; and authority, 161-2; English, 172, 173; *see also* Liberty
Freud, 216
Friendship, 145
Frustration, 29, 113
Future, 28, 34

General will, *see* Will
Geneva, 2: as a model civilization, 7, 14, 100, 117; magistrates of, 8, 91, 104, 105, 106-7, 189; *Social Contract* a warning to citizens of, 8, 104, 208; Rousseau's attitude to, 12-13, 102, 104, 105-6, 115, 117; his exchanges with authorities of, 103, 104, 105-6, 106-7, 109, 230; 'cercles' of, 93-4; religion in, 115-16
God, 2, 71, 72, 100, 118, 132; indifference

of, 10; belief in, 60, 108, 121, 122; does not punish 68; will of, 72, 168; Wolmar resembles, 128, 135, 136, 151, 162; agents of, 146, 157
Golden Age: ideal of, 5, 51, 52, 65, 111, 212; never yet achieved historically, 6, 12, 51, 52, 58, 197, 213; an expression of nostalgia, 8-9, 11, 57; man's state before inequality, 11, 25; familial society in, 22-7, 85, 133; intellectual limitations in, 23-4, 29, 31, 56; paternal authority in, 25, 133; economic limitations of, 28, 48; an exercise in indignation, 30; competition foreign to, 52, 57; privately created, 53, 59, 120, 127, 148, 187, 193, (at Clarens) 63, 151, 154; exists without religion, 119, 120
Goodness, 36, 59, 60-5, 66, 69, 70, 73; *see also* Virtue
Government, 8; as opposed to sovereignty, 19-20; aristocratic, 19, 210; and civic order, 21; politics, the study of, 104-7; despotic, 109; monarchical, 168, 199, 202, 208; illustrated, in metaphor of body politic, 197-214; autocratic, 202; *see also* Democracy; Republic
Great Legislator, 20, 127, 128, 129, 133, 151; the image of public authority, 154-8, 160, 161; and the practice of preventive politics, 165, 166, 170, 171, 172, 174, 176, 179, 181, 182, 183, 185, 186, 187, 189, 192, 201
Greek language and drama, 84
Grotius, 179, 207, 218

Habit(s), 34, 71, 87, 147; *see also* Custom
Happiness, 22, 23, 25, 63, 73; man's failure to find, 39, 40, 70-2; public, 165, 169, 193-7; *see also* Felicity
Hegel, 78
Helplessness, *see* Dependence
Helvétius, 37, 45, 83; and theory of ideology, 78-81, 82, 83
History, 6, 9, 80; Rousseau's indifference to, 1, 2, 3, 7, 53, 110; and utopia, 11, 12, 30; of the species, 33-4
Hobbes, 79, 82, 133, 219, 220, 227; on opinion, 77; on government, 170, 176, 198, 199; absolutism of, 200; Diderot on, 218; *see also* Leviathan
Holland, 127, 158
Homer, 157

239

Index

Hope, 10, 29
Hume, 130

Ideology, 78, 80
Ignorance, 23–4, 71, 79, 80
Imagination, 34, 54; and memory, 10, 28, 75, 139, 147; control of, 34; creative, 54–5
Immorality, 34
Inclination: and duty, 50, 64, 166, 182, and situation, 58, 63
Independence, 34–5, 46, 60, 63, 129–30, 159
Individual: rights of, 16–17; integrity of, 30; experience, in social situations, 34, 172; inclination, indicates that of group, 35–6, 53–4; sufferings of, 39–40; strength and weakness of, 40–1; personality, development of, 45, 55–6; Rousseau's sympathy for the, 54; freedom of the, and opinion, 91–5; education of, 160; a composite 'man in general', 166, 167, 183, 203; happiness of, 194, 197–8
Inequality, 10–11; inevitability of, 17–18, 22, 45, 153–4, 170; elimination or avoidance of, 18–19, 28, 169, foreign to Golden Age, 25, 48; between masters and servants, 25–6; between poor and rich, 26, 95; and material progress, 28; urban, 29, 55; Rousseau's hatred of, 30, 35, 131; civilization a system of, 44, 52; natural, 44–5, 50, 162; produces indifference, 47; and dependence, 48; and work and property, 50–1; desire for, 50, 52; produces deceptions, 56, 76; and amour propre, 82, 97; and associations, 93, 94, 95; and injustice, 105, 176; politics of, 107; social, 105–6, 108, 110, 111, 163; institutionalized, 166, 'general will' opposes, 184–97; moral, 203–4
Injustice, 49, 105, 110, 126
Innocence, 4, 21
Inner: conflict, 23, 167; balance, 55; compulsion, 162
Instinct(s): natural, 20, 61, 62, 72, 76; for survival, 55, 58; see also Conscience
Intellectuality, 64, 139
Intellectuals, 101–3, 125, 201, 202, 206, 214
Intelligence, 36, 37, 54, 71

Intolerance, 114
Introspection, 39, 40, 58, 70
Introspective psychology, see Psychology
Isolation, 47, 48, 58, 170, 171

Jansenists, 12
Jesuits, 12, 80, 97–8, 112, 116
Jesus Christ, 122, 138
Jews, 161, 172
Jouvenel, Bertrand de, 230
Judgment, 30, 61, 76
Julie (N.H.): in Golden Age surroundings, 22, 65, 86, 154; as a mother, 34, 147, 148; relationship of, with Wolmar, 61, 62–3, 143; relationship of, with Saint-Preux, 66, 67, 99, 137, 138, 139 141, 142; and will power, 73; and opinion, 87, 90; suicide of, 87, 120, 138, 144; and father, 89; and politics, 106; and Claire, 145
Jurisprudence, 110
Justice, 20, 38, 96, 167, 193, 210–11; importance of, 48 9; Emile and, 49, 50, 186; illustrated by Wolmar, 153; and amour propre, 175; conditions required for, 176–83; and the individual, 186–7, 188; not concerned with war, 189; see also Contract; Mutuality

Kant, 73, 220
Keith, George, 63, 130
Kings, 132, 133; see also Monarchy
Knowledge, 24, 79

Language, and music, 84, 156–7
Laws(s), 8, 173, 181, 182, 201; and magistrates, 51, 151, 205; rule of, 132, 155–6, 200; of nations, 206–8
Laziness, 24, 45–6, 72
Legislation, 79, 81, 122
Legislator, see Great Legislator
Leigh, R. A., 231
Leviathan, 169, 198, 199–202, 209; see also Hobbes
Liberty, 18, 46, 112, 130, 176; see also Freedom
Literature, and society, 80
Locke, 145, 217, 221, 222; sensationalist psychology of, 33, 82, 83; and intellectual growth, 37–8, 39, 40, 54; and individualism, 41, 53, 54; on property, 49, 50; on the will, 70, 71, 73;

240

Index

Opinion—*cont.*
conflict of, with nature, 85; and marriage, 85–9; subjugation of self to, 90–5; moulded from above, 97–100, 103; a form of memory, 140
public: false, 3, 73–4; in Spartan republic, 17, 31; and marriage, 85; and power, 90; despotism of, 95–7; and religion, 108; and the arts, 110; and honour, 111; altering of, by Legislator, 157–8
Oppression: psychic growth of, 34; evils of, 35, 36, 74, 84, 192; and inequality, 50, 51; avoidance of, 56, 60, 182
Orators, oratory, 84, 201
Originality, 55, 56
Orthodoxy, 108, 109, 114

Pain: and remorse, 38; is evil, 59, 70, 71; retreat from, 60; freedom from, 60, 62, 85
Paoli, General, 157
Paris, society in, 5, 13, 26, 29, 77, 86, 91, 98–9, 104, 144, 174, 175; emergence in, of 'empire of opinion', 78, 96; literary life of, 109, 110; Archbishop of, 116, 117, 122, 230; religious climate of, 115–16
Parliamentary institutions, 94–5
Party, spirit of, 96
Pascal, 77, 97
Passion(s), 38, 66, 79, 81, 84, 85; mastery of, 41, 62, 71
Passivity, 7, 107, 119
Past, 28, 34, 158
Paternal authority, 21, 25, 86, 128, 145
Patriotism: Spartan, 21, 28, 160; ancient, 156; policy of, 175–6, 188; a military virtue, 189, 201, 203–4
Patronage, 109, 113, 130
Peace, 30, 163, 167, 185; and war, 113, 188, 189, 207
Peasants, 23, 113, 118, 163; utopian, 63, 104, 153, 213; attracted to Paris, 91, 100, 152; welfare of, 168, 169
People, the: definition of, 107, 165–8; sovereignty of, 168; will of, 184–97; real interests of, 185–8
Perfectibility, 10, 18, 45, 54
Perfection, 9, 10, 12, 17, 26
Personifications, political, 165–70, 176–7, 183
Peter the Great, 161

Philosophers, 39, 138–9, 170–1
Philosophes, 102, 169; control opinion, 96; and 'counter-church', 97–8; Rousseau's relations with, 108–13, 222, 223; *see also* Men of letters
Philosophy, classical, 12, 84, 110, 139
Piaget, 216
Pity, 21, 26, 38, 46–7, 54; *see also* Compassion
Plato, 3–4, 9, 11, 218, 224, 225
Pleasure, 38, 59, 61–2, 75, 85, 88
Plutarch, 12, 53, 154, 155, 227
Poland, political plans for, 14–15, 16, 20, 95, 133, 161, 176
Political: participation, 18; economy, 151
Politics, 30; opinion dependent on, 76–8; Rousseau's view of, 104–7, 123; preventive, *see* Great Legislator
Pompadour, Mme de, 110
Poor, 11, 26, 99, 104, 168, 204; 'too stupid to feel', 47, 124; inequality between rich and, 50–1, 52, 92, 95, 179–80, victimhood of, 125
Potentialities, potentiality, 36, 37–8, 44–5
Power, 79, 80, 98, 106–7
Prejudice, 73, 77, 86, 88–91, 158
Priesthood, 77, 80, 124–5; *see also* Clergy
Privilege, 93
Progress, 16, 28, 29, 101
Property, 49–51, 178
Protestant writings, of Rousseau, 116, 118
Protestantism, 114, 115, 121
Psychology: introspective, 9–10, 33, 38; sensationalist, 33, 37, 39–40, 81–2, 83; of learning, 33, 37; moral, 35, 37, 165, 167, 184

Racine, 66
Rameau, 221
ranz de vaches, 141
Reason, 38, 61, 64, 72, 157
Recovery, inner, 65
Reflection, 139, 160
Reform, 'useless and impossible', 7
Reformation, 121
Religion, 80, 108–9, 113; Rousseau's attitude to, 108–9, 113–25; civil, 117; *see also* Calvinism; Catholicism; Protestantism
Remorse, 38, 60, 67, 68
Republic(s), 19, 20, 201–2; fate of, 8, 104, 105, 159; virtues of, 66
Resignation 12, 19, 30, 40, 60, 62, 163

242

Index

Rich, 11, 99, 103, 168; lack sympathy, 26, 47, 92, 125; inequality between poor and, 50–1, 52, 92, 95, 125, 179–80, 204; power of, 76, 77, 113; *see also* Wealth

Richards, I.A., 227

Richelieu, duc de, 110

Roman society, *see* Spartan–Roman society

Rousseau, Jean-Jacques: indifferent to history, 1, 2, 3, 7, 11; an 'homme revolté', 1, 2–3, 7–8, 9, 127, 184; his utopian models, designed to induce moral recognition, 2, 11–12, 30, 32 (*see also* Golden Age, Spartan city, Spartan–Roman society); need of, for self-revelation, 2, 41, 99–104, 114; as an introspective psychologist, 9, 33, 39–53, 58, 59; addicted to fantasy, 12, 13, 44, 55, 117; as a citizen of Geneva, 12–13, 100, 102, 103, 104, 105, 115, 116–17; admired military valour, 14, 15; identifies with the individual, 30, 33, 41; illustrates autobiographically life of man in general, 41–4, 46, 52–3, 58; 'moral strategies' of, 57–74; despises priesthood and men of letters, 77, 101, 109–26; points of agreement between Helvétius and, 78–83; and sensationalist psychology, 83–4; on the conflict of nature and opinion, 84–91; on corruption of opinion-making, 91–103; on conspiracy, 91, 95–7, 130; despised ruling classes, 91, 130–2; on Genevan 'cercles', 93–4; a professional victim of oppression, 105–8; religious experiences of, 114–15, 117; personal philosophy of, 124–6; on authority, 129–33 (*see also* Authority), his use of metaphor, 165–70, 226, 227; debt of, to Montesquieu, 174; on citizenship, 174–84; his use of term 'general will'; 184–97; on the body politic, 197–214; problems of interpretation of, 215–31

Works of:

Confessions, 41, 208, 219, 234

Considerations on the Government of Poland, 14–15; *see also* Poland

Discourse on the Arts and Sciences, 12–14, 208

Discourse on Inequality, 36, 105, 179, 206, 208

Economie Politique, 16, 176, 199–208

Emile, 24, 36, 37, 38, 223–4, 234, 235; *see also individual entry*

Emile et Sophie, ou Les Solitaires, 234–5; *see also individual entries*

First Discourse, 13, 14, 199

La Nouvelle Héloise, 24, 37, 41, 45, 53, 106, 128, 172, 173, 224, 228; message of, 87–8, 222–3; summarized, 232–4; *see also entries for individual characters*

Letter to d'Alembert, 117

Lettres Morales, 37, 38, 229

Rousseau jugé de Jean-Jacques, 96

Second Discourse, 36

Social Contract: 19, 27, 28, 165, 185; a yardstick for society, 17, 208; a warning to citizens of Geneva, 8, 104, 208–9

Routine, 147

Ruling, art of; exemplified by Wolmar, 150–4; exemplified by Great Legislator, 154–8; among the ancients, 156–7

Saint-Preux (*N.H.*), 25, 66, 83, 132; relations of, with Julie, 22, 62–3, 85, 86, 87, 141, 142; on Paris, 26, 98–9; Rousseau identifies with, 45, 130, 134 on Helvétius, 45, 81; and conscience, 67–9; relations of, with Lord Eduard, 68–70, 136, 137–8, 142, 143, 172, 173, and Baron d'Etange, 73, 89; passivity of, 90; a man destroyed by society, 136–144; Wolmar's care of, 141–4, 150; as tutor to Wolmar children, 143, 146–7

Salante, (*Télémaque*), 5

Salisbury, John of, 198–200

Sartre, 216

Savage, nature of, 36

Schinz, 231

Science, 110

Scoundrels, 'all valets are', 43–4, 112

Self: and citizenship, 16; civic, 20; artificial, 34; original, 34; injury to, 38; fragmented, 72; natural, 88; 159; socialized, 88; inborn, search for, 159–60

Self-absorption, 2

-appreciation, 48

-awareness, 37, 140

-communion, 26

243

Index

Self-confidence, 140, 141
-consciousness, moral, 140
-control, 63
-deception, 41, 107
-delusion, 107
-destruction, 104, 183
-determination, 28, 182
-enslavement, 127
-esteem, 111, 159, 160, 187
-expression, 6, 17, 18, 24, 25-6
-fulfillment, 5
-government, 19
-healing, 26
-inspection, 71
-interest, 50, 79, 80, 81, 82, 83, 96
-justification, 41
-knowledge, 39, 41, 88, 108
-liberation, 107
-love, 21, 23, 31, 36, 48, 61, 63, 66, 67,
72, 202
-perfection, 38
-possession, 73
-preservation, 50, 202
-repression, 6, 16, 72
-restoration, 127
-revelation, 2
-righteousness, 125
-sufficiency, 27, 34-5, 55, 171
-understanding, 88
-vindication, 2
Semi-socialized state: the cause of all
misery, 5, 16, 51, 206; consequences
of, 62, 186, 188, 207, 208; avoidance
of, 171
Seneca, 3-4
Sensationalism, see Psychology
Sensitivity, moral, 61; see also Conscience
Serfdom, 18
Servants, 112, 127, 131, 152-4
Servius, 94
Sexuality, 22, 84-5, 86, 139
Simplicity, 22, 23, 56
Sincerity, 1, 41
Slavery, slaves, 18, 60, 112, 132
Soboul, André, 216
Social: state, as opposed to natural, 5, see
also Semi-socialized state; change, 11,
183; equality, 18; contract, 20-1, 23,
176-81, 187, 189; immobility, 29;
complexity, 29-30; prejudice, 73;
scale, 77; criticism, 77; class, 81-2,
85-91, 132; humiliation, 138; differ-
ence, 153, 154

Socialization: in Sparta and Rome, see
Spartan-Roman society; in village
society, 31; see also Semi-socialized
state
Society, 2, 9; education against, 5, 163;
civic, civil (as portrayed in Spartan
city), 11, 12-22, 51, 165-6, 167, (a
legitimate) 177-97, 210; and the individual, 16-17, 29-30; familial, as
portrayed by Golden Age, 21-8; disasters of, 52, 72, 73; institutions of,
51, 174; failure of, 55; a moral prison,
59; political mores of, 92-3; 'pure',
100, 159; and character of a people,
174; importance of a small, 174-6;
see also Civilization
Socrates, 67, 80, 199, 205
Solitude, 24, 58, 88, 159
Solon, 94, 156
Sophie (Emile), 86, 145, 150, 154
Soul: 33, 63, 81, 92, 157, 159; of Everyman, represented in Rousseau, 34, 40,
41-3; of the body politic, 198-9
Sovereign, the: political personification of,
165, 166, 176-7, 180, 181, 182, 187,
191, 199, 200-1; impersonal rules
decided by, 191-3
Sovereignty: and government, in Social
Contract, 19; ends of, 20; 'of the
people', 168, 176, 181, 182, 184, 185
Spartan city: a model of Utopia, 3, 5, 58,
127, 133, 184; model of, an instrument of condemnation, 7, 8, 11-12,
30, 101-3, 213; and inequality, 11,
18; organization of, 12-22; version of
classical military heroism, 13-14, 101-
2, 160, 187; and redirection of amour
propre, 19, 160, 182; unintellectual
and unreligious, 31, 119, 160; communal will in, 19, 56, 57, 58, 64, 65,
81; collective satisfaction of human
needs in, 59, 193, 196, 197; denaturation in, 66, 197; as described in
Economie Politique, 199-200
Spartan-Roman society: virtues of, 6, 8,
64, 156, 173, 203, 205, 208-9; ideal
of, 7, 59, 94; socialization in, 13-14,
21, 87, 100, 159, 193, 202
Spontaneity, 66
Stability, 30
Starobinski, 230
Stupidity, varieties of, 10, 31, 36, 51, 73,
192, 212, 213

244

Index

Subjection, 182

Suffering, 3, 51, 59; an elemental fact, 12, 39–40, 54; of the individual, 16, 39, 44, 52; of others, pity for, 21, 38, 46–7

Suicide, 68–70, 73

Superstition, 80, 97, 114, 118, 123

Suspicion, 24, 97

Switzerland, 127, 158; intimations of ideal rural life in, 6, 7, 8, 25–6, 27, 28; folk music of, 83–4, 141; *see also* Geneva; Neufchatel; Valais

Theism, 115

Thucydides, 53

Truthfulness, 1

Tutor, function of, 146–50

Tyranny, 80, 97, 113, 118, 201

Unanimity, 188, 190

Understanding, 54

Utopia: varieties of, 1–12, 164; Rousseau's two models of, *see* Age of Gold; Spartan City; Spartan–Roman society

Vagrancy, 46, 69

Valais, 23, 25, 85, 87

Valets, 43, 44, 111–12, 124

Vanity, 16, 112, 147

Venice, 8, 105

Vercellis, Mme de, 26

Vicar, Savoyard (*Emile*), 60–2, 72, 73, 114, 121, 123

Victimhood: resulting from inequality, 29; Rousseau's sense of, 38, 106, 107, 130; common experience of, 54, 86, 90, 125; and choice, 57; escape from, 58, 59, 69

Village society, in the Golden Age, 23, 27, 29, 31

Vincennes, 78, 101

Virtue, 31, 46, 212; civic, 5, 7, 61, 73, 81, 203, 204; and the power of the will, 63–4, 69; search for, 65–7; and politics, 79; *see also* Goodness

Voltaire, 3, 105, 113, 121, 196; champion of civilization, 7, 169; followers of, 82, 97, 113, 115; Rousseau's hostility to, 101–3, 104, 108–9, 110, 114, 116, 117, 123–4, 221–2, 229

War(s), 74, 99, 110, 118, 122, 196, 206; and peace, 113, 188, 189, 207

Warens, Mme de, 130, 134

Weakness, human, 41, 52, 56, 58, 62, 77, 112, 163

Wealth, 95, 204; *see also* Rich

Wickedness, 34

Will (power): individual, 56; and goodness, 57, 62, 69; Emile's, 59–60, 64; Julie's, 65; importance of, 70–4; new, creation of, 157; general, 165, 166, 168–9, 184–97, 198, 204, 205

Wisdom, 12

Wolmar (*N.H.*): children of, 24, 34, 143, 146–7; and neighbours, 29; on individual personality, 45; and reason, 61; and duty, 65; and atheism, 81, 120, 121; and class barriers, 81–2; excellence of, 86, 87, 89; god-like qualities of, 90, 121, 128, 129, 134, 135–6, 137, 138, 142; cures Saint-Preux, 141–4; relationship of, with Julie, 142, 144; as the master of Clarens, 150–4

Woman, 138

Women: of Sparta, 15, 21, 65, 66, 172; of Rome, 15; in the Golden Age family, 25; Rousseau's attitude to, 144–5

Work, 50–1; *see also* Division of labor

Xenophobia, 16, 31, 169, 171

245

CAMBRIDGE STUDIES IN THE
HISTORY AND THEORY OF POLITICS

TEXTS

LIBERTY, EQUALITY, FRATERNITY, *by James Fitzjames Stephen.* Edited, with an introduction and notes, by *R. J. White*

VLADIMIR AKIMOV ON THE DILEMMAS OF RUSSIAN MARXISM 1895-1903. An English edition of 'A Short History of the Social Democratic Movement in Russia' and 'The Second Congress of the Russian Social Democratic Labour Party', with an introduction and notes by *Jonathan Frankel*

TWO ENGLISH REPUBLICAN TRACTS, PLATO REDIVIVUS or, A DIALOGUE CONCERNING GOVERNMENT (*c.* 1681) *by Henry Neville* and AN ESSAY UPON THE CONSTITUTION OF THE ROMAN GOVERN-MENT (*c.* 1699) *by Walter Moyle.* Edited by *Caroline Robbins.*

J. G. HERDER ON SOCIAL AND POLITICAL CULTURE, translated, edited and with an introduction by *F. M. Barnard.*

THE LIMITS OF STATE ACTION, *by Wilhelm von Humboldt.* Edited, with an introduction and notes, by *J. W. Burrow.*

STUDIES

1867: DISRAELI, GLADSTONE AND REVOLUTION. THE PASSING OF THE SECOND REFORM BILL, *by Maurice Cowling*

THE CONSCIENCE OF THE STATE IN NORTH AMERICA, *by E. R. Norman*

THE SOCIAL AND POLITICAL THOUGHT OF KARL MARX, *by Shlomo Avineri*

MEN AND CITIZENS: ROUSSEAU'S SOCIAL THOUGHT, *by Judith Shklar.*

IDEALISM, POLITICS AND HISTORY: SOURCES OF HEGELIAN THOUGHT, *by George Armstrong Kelly.*